Successful Governance Initiatives and Best Practices

Experiences from Indian States

Successful Governance Initiatives and Best Practices

Experiences from Indian States

सत्यमेव जयते

Planning Commission
(State Plans Division)
GOVERNMENT OF INDIA

in association with

HDRC
Human Development Resource Centre

UNDP
India

Human Development Resource Centre,
UNITED NATIONS DEVELOPMENT PROGRAMME

Published by

AF

ACADEMIC FOUNDATION
NEW DELHI

Published in 2003 by
ACADEMIC FOUNDATION
4772-73 / 23 Bharat Ram Road,
(23 Ansari Road), Darya Ganj,
New Delhi - 110 002. INDIA.

Phones : 23245001, 02, 03, 04.
Fax : 011-23245005
e-mail : academic@vsnl.com
www : academicfoundation.com

Successful Governance Initiatives and Best Practices: Experiences from Indian States

ISBN 81-7188-306-0

Printed at Print Perfect, Mayapuri Industrial Area, New Delhi.

Acknowledgements

This documentation of Successful Governance Initiatives and Best Practices was prepared by a joint Planning Commission-HDRC team consisting of

Planning Commission
State Plans Division

Rajan Katoch

C. Laldinliana
Santosh

United Nations Development Programme
Human Development Resource Centre

K. Seeta Prabhu

Alka Narang
Suraj Kumar
Aparna Pande
Nitya Mohan
Kalpana Chaudhary

The preparation of the document was greatly facilitated by the support and invaluable inputs by the State Governments of Andhra Pradesh, Assam, Himachal Pradesh, Karnataka, Kerala, Madhya Pradesh, Maharashtra, Punjab, Rajasthan, Tamil Nadu, Tripura, Uttar Pradesh, Uttaranchal and West Bengal.

Background reports, case studies and papers prepared to document the initiatives highlighted in this volume were contributed primarily by L.N. Vijayaraghavan and Alok Sinha. Editing support was provided by Usha Tankha and Sandhya V. Iyer. We also acknowledge the support provided by AusAID.

कृष्ण चन्द्र पन्त
K. C. Pant

उपाध्यक्ष
योजना आयोग
भारत
DEPUTY CHAIRMAN
PLANNING COMMISSION
INDIA

October 17, 2002

Foreword

The Mid Term Appraisal of the Ninth Plan had noted that, along with shortfalls in public investment, it is often design weaknesses and poor implementation of schemes at the grassroots level that tend to restrict the benefits of Government programmes from reaching the intended beneficiaries. At the same time, some States have taken up initiatives that have successfully addressed these weakness; many other States have been seeking to improve implementation, and have expressed the desire to know more about successful models of implementation in other States.

In an effort to respond to this felt need, encourage best practices in governance and implementation, and disseminate information relevant to raising standards of implementation across States, Planning Commission has prepared, in cooperation with the United Nations Development Programme (UNDP), a compendium of successful Governance Initiatives and Implementation Practices. This compendium attempts to identify and highlight models of effective implementation and delivery of public services in the Government sector. We have restricted ourselves to the Government sector, where the impact of better implementation is enormous, and where there is a paucity of such documentation, in contrast to the considerable material published on successful models in the non-Government sector. The objective is to document replicable success stories, which can be used for experience sharing both at the national level as well as between State Governments.

The priority areas that have been taken up in this compendium are interventions in the delivery of social services, land and water management and areas of major public interface with the government. This is a Tenth Plan initiative of the Commission, and while selected initiatives have been incorporated in this volume, we see this as a continuing exercise and during the course of the Tenth Plan, we plan to bring out further editions including subjects and initiatives not covered here.

This compendium is special also because it is the product of a collaborative endeavour. The State Plans Division of the Planning Commission and the Human Development Resource Centre (HDRC), UNDP India Country Office, have worked together to prepare this compendium. I do hope that the compendium will be of value to State Governments as well as development practitioners, as it is intended to be, and will help all of us assimilate the lessons of these best practices and catalyse systemic changes for the better.

(K.C. Pant)

Introduction

Successful Governance Initiatives and Best Practices - Experiences from Indian States is a compilation of case studies of Government's development initiatives that have successfully achieved their intended goals and made a signal contribution to improvement in governance and implementation practices. The compendium aims to highlight these initiatives, facilitate inter-temporal and inter-state comparisons and to encourage their replication in other parts of the country.

This compendium has been prepared by the State Plans Division of the Planning Commission of India in collaboration with the Human Development Resource Centre (HDRC), United Nations Development Programme, New Delhi. For the preparation of the compendium, consultations were held with State Government officials from the district and State levels, as well as from the nodal ministries at the Centre and the Planning Commission. Information pertaining to various schemes in rural and urban areas was received from a number of districts from many States. The effort was to bring out a well documented representative selection from the information available.

The present volume focuses on three key areas—human development and social services, land and water management and areas of major public interface with Government. The objective is to describe practices and experiences in the implementation of programmes and projects that have successfully addressed real-life problems. It is hoped that the case studies discussed in this volume will serve as a basis for facilitating an exchange of ideas, experiences, policies and practices among States of India as well as similarly placed developing countries.

Land and water management interventions are linked to livelihood security for the poor and the marginalised. Hence there is a need to review and bring out successful strategies adopted for using land and water more productively, which ensure the reduction of poverty and improved food security.

Human development indicators relating to education, health and the empowerment of women, especially in the Indian context, are important for several reasons. The nexus between illiteracy, under-nutrition, morbidity and fertility implies low productivity of human resources and levels of poverty in the country. These quality of life indicators are also relevant from the perspective of human development. Initiatives that have successfully sought to tackle these problems have therefore a special relevance to the country's development effort.

The decentralisation of funds, functions and functionaries, mandated by the 73rd and 74th Constitutional Amendments of 1992-93, has facilitated the transformation of communities from being passive beneficiaries to proactive stakeholders. This transition has been evident in different contexts including municipal governments, markets for agricultural produce and increasing role of people's institutions. Information and communication technology has also proved to be an efficient and transparent medium for administrative activities and the dissemination of information.

Some of the key criteria used for identification of initiatives that have been incorporated into the compendium have been:

- Relevance to the poor
- Benefits to maximum number of people
- Quantum of funds being deployed
- Potential for productivity enhancement of the participating population
- Viability
- Level of community participation and commitment
- Sustainability of interventions
- Potential for replicability
- Well documented

Information is provided to the extent possible on the geographical coverage, allocation of funds, target achievement, activities undertaken, institutional arrangements and evaluations as applicable. Contact details have been provided at the end of each case study to help interested persons to obtain information in greater detail from the authorities in charge of the project. Efforts have been made to emphasize those projects whose success are attributable to effective partnerships between the Government and the people and are not purely individual oriented. The compendium is illustrative, and not prescriptive.

Broadly, several factors seem to have played a critical role in determining the effectiveness of initiatives such as those included here. Most of these initiatives seek to help people empower themselves. Consequently increased community involvement in the planning and implementation stage have effected a paradigm shift from a supply driven model of service delivery to a demand driven approach and have led to transparency and flexibility in operation. Most projects seek to tackle a concrete problem e.g. the issue of water scarcity, display potential for replicability and expansion to other villages or cities, offer hope of sustainability and build on community involvement or promoting a spirit of entrepreneurship.

Dissemination of information is a key objective of the compendium, and dissemination is an ongoing exercise. The expectation is that information on specific initiatives by some States on better ways of doing things and delivering results would provoke and encourage some others to find their own variants of better ways of delivering results and forge their own path-breaking initiatives. More such initiatives would help ensure that the benefit of development programmes reach those for whom they are intended, and touch the lives of the people positively. These would perhaps form the content of the next edition of the compendium on successful governance initiatives and best practices in States.

Brenda Gael McSweeney
UNDP Resident Representative
& UN Resident Coordinator

Contents

Section I Land, Water and Livelihood

Section II Human Development and Social Services

Section III Public Interface with Government

Contents

Section I

Land, Water and Livelihood

Introduction

Access to land and water resources is critical for improving the economic status of the poor and the marginalised. It is necessary to look at options that have been tried and tested for more productive use of available land and water, in order to ensure enhanced food security and bring about reduction of poverty.

Clearly, a part of the land and water problem is the increasing demand for these resources for domestic, industrial and agricultural purposes – a direct response to an increasing population and more intensive use and consumption. In India, agriculture alone accounts for 70 per cent of total water usage–mainly for crop irrigation. Land and water are going to be constraints in the future for improving productivity in agriculture. Recognising this, the Approach Paper to the Tenth Five-Year Plan recommends a major revival of public investment in irrigation capacity and water management. Initiatives in watershed development, water management, sustainable land practices based on community participation and institutional improvements are therefore important.

Globally, land and water management have emerged as crucial issues for ensuring the sustainability of livelihoods of people depending on them. GEO-2000, a specially commissioned survey by the United Nations Environment Programme, envisages a holistic approach towards the management of land and water mechanisms. This includes the coordination of the management of land and water resources, establishment of secure land and water property rights where these do not exist, reorganisation of policies at the river-basin level, introduction of concepts of shared and equitable water use, and alternatives to the use of marginal land.

This section covers integrated watershed development projects in Himachal Pradesh, Madhya Pradesh and Rajasthan. The Indo-German Changar project, located at the foothills of the Himalayas in Himachal Pradesh, represents a good example of successful harmonisation of socio-economic development with ecological sustainability. The Rajiv Gandhi Watershed Management project in Madhya Pradesh is a successful example of a mission approach that effectively connects policy-makers at all levels with the beneficiaries. The Bundi Canal project in Rajasthan highlights the criticality of redesigning existing canal systems to ensure the availability of water for irrigation to the tail-enders.

The Swajal experiment, from Uttar Pradesh and Uttaranchal, seeks to build community participation for the effective management of rural water and sanitation schemes. The benefits of resorting to cost-effective and farmer-owned-and-operated minor irrigation systems, such as shallow tube wells in regions with high groundwater tables, have been brought out in the case of Samridha Krishak Yojana of Assam. Tripura's Rubber Block Plantation experiment has emerged as an example of an initiative where the cohesive development of the rubber sector has helped in improving livelihood security as well as stabilising previously environmentally unfriendly cultivation practices.

The role of women in ensuring sustainable livelihoods has been demonstrated in two examples from Tamil Nadu and Kerala. The Tamil Nadu Women in Agriculture project is an innovative scheme that aims at improving living standards of poor farm households by imparting training to farm women on the latest agricultural techniques, while the participatory poverty reduction model, which identifies women as key actors, has been highlighted in the study of Kudumbashree in Kerala.

Interventions discussed in this section tend to share the following characteristics:

- A sense of community ownership and responsibility.
- A participatory bottom-up approach in which communities exercise control.
- Transparency in operations and effective dissemination of information.

The need is to learn from the success stories, and look at the best context-specific options for up-scaling and replication of these models where conditions are appropriate in other states.

CHAPTER 1

Community Contracting in Rural Water and Sanitation

Swajal, Uttar Pradesh & Uttaranchal

Introduction

The Swajal approach of integrating rural water supply and environmental sanitation is implemented jointly by the Government of Uttar Pradesh and the World Bank. This six-year project (1996-2002) represents a paradigm shift in terms of delivery of sustainable water supply and environmental sanitation facilities. The project is being implemented in 1000 villages in seven districts of the Bundelkhand region, 19 districts across the rest of Uttar Pradesh, as well as 12 districts of the Kumaon and Garhwal region in Uttaranchal state. The project has been planned to support a package of investments and a process of policy reforms intended to deliver sustainable health and hygiene benefits to the rural population. The investments are designed to improve knowledge, attitude and practices in the linkages between health and hygiene, improve water supply service levels (quantity, quality, equity, reliability, coverage and access), and improve the environment through safe disposal of human waste. The project is demand-responsive and community-driven. It ensures the active participation of community, especially women, in all activities of the project cycle.

Background

Many areas of Uttar Pradesh suffer from water scarcity, nearly one-third of the habitations not even receiving the basic service level of 40 lpcd prescribed by the Government of India. The rural water supply system includes traditional open wells, hand pumps, piped water supply schemes with treatment plants and private connections. Over one-third of these are out of order at any given time due to lack of maintenance. The process of decentralisation of rural water supply systems has been confined to handing over of hand pumps to village panchayats, which are responsible for repairs as well. Further, sanitation level in the state is considerably lower than the national average, with only about 2.5 per cent of the total population using latrines.

The Swajal project was the first initiative in Uttar Pradesh that involved rural communities assisting non-governmental organisations (NGOs) in planning, implementing and maintaining water supply and sanitation systems at the village level. Village selection is transparent and is based on criteria such as demand, need, technical feasibility, economic viability and social and environmental soundness. The project cycle is for a period of 33 months, and consists of three distinct phases: pre-planning, planning and implementation, each overlapping the other.

All project components are implemented by the Project Management Unit (PMU) of the Department of Rural Development, government of Uttar Pradesh. The PMU is assisted by 10 District Project Management Units (DPMUs), eight in the hills (Pithoragarh, Bhimtal, Srinagar (Garhwal), Almora, Bageshwar, Chamoli, Uttarkashi and Dehradun and two in the Bundelkhand region (Jhansi and Banda).

Objectives

The specific objectives of the project are to:

- Assist the government of Uttar Pradesh in identifying and implementing an appropriate policy framework to promote long-term sustainability of the rural water supply and environmental sanitation sector.
- Deliver sustainable health and hygiene benefits to the rural population through improvements in water supply and environmental sanitation services.
- Improve rural incomes through income-generating opportunities for women.
- Test alternatives to the current supply-driven delivery mechanism.
- Promote sanitation and gender awareness.

Salient features

Pre-planning

Selection of support organisations

The project starts with a pre-planning phase that lasts a year, and includes the selection of villages and support organisations (SOs), i.e. the shortlisted NGOs who act as social intermediaries, and mobilise the community. Field visits are undertaken by the DPMUs to ensure that each SO (1) is legally registered; (2) has a constitutional provision to engage in rural water supply and environmental sanitation service delivery and related activities; (3) has audited and certified accounts; (4) has a proven track record of at least three years' experience in rural water supply and environmental sanitation or community development activities evidenced by the satisfactory completion of a participatory and demand-driven project; and (5) has demonstrated staffing capacity to carry out the proposed services or ability to procure such staffing capacity.

Panchayati Raj institutions (PRI) model

To promote sustainability of rural water supply and sanitation systems, the project has involved the rural communities in planning, constructing and maintaining these facilities. Panchayats provide assistance both for community development and engineering support to the communities at all stages of the project. Public sector organisations like the Uttar Pradesh Jal Nigam, private firms, NGOs, etc., act as SOs. The project has also tried gram panchayats as SOs. Involvement of panchayats is expected to reduce the cost of implementation, making the project replicable on a wider scale.

Planning

Community mobilisation activities

Community mobilisation activities form an essential part of the project planning phase and are expedient to the formation of the village water and sanitation committee (VWSC), which consists of 7-12 members. The committee is democratically elected and is representative of the user community, with a minimum of 20 per cent reservation for scheduled caste/ scheduled tribes and a 30 per cent reservation for women.

Another feature in the community participation process is the formulation of three community action plans (CAPs). These outline the process by which communities would implement the project, based entirely on their needs.

- The *Technical Plan* incorporates the construction of the water supply scheme, latrines and drainage, and the village environmental action plan (VEAP).
- The *Contribution and Management Plan* includes monitoring and evaluation, operation and maintenance, and cash and labour contribution plans.
- The *Community Empowerment Plan* involves hygiene & environmental sanitation awareness, women's development initiatives and non-formal education plans.

These plans are discussed in a community-wide 'agree-to-do meeting', where consensus is sought by the VWSC from all sections of the community. The SO and DPMU staff place the choice of technologies for the water supply and sanitation (WSS) scheme before the community, which selects the most suitable process based on availability of resources.

Box 1.1 **SARAR**

The men folk of village Sinwalgaon have proved that they are equal partners in managing household chores. Sundays have been declared a holiday for women. For men, it is a day to prove their ability to manage household chores, and they are busy fetching water, firewood and fodder. This reversal of roles is a result of the participatory technique called SARAR. It is a tool introduced in the Swajal project by the SOs to mobilise the community and get the beneficiaries to act together in group activities. The SARAR kit consists of games and other implements aimed at motivating the community, especially women, to take charge of their situation and come up with creative solutions to problems. This tool is being used effectively by an NGO, Parvatiya Jan Kalyan Samiti, Ranichauri, Tehri. It has helped to empower the village women and given them a voice in managing the affairs of their village.

Source: Government of Uttar Pradesh, Swajal Project, Uttar Pradesh/Uttaranchal Rural Water Supply and Environmental Sanitation Project, Department of Rural Development, Lucknow

During community mobilisation, an important tool used for gender sensitisation is SARAR (self-esteem, associative strength, resourcefulness, action planning and responsibility), where the communities engage in games based on problem analysis, investigation, sensitisation and community decision-making (Box 1.1).

Community empowerment plan

The community empowerment plan (CEP) accords greater decision-making powers to communities in the management of their water supply and sanitation schemes. Components of the CEP are outlined below:

- Non-formal education (NFE): NFE provides the community with information and functional literacy according to the needs expressed by them. The SOs generally use this as an entry tool in the planning phase. The community is divided into geographical clusters and activities are carried out cluster-wise.
- Hygiene & environmental sanitation awareness (HESA): HESA aims to reduce morbidity levels in the village by increasing awareness about disease and its prevention and by generating a demand for safe water and sanitation. Here the community decides health and hygiene standards to be adopted by them by evaluating local behaviour in aspects related to personal, domestic environmental hygiene and sanitation. The community also fixes certain performance indicators for itself after conducting periodical 'healthy home' surveys. Subsequently, it sets certain targets with regard to each of these indicators and proposes interventions to attain these targets.
- Women's development initiatives (WDI): These aim at empowering women by enhancing their capacities through the formation of representative grassroots bodies like self-help groups (SHGs) and Swajal Saheli Samoohs. These organisations support the VWSC in incorporating a gender perspective into water supply schemes. Women are trained to utilise the time saved from hitherto time-consuming activities such as collection of water and participate in economic activities. In May 2001 there were 1,435 SHGs in Swajal villages, which had mobilised savings of over Rs. 72 lakh. The aim of these community empowerment activities is to build the

capacities among village communities, who will then be in a position to take care of their development, not only in the water and sanitation sector but also in all spheres.

Project implementation

Village water and sanitation committees (VWSCs)

VWSCs are formed through a process of consensus. Clean-up campaigns are organised, along with sensitisation of the community on environmental sanitation issues. Engineering surveys are done and various water supply options are worked out. In a community-wide 'agree-to-do meeting', a water supply option is chosen by the community. A project report detailing the engineering design of the chosen water supply and sanitation systems is prepared by engineers of the SO with full participation of the community at every step. Apart from engineering design, the community draws up a set of community action plans detailing the ways in which the community proposes to tackle the sanitation issues, skill training, and non-formal education. The community also draws up the plan for contribution of cash or labour and construction of water supply and sanitation systems. Implementation is by all the three partners in the project – village community, SO and the PMU. A tripartite agreement clearly defines the roles and responsibilities of each partner. All capital funds of the PMU and the community are transferred to a joint account operated by the VWSC and SO.

Box 1.2 **Women's self-help groups**

The women in Sirauli Khan village were confined to household chores and were economically dependent on the household. The Swajal Project created awareness in the village through various methods like PRA mapping, games and other innovative ways. Women became aware that they had rights, and took a forthright step in fulfilling their aspirations by forming a self-help group (SHG) called Bibi Fatima SHG. It consists of 20 members who save Rs. 50 every month. The SHG has opened a bank account in the Oriental Bank of Commerce in Kichcha. Their motive for forming the SHG was initially to be trained in an income-generating activity and to avail of the facilities under the Private Rural Initiative Programme (PRIP) to increase their earnings.

The experience of one SHG member was that when her spouse was arrested by the police on a false allegation of robbery, she had to borrow Rs.3000 from the SHG in order to bail him out. Such a sum would have been unthinkable for anyone in the village community, which comprises labourers whose wages barely suffice to buy provisions for the family's daily meals. The women have resolved to make their SHG a life-long activity.

Sheetla SHG of Simayal village, Ramgarh block, headed by a woman Pradhan, is a success story in vegetable growing on a commercial basis. Besides being trained in vegetable production, the women also learned fruit and vegetable preservation methods, so that the excess produce was not wasted. The group, after all investments and expenses, has now saved Rs.11,000 in its account. Other SHGs from surrounding villages are drawing inspiration from them and also increasing their earnings by having their produce marketed by Mother Dairy.

Source: Government of Uttar Pradesh, Swajal Project, Uttar Pradesh/Uttaranchal Rural Water Supply and Environmental Sanitation Project, Department of Rural Development, Lucknow

Strategies

Cost sharing

One of the most innovative and significant features of the Swajal Project is that communities demonstrate their demand for the water and sanitation facilities by sharing the capital cost of the facilities. Cost sharing includes: (i) a 10 per cent share in the capital cost, contributed in the form of cash and labour in varying amounts, depending on the region and type of technology selected; and (ii) operation and maintenance (O&M) financed entirely by the community, of which 50 per cent is collected during the planning phase as testimony of their commitment to the scheme. The following methods have been used to raise additional resources and facilitate O&M:

- VWSC has generated revenue for the O&M fund by selling water, purchasing tent-house equipment and renting it out at a fixed charge.
- In some villages, when a substantial O&M amount is collected, it is deposited in a fixed deposit in the bank and expenses are met from the interest accrued.
- VWSC bye-laws for this activity are framed and adopted by the village community and made known to all so that there is no confusion in their administration.
- Regular cluster-wise meetings are held to review O&M collection and address all problems.
- Printed receipts are issued to all payees and records are maintained.
- The village maintenance worker is trained in O&M and paid a monthly fee, which is decided by the community and monitored by the VWSC.
- Women and SHGs actively assist the VWSV in O&M collection by motivating defaulters and giving loans to those who cannot bear the expenses.

The cost-sharing component of Swajal has generated a sense of ownership of the WSS scheme in the community and has enabled them to operate and maintain the facilities that have been created.

Community contracting

Another unique feature of the project is community contracting, whereby the project has to come up with innovative methods of facilitating community procurement of goods, works and services. The village community, DPMU and SO engineers arrive at the best possible rates for material and labour based on a market survey. All the materials are procured from authorised dealers or manufacturers to ensure quality and quantity (Box 1.3).

Box 1.3 **An example of community procurement**

The all-woman VWSC of village Kamtoli in Almora district has set an exemplary record in community procurement. The chairperson, Shanti Malda, went with the engineer of the concerned support organisation to ascertain the quality of goods purchased for construction. On examination of the procured pipes, she found that those on the top were of good quality whereas those underneath were relatively inferior. She insisted on opening all the sealed packages and returned all the goods that were not up to the standard. This procedure has since been adopted by several VWSCs during procurement.

Source: Government of Uttar Pradesh, Swajal Project, Uttar Pradesh/Uttaranchal Rural Water Supply and Environmental Sanitation Project, Department of Rural Development, Lucknow

Choice of technology

The rural water supply (RWS) and latrine components of the project provide choices to consumers in terms of type of technology and service level. In the hilly region, this includes piped water supply schemes, captured springs with hand pumps, rainwater harvesting and spring development (including combinations of technologies most suited to local conditions). In the Bundelkhand region and foothills, water supply choices include piped water schemes from tubewells, dug wells, surface sources (where required) and hand pumps. A typical choice for latrine technology is twin pit pour flush system. The environmental sanitation component focuses on local behaviour change, personal, domestic and environmental sanitation improvements, including drainage, garbage, soak and compost pits, and catchment protection.

Training

Three agencies impart training and ensure smooth functioning of the water supply and sanitation schemes—the Centre for Development Studies, Uttar Pradesh Academy of Administration, Nainital, for community development training initiatives; the University of Roorkee on behalf of the Project Management Unit (PMU) organises training of technical components like survey and design; and in the villages the SOs organise various training programmes on community development activities.

Impact

According to a sample survey conducted by the PMU, Department of Rural Development, government of UP, the Swajal project has ensured direct benefits to about eight lakh rural inhabitants. It is estimated to cover about 12 lakh inhabitants as populations rise to design levels. The project has also made considerable impact both at the policy and the project level. The following are a few highlights:

- Increased access of women and young children to improved, adequate, and safe water and sanitation facilities, which in turn have had a positive impact on their health and productivity.
- A positive effect on the environment, arising from improved ecological conditions in watershed areas, which has increased the availability and quality of water.
- Reduced bacterial contamination of the environment due to improved hygiene and sanitation practices, controlled disposal of human wastes and better environmental management.
- Improved quality and sustainability of water sources due to catchment protection.
- Community capacity for self-reliance and independence for VWSCs developed as a result of training.

Short-term impact

- Women's representation in VWSC has been consistently above the norm of 30 per cent reservation for them.
- The drainage systems built in each village serve as source protection, as well as help in mosquito and disease control.
- Net coverage of latrines has risen from 7 per cent to 34 per cent after the introduction of Swajal.
- Catchment protection prevents contamination from surface pollutants, potentially recharging the source and preventing erosion.

Long-term impact

- The number of NGOs involved in the project has increased from 19 to 80 over the past five years. In the process of project implementation several NGOs have also built their capacity and infrastructure. In the long run, such capacity building and strengthening of the NGO sector will lead to healthy pressure on government delivery systems and also stimulate private initiative in various development sectors.
- The VWSC has developed as a novel responsibility centre in the village without upsetting the institution of gram panchayat.
- The Uttar Pradesh Jal Nigam has agreed to take up several villages and execute the water supply systems on the Swajal pattern.
- In the proposed experimental batch-3X, two private organisations are being involved as SOs. Experience gained from this will be a major input to the proposed sector study/reforms in terms of identifying the level and nature of private sector participation in the rural water supply and sanitation sector.
- At government of Uttar Pradesh level, the responsibility of rural water supply has been transferred from the Department of Urban Development to the Department of Rural Development, and consequently there has been devolution of several development functions to the gram panchayat level.
- NGOs that work as SOs in the project areas have been major beneficiaries of Swajal. There has been a phenomenal increase in the their fund-handling capacity. As of the year 2000, an average of about 80 lakh per annum was being handled by the NGOs. SOs have built good capacity to keep accounts, which will have long-term benefits while working with similar government-funded projects.

The macro-level impact of the Swajal project can be analysed from the project as well as policy level.

Project-level impact

- *Changing village dynamics:* Women, as key stakeholders, have begun to express themselves more vociferously. Communities, independent of their headmen, have begun asserting their rights and are more aware of their needs.
- *Transparency and reduction in corruption levels:* The transparency in dealings that characterises the Swajal project has led to unanimous demand that all village dealings be conducted along similar lines, leaving little room for corrupt practices and the misappropriation of village funds.
- *Sensitisation of PMU staff:* The process of dealing with SOs and village committees has inculcated a degree of sensitivity within government units, fostering a demand-driven, people-centric approach.

Policy-level impact

- *Influence on national policy:* The Swajal project represents a paradigm shift in terms of delivery of sustainable water supply and environmental sanitation facilities. Key policy makers have been taking notice of the capacity building and partial cost recovery angles of the project. The Rajiv Gandhi National Drinking Water Mission of the government of India is designed on similar lines as the Swajal model.

- The success of the Swajal project has prompted the government of India to earmark 20 per cent of funds provided to state governments for implementing projects on similar lines.
- *Influence on the Uttar Pradesh Jal Nigam:* The UPJN, a centralised government organisation, responsible for the existing delivery of rural water supply in Uttar Pradesh, is making efforts to strengthen its community development activities, as well as to become more responsive to its beneficiaries, as demonstrated by the success of Swajal.
- *The PMU model being used for joint forest management:* The PMU model is being used as the basis of joint forest management projects in Uttar Pradesh. The use of NGOs as an interface between local communities and the government, formation of village communities and community participation methods are some of the strategies replicated from the Swajal project.

By developing procedures for the public funding of demand-driven, community-based development, the Swajal project will enable wider replication of sustainable rural water and sanitation facilities, which has not been possible through top-down public programmes.

Summary

Swajal was initiated in 1996 as a six-year project in 26 districts of Uttar Pradesh and 12 districts of Uttaranchal. The main objectives of the project were to identify and implement an appropriate policy framework to promote long-term sustainability of the rural water supply and environmental sanitation sector and deliver sustainable health and hygiene benefits to the rural population through improvements in water supply and environmental sanitation services.

The project has not only improved rural water supply and sanitation facilities, but also empowered village communities, and enhanced community participation through confidence building. It has improved female participation in various economic activities through the formation of women's SHGs. Components of Swajal such as SARAR, integration of the PRI model, and community mobilisation activities have helped generate a sense of ownership in the minds of the villagers and empowered women.

The cost-sharing strategy is the most innovative and significant feature of the project, in which communities have to demonstrate the demand for the water and sanitation facilities by sharing the capital cost of the facilities. This generates a sense of ownership of the WSS scheme in the community and enables them to operate and maintain the facilities.

Replicability

The Swajal model highlights the benefits of partnership between the village community, NGO and the government. The government mainly takes on the role of facilitator. The fact that the communities were taken into confidence has created a demand for the water supply and sanitation facilities and contributed towards capital cost and maintenance. There is an enormous amount of capacity building in communities and NGOs.

By introducing several innovations in a hitherto stagnant situation, the project has proved to be not only applicable but also replicable (Box 1.4).

Box 1.4 **Community mobilisation at its best**

A scheduled caste family in Kafalkot village (a Swajal village) was too poor to fix the doors and windows or the flooring of a house allotted to it under the Indira Awas Yojana. Hence the family was living in a cattle-shed. All households had submitted their up-front contributions. However, as this household did not have the resources to pay this amount, they were excluded from the list of beneficiaries.

When the pipeline excavation commenced in the village, the woman of this poor household valiantly came forward and contributed her labour even though she was not part of the scheme. She argued that even though she could not become part of this scheme she at least could contribute her share of the labour, if not the cash. The women of the village were deeply impressed by her reasoning and immediately called a cluster group meeting and collectively decided to bear the expenses of her cash contribution. In this way, they ensured that this family also became part of the scheme. In the same meeting, the woman also pledged that even after contributing her share of work as part of the up-front amount, she would continue to work as a construction labourer, so that she could pay back the amount incurred on her behalf by the other women.

The SO involved, Jan Sewa Sansthan, was highly appreciative of the woman's commitment as well as of the community's efforts in including this poor family in the scope of the project. This is a good example of positive community action and social mobilisation and a lesson on how all communities and VWSCs should function ultimately as grassroot level institutions.

Source: Government of Uttar Pradesh, Swajal Project, Uttar Pradesh/Uttaranchal Rural Water Supply and Environmental Sanitation Project, Department of Rural Development, Lucknow

A demand-responsive and community-based programme driven by transparent criteria and based on three pillars—community ownership; cost-sharing in capital and operation and maintenance; and community labour and community contracting can make grassroots governance a reality. The methodology of the project can be successfully replicated in other development areas. The project has succeeded in propagating the following best practices:

- Bringing water supply and environmental sanitation to the forefront as an extremely pertinent issue in improving health and hygienic conditions in rural areas and generating awareness among the opinion leaders of the state, as well as showcasing the programme for others to emulate.
- Creating a positive environment to facilitate the assimilation of grassroots-level efforts.
- Providing inputs to empower women and enhancing their decision-making role.
- Motivating community members to achieve programme goals, i.e. ownership and self-maintenance of water and sanitation facilities.
- Developing an innovative participatory approach that provides communities with a major decision-making role in development planning.
- Introducing partial capital cost recovery and full cost recovery for operation and maintenance.
- Integrating water supply service delivery with environmental sanitation by developing beneficiary awareness of the linkages between health and sanitation.
- Swajal project has also highlighted the issue of transparency in dealings and dissemination of maximum information. Transparency at all levels is believed to be the key to community

empowerment and sustainability—within PMU, within DPMUs, between PMU and DPMUs, DPMUs and SOs, SOs and VWSCs, and between VWSCs and user communities.

Contact

Director
Project Management Unit
The Swajal Project (Department of Rural Development, Government of Uttar Pradesh)
3, Fawn Brake Avenue
Sarojini Naidu Marg
Lucknow – 226001
Tel.: +91-522-239 428
Fax: +91-522-237 709
E-mail: swajal@lwl.vsnl.net.in
Website: www.swajal.org

CHAPTER 2

Integrated Watershed Development

Rajiv Gandhi Watershed Management Mission, Madhya Pradesh

Introduction

Watershed development in Madhya Pradesh dates back to the 1950s. Madhya Pradesh was one of the states chosen after Independence for centrally sponsored programmes under the River Valley Project (RVP) and ravine reclamation. Later, programmes such as the Drought Prone Areas Programme (DPAP), Integrated Watershed Development Programme (IWDP) and National Watershed Development Project for Rainfed Areas (NWDPRA) were also initiated in the state. Programme activities typically concentrated on constructing structures to arrest soil and water erosion, water harvesting and reducing biotic pressure to enhance land productivity. People's stake and their participation in planning and management of watershed development activities were not central to the process.

It was only in 1994 that a change in strategy was adopted. All the programmes being implemented in the state were combined under the umbrella of the Rajiv Gandhi Watershed Management Mission (RGWMM). The world's largest watershed programme, RGWMM covers 3.4 million hectares in undivided Madhya Pradesh, pooling resources from a range of centrally sponsored schemes.

Background

The links between poverty and environmental degradation have been identified as being crucial to improving the productivity and income of the people residing in rural areas. The Rajiv Gandhi Watershed Management Mission, initiated in 1994, aims at improving the land and water resources in environmentally degraded villages. The larger goal is to move watershed management from being a technocentric programme to a people's movement. RGWMM has, therefore, adopted direct people's participation as a core element of its strategy. The institutional arrangements, procedures and processes adopted for programme implementation mark a reversal from the past, and are geared to a participatory bottom-up approach, in which communities exercise control over programme activities at each stage and government and non-government agencies play catalysing, facilitating and coordinating roles. An easily accessible repository of inter-disciplinary inputs drawn from line departments, NGOs, sectoral experts and research and academic institutions has been prepared to inform planning and implementation.

Objectives

The specific objectives of the programme include:

- Environmental regeneration and improvement of environmental resource base as a source of labour-intensive growth, while augmenting productive capacities, increasing resource-use efficiency and correcting regional and rural-urban imbalances.
- Integration of poverty reduction and environmental regeneration through participatory watershed management.
- Provision of livelihood security to resource-poor households through just and sustainable access to basic needs such as food, fodder, fuel and water.
- Location-specific interventions, given the diverse natural resource and socio-economic conditions across the state.

Salient features

Project set-up

The Rajiv Gandhi Watershed Management Mission is registered as a society under the Madhya Pradesh Societies Registration Act, 1973. As a registered society, it is mandated to coordinate the watershed development efforts of various line departments in the state; pool resources and expertise readily available to create synergy and lend focus to interventions; and work towards building an appropriate environment for sustainable people-centred interventions.

There are institutions for watershed development at three levels: the state, district and village. At the state level, the Mission Coordinator is the Secretary to the Chief Minister and therefore, the project is supervised directly by the Chief Minister himself. In addition, an Empowered Committee chaired by the state's Chief Secretary ensures inter-departmental coordination and administrative support. A full-time Director heads the RGWMM. The Director is assisted by personnel deputed from various departments (Fig. 2.1).

At the district level, the Collector is the mission leader and is responsible for fund flow and project progress. The Chief Executive Officer (CEO) of the Zilla Panchayat (District Council) is directly responsible for the project and reports to the Collector. There are two committees at the district level—the District Watershed Advisory Committee (DWAC) and the District Watershed Technical Committee (DWTC).

The milli-watershed is the planning unit for RGWM activities and is identified by the DWAC. At the level of the planning unit, programme activities are managed by a Project Implementation Agency (PIA) selected by the DWAC. The PIA is normally a government department or an NGO, and is responsible for operationalising the programme at the level of the planning unit. The PIA Project Officer (PO) is either a class II government official or drawn from the NGO PIA. PIA members from various line departments assist the PO. The PIA members facilitate and coordinate village-level activities.

At the village level, village watershed committees (VWCs) plan and execute the programme. VWC members are usually from user groups (UGs), self-help groups (SHGs) and water thrift and

Fig. 2.1 **RGWMM institutional structure**

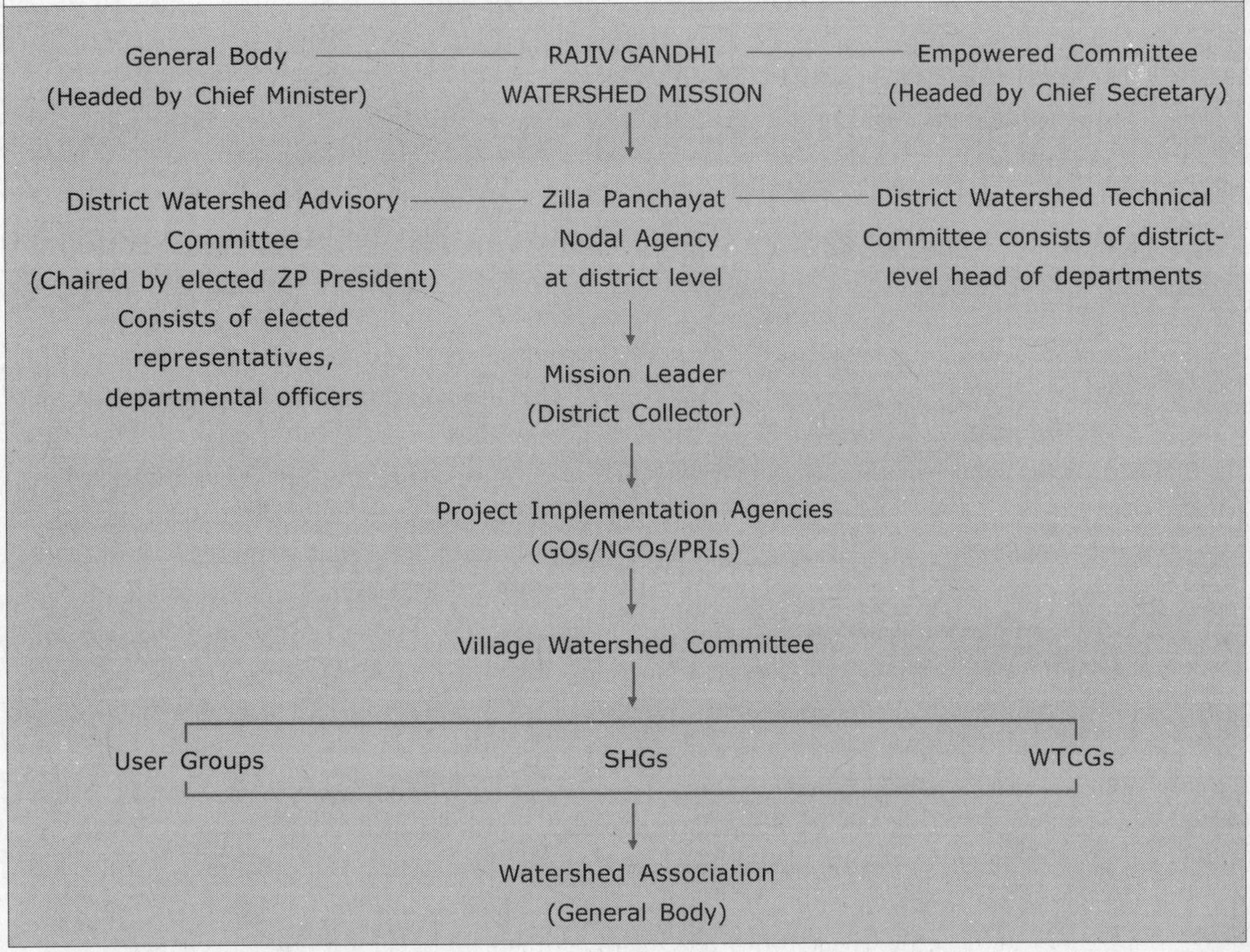

credit groups (WTCGs), as well as from the panchayat. The UGs, SHGs and WTCGs also plan and undertake various components of the programme at the village level.

Programme activities and management

Programme activities in a district commence with the formation of DWAC and DWTC. The DWAC plays a central role in selecting milli-watersheds for intervention. Milli-watersheds span an area of 5,000-10,000 ha and are divided for operational purposes into micro-watersheds of 500-1,000 ha. They are selected on the basis of low availability of drinking water, declining agricultural productivity, increasing fallow lands, higher SC/ST population and lower wage rates, using geo-coded maps. Proximity to treated watershed areas is another recommended criteria for milli-watershed selection. The PIA manages programme activities at the milli-watershed level. There is provision for undertaking entry point activities in the village during the preparatory phase, in which immediate and pressing village-level concerns are addressed, to gain public confidence. The entry point activities have to be proposed by the gram sabha.

Participatory rural appraisal (PRA) is instrumental in identifying programme activities at the village level and individuals likely to benefit from them. These individuals are organised into groups. Typically, three types of groups are identified: UGs of beneficiary farmers; SHGs; and WTCGs of women who wish to undertake savings, credit and income-generation activities.

The VWC is the key programme-specific institution at the village level and is registered with the District Rural Development Agency (DRDA). Among its key activities are the preparation and implementation of village-level plans; collection of contributions from villagers for a fund created for maintenance of programme assets; developing appropriate benefit-sharing arrangements; promotion of WTCGs; and assisting community mobilisation and other efforts of PIA members.

Available sectoral funds from the DPAP, IWDP and 50 per cent funds from the Employment Assurance Scheme are pooled at the district level. The programme guidelines stipulate a norm of about Rs. 4,000 per ha. About 75 per cent of this amount is to be expended by the VWCs. The remaining amount is released in instalments over three years to the PIAs. Allocations earmarked in the first year are the highest since these include expenditure on entry point activities (about 5 per cent), community mobilisation (4 per cent), village-level training and administrative expenses (3 per cent). It is interesting to note that the relative share of allocations towards administrative head is maintained in the first two years and increased in the third to 4 per cent. Allocations on community organisation and village training are reduced from the second year to one per cent each. Thus, the PIA budgetary allocations are considerably lower in the subsequent years.

Villagers make a certain minimum contribution, in the form of cash, labour or material, to the programme activities. Contributions for community works on public lands are provided for at 5 per cent of the estimated cost of works. A similar contribution is expected from SC/STs and persons below poverty line (BPL) for works on private lands. Contributions expected from other categories are higher, at about 10 per cent. The contribution is deposited into a development fund for maintenance of programme assets.

Impact

RGWMM is currently operational in all districts of Madhya Pradesh. By March 2000, an area of about 3.6 million ha, spread over 8,300 villages had been selected for treatment. The area earmarked for treatment, about a tenth of the total state area, is being covered largely under DPAP and EAS. Of this area, about 2.6 million ha had already been fully treated by March 2000 and programme activities were in various stages of completion in the remaining area. At the village level, about 1,10,000 UGs and 9,400 WTCGs had been formed as on March 2000 (Table 2.1).

RGWMM has contributed to increase in cultivated area, crop yield, and fodder and fuel availability in most districts. The total number of families to have benefited directly from programme activities is estimated to be about 1,63,000.

TARU, a consulting group, carried out an evaluation of RGWMM in Madhya Pradesh in the year 2000. A total of 58 project villages spread across 12 major agro-ecological zones of the state were covered. In addition to the project areas, 13 control villages spread over seven agro-ecological

Table 2.1 Area under RGWMM operation: an overview of coverage in March 2000

Item	Programme		Total
	EAS	DPAP	
Area selected for treatment ('000ha)	2,663	824	3,602
Area treated ('000 ha)	1,861	634	2, 577
No. of milli-watersheds selected	624	173	839
No. of micro-watersheds selected	4,461	1,253	5,961
No. of villages selected	6,057	2,016	8,318
No. of milli-watersheds covered	468	143	644
No. of micro-watersheds selected	3,201	976	4,343
No. of villages selected	3,927	1,516	5,607

Note: Figures for IWDP are not reported above but included in the total

Source: RGWMM, 2000

zones/ districts were also studied. The results of the study can be classified under environmental impact, livelihood-related impact and socio-political impact, the details of which are as under:

Environmental impact

- There has been an appreciable increase in cropped area in 46 of the 58 project villages compared to only eight of the control villages. Further, 13 out of 23 villages experienced an increase in both kharif and rabi cropped area were in the upper reaches, where the agriculture is risky due to poor soil and moisture conditions. Improvements in kharif crop areas in most project villages suggest that RGWMM interventions have contributed significantly.
- An increase was also reported in non-crop biomass area in eight of the 58 project villages, a phenomenon not evidenced in any of the 13 control villages. This is an indication of the contribution made by RGWM interventions. The increase in non-crop biomass area as a proportion of village area ranged from one to seven per cent of the total village area in most of these instances (Table 2.2) All the 17 project villages that reported a decline in non-crop

Table 2.2 Number of villages reporting change in non-crop biomass area (1994-99)

Reported change	Project villages		Control villages	
	Nos.	%	Nos.	%
Increase in non-crop biomass area	8	14		
No significant change in non-crop biomass area	33	57	10	77
Decline in non-crop biomass area	17	29	3	23
Total	**58**	**100**	**13**	**100**

Source : TARU Primary Study, 2000

Table 2.3 **Number of villages reporting change in well and handpump drying over March –June (1994-99)**

Month	No. of project villages reporting dry wells & hand pumps		No. of control villages reporting dry wells & hand pumps	
	1994	1999	1994	1999
March	22	14	5	5
April	37	31	7	7
May	52	51	12	12
June	47	47	12	12
Sample Base	58		13	

Source: TARU Primary Study, 2000

biomass area witnessed an increase in either kharif or rabi cropped area. This suggests that at least a part of the increase in cropped area in these villages has been at the expense of non-crop biomass area. The 8 project villages reporting an increase in non-crop biomass area witnessed increases in cropped area as well.

- There were 50 project villages where there was no positive change in non-cropped biomass area was reported. It could either be due to afforestation or fodder development interventions or both in all these villages.
- Water availability has been reported with reference to the period for drying up of wells and hand pumps. It is during this period, extending over March-June, that drinking water shortages are experienced in almost all study villages. RGWMM interventions appear to have contributed to the improvement in water availability (Table 2.3). The seven project villages, where no drying up of wells and hand-pumps took place, are spread over six study districts, indicating that their relatively better situation owes mainly to local factors. There has been no significant change in the number of project villages reporting drying of hand pumps and wells during May and June. This would suggest that while periods of well and hand pump drying have reduced significantly in some project villages,. problems experienced in May and June persist.
- An increase in irrigated area has also been reported in 38 of the 58 project villages (Table 2.4). Crop-mix change over the period of five years has been reported by about a fourth of the landed respondents in the project villages.

Livelihood-related impact

Traditional watershed programmes have been critiqued as being fundamentally inequitous as their benefits have been higher among medium and large farmers. Small and marginal farmers, with lands typically located in upper reaches, benefited to a lesser degree from earlier interventions and still fewer opportunities emerged for the landless. Under RGWMM's watershed-plus paradigm, opportunities have been created for these groups through afforestation and fodder development interventions. These are geared to augment employment opportunities in addition to direct wage employment opportunities during works. One of the major direct impacts on women has been in

Table 2.4 **Reported reasons for increase in irrigated area (1994-99)**

Reported reasons for increase in irrigated area in Last 5 Years	Project villages		Control villages	
	No.	%	No.	%
Watershed activities	23	40		
Private investment in irrigation facilities	9	16	7	54
Schemes other than RGWMM	6	10	2	15
No significant change in irrigated area	20	34	4	31
Total	**58**	**100**	**13**	**100**

Source: TARU Primary Study, 2000

terms of equal wages for labour provided under RGWMM. SHGs and WTCGs are intended to provide opportunities for investment in the non-farm sector, besides providing greater control over household level resources and decision-making power to women.

The direct wage employment opportunities provided through the RGWMM have provided immense relief to the landless and small and marginal farmers. These opportunities have made a significant contribution to household income, addressed immediate concerns at the household level and checked daily movement to urban centres in search of work. Direct wage employment availability for about 40-60 days per household per annum was reported by about half the landless respondents, translating into an annual income of Rs. 1,600-2,400 and leading to a temporary decline in daily movement to neighbouring urban centres in search of work.

Socio-political impact

RGWMM has created village-level institutions to plan, implement and manage interventions. These institutions have been created with the specific purpose of entrusting substantive responsibilities to the villagers so as to ensure location-specific, need-based planning that balances the concerns of multiple interest groups within the village; restore parity in government official-people relations; and build resource literacy and permanent interest in maintenance of assets. This approach is linked to the larger agenda of the Government of Madhya Pradesh for people-centred development, which includes empowerment of panchayats. SHGs and WTCGs are crucial instruments in this context, not only for economic benefits but also for the realisation of self-potential both as individuals and collectives.

One of the major achievements of RGWMM has been the emergence of leadership and management skill pools at the village level, which can potentially challenge established power structures and complement the Panchayati Raj agenda of the Government of Madhya Pradesh. Improved resource literacy is a key change ushered in the project villages by RGWMM activities. This is a result of the significant attention the RGWMM has received from public representatives and government officials, and numerous Jal Sammelans, government official-people interactions and training programmes. There is also an increased appreciation of the agenda for sustainable natural resource management in select quarters, especially among VWC presidents and secretaries.

The programme has led to increased control of women over household resources and decision-making through several measures, including formation of WTCGs and SHGs; reduced drudgery (in fetching water, fuel and fodder) through drinking water improvements, afforestation and fodder development interventions. Another key gain for women has been the parity in wages received.

Summary

The Rajiv Gandhi Watershed Management Mission, initiated in 1994, was designed to improve the land and water resources in environmentally degraded villages. The larger goal of the mission was to move watershed management from being a technocentric programme to a people's movement. RGWMM, therefore, adopted direct people's participation as a core element of its strategy. The programme is mandated to coordinate the watershed development efforts of various line departments in the state; pool resources and expertise readily available to create synergy and lend focus to interventions; and work towards building an appropriate environment for sustainable people-centred interventions. There are institutions for watershed development at three levels: the state, district and village. PRA is instrumental in identifying programme activities at the village level, as well as beneficiaries, who are organised into groups. Villagers have to make a certain minimum contribution, in the form of cash, labour or material, to the programme activities.

The programme has led to substantial improvements in environmental conditions, irrigation facilities and land-use patterns, which have led to an improvement in overall agricultural productivity. The direct wage employment opportunities provided through the RGWMM have provided immense relief to the landless and small and marginal farmers. These opportunities have made a significant contribution to household income, addressed immediate concerns at the household level and checked daily movement to urban centres in search of work.

One of the major achievements of RGWMM has been the emergence of leadership and management skill pool at the village level, which can potentially challenge established power structures and complement the Panchayati Raj agenda of the Government of Madhya Pradesh. Land-use changes and improved water availability as reported in some project villages may be expected to affect livelihood favourably, especially agriculture. On the other hand, there remain project villages where changes have been witnessed on a lower scale. Some of these can be ascribed to reasons which cannot be addressed in the current RGWMM framework, such as encroachments, migration, grazing and the declining stakes of small and marginal farmers in agriculture.

There are, however, other issues related to competing land-use claims, funding delays and adequacy of allocations, planning and efficacy of water-harvesting structures and the scale and protection of afforestation and fodder development interventions that the RGWMM is in a position to address. Terrain and land ownership patterns admittedly are key constraints for RGWMM interventions and would require development of location-specific technologies and interventions over time

Box 2.1 **The Jhabua experience**

Jhabua district of Madhya Pradesh borders Rajasthan and Gujarat. It is a district with great variations in social conditions, terrain and resource endowment. While parts of it through which the Narmada flows are reasonably well endowed in terms of soil quality (Deccan black soil suitable for cotton cultivation), water resources and settled agriculture (practised by the Bhils, Bhilalas and Patelias), the rainshadow region is extremely underdeveloped, largely due to soil erosion.

As a result, agriculture gives way to seasonal migration (*chait kaatana)* in search of livelihood for the small and marginal farmers. The emergence of canal-irrigated areas in the neighbouring regions and states has created pull effects that reinforce the push effect from degrading and marginal holdings in rainfed areas. The net effect of these phenomena is the increasing marginalisation of agriculture and high fluctuations in agricultural productivity in the rainfed areas of Jhabua. A significant proportion of the small and marginal landholders' time is spent away from the village, leading to low stakes in land improvement. With agricultural income deemed uncertain, it is indeed a daunting task to check seasonal migration, especially among small and marginal farmers.

Given this situation, it is remarkable that the Jhabua experience in watershed management has been widely hailed as a success story, where the arid and semi-arid regions have been transformed with improved water levels, cropping patterns and intensity. The obsession with reporting success stories and lack of systematic evaluation of process and impact is not borne from the experience in Jhabua. Jhabua marks an instance where independent evaluation studies have been undertaken. The inputs from such studies have been well received within the district leadership, and attempts are being to reformulate strategies in the light of findings. These have also been supplemented with discussions and workshops, where crucial issues pertaining to programme implementation have been highlighted, problem areas discussed and action points formulated.

through constant experimentation. These assume importance in the light of limited impacts in select locations, particularly with respect to increases in cropped, non-crop biomass and irrigated areas. A more direct approach to ensure increased control of women over household resources and decision-making has been in the form of WTCGs. These WTCGs, much like SHGs, have suffered from myriad problems, notwithstanding isolated successes in Jhabua and elsewhere (Box 2.1).

Replicability

Replicability of a development project is ensured only if proper systems and procedures are put in place to ensure its smooth implementation. Such systems help in making the project sustainable and self-reliant. The following features guarantee these characteristics to the RGWMM.

Monitoring mechanisms

RGWMM has sought to institutionalise a rigorous reporting system of gathering village-level data on a monthly basis and compiles it at the milli-watershed and district level to assess progress and shortcomings. The standard reporting format developed earlier has been adapted at the district level to reflect the priorities of the district leadership but typically contains information on area treated, progress of works, financial allocations and expenditure, and number of village-level groups formed. There also is a culture of introspection, and field data is considered to have utility beyond mere reporting.

The management of RGWMM activities is crucially dependent on the district leadership, availability of human and financial resources, quality of training and capacity building efforts, and monitoring, control and feedback mechanisms. Cumulatively, these are expected to ensure pursuit of the stated objectives in the right spirit, prepare programme functionaries and village-level institutions for the anticipated challenges and current and future roles, and ensure opportunity for identifying shortcomings and effecting mid-course corrections. Analysis on these aspects indicates significant achievements with respect to internalisation of programme spirit, attunement to unconventional demands, emphasis on training and capacity building and institutionalisation of monitoring mechanisms.

Entry point activities

Before starting a project, a conducive environment needs to be developed, which not only gives credibility to the project but also generates adequate interest among the participants. This is where the entry point activities play a crucial role.

In RGWMM, entry point activities are commonly undertaken parallel to VWC selection. These activities were envisaged to address pressing needs at the village level, build PIA credibility and set the tone for future action. There are indications that these objectives have been fulfilled at the village level with investment in community infrastructure such as hand pumps, ponds, and buildings in most of the project villages.

Innovative attempts to address the situation are in evidence. These include ensuring villagers' contribution for community infrastructure; baseline data collection at the household level so as to identify household-level problems; and hiring of female professionals to interact with women. These have helped in creating the right environment for the future and indicate the willingness of programme functionaries to alter functioning styles in the context of emergent realities.

Equity and transparency

Equity and transparency are key emphasis areas for the RGWMM. Learning from past experience of watershed programmes, RGWMM envisages arrangements which allow the poor and women a greater say in activity selection, planning and representation in the VWCs. Transparency has been ensured through requirements to present action plans, accounts and progress statements to the Gram Sabha. The emphasis on equity and transparency has been premised on the fact that the involvement of the larger village community is necessary to ensure that benefits reach a wide constituency and genuine stake is developed among them for the future.

The Rajiv Gandhi Watershed Management Mission has succeeded in highlighting the following features for its success:

- Creation of a right environment for the people to participate and take adequate interest in the activities.

- Involving people from different fields, including politicians, bureaucrats, technical experts, NGOs and the beneficiaries, thus lending credibility and accountability to the programme.
- Ensuring equity by involving and addressing the specific needs of different groups like the landless labourers and women.
- Emphasising transparency through robust monitoring mechanisms like periodic reporting and accounting system.
- Stressing the need for continuous training and capacity building activities.
- Empowering people by generating awareness and developing leadership.

Contact

Mr. Manish Rastogi
Mission Director
Rajiv Gandhi Watershed Management Mission
E-mail: rgmwm@vsnl.com, directwater@hotmail.com

CHAPTER 3

People Centred Eco-Development in the Himalayan Foothills

Indo-German Changar Project, Himachal Pradesh

Introduction

Forest cover in Himachal Pradesh is an extremely important factor in determining the environmental balance, economic growth and economic well-being of north-western India at large. Besides allocating plan outlays for the forest sector towards maintenance and afforestation programmes, the government is attempting to involve the local population in the process of afforestation. The Changar area has a substantial proportion of underutilised rainfed but degraded land. The poor and weaker sections in most villages own such land as their only assets. In contrast, there are regions with rich pockets of mixed forests and fruit trees on village common lands. These regions have been fulfilling the nutritional, medical and fodder needs of local villages for many years. However, most of the surplus fruit output is wasted.

The Indo-German Changar Eco-Development Project (IGCEDP), Palampur, identified the availability of such surplus produce as a comparative advantage for the area, which could be converted into the centre of an income-generation initiative. The Eco-Income Generation Programme of the project involved two voluntary organisations—New Hope (Kangra) and Himalaya Bachao Samiti (Chamba)—in demonstrating a possible alternative. The IGCEDP is jointly implemented by the Duetsche Gesellschaft fuer Technische Zusammenarbeit (GTZ), German Agency for technical cooperation and the Himachal Pradesh Eco-Development Society (HPEDS). The financing of the programme is by the Government of Himachal Pradesh and the Government of the Federal Republic of Germany.

Background

Eco-development has become the key to diversification of sustainable livelihood options for the poor villagers of Changar region, located in Kangra district of Himachal Pradesh. The villagers, who depend heavily on natural resources from common/forest lands, face innumerable problems, including scarcity of drinking water, fodder and fuel, low production on cultivated lands, low milk production, labour shortages, poor technical back-stopping by government departments, massive soil erosion and inadequate infrastructure. Additionally, the mountainous terrain of Kangra district is characterised by geomorphologic instability, rugged topography, and extreme water scarcity during summer, which has rendered agriculture an unsustainable livelihood option.

Table 3.1 Socio-economic features of the Changar project area

Indicator	Units
Project Area	428 sq. km
Number of villages	578
Total population	130,000
Population growth p.a	8 per cent
Average land holding	0.74 ha
Livestock population	80,000
Household size	4.8 persons

Source: Indo-German Changar Eco-Development Project, November 1996

The problems perceived during implementation of the project were a lack of cohesion in the community, high dependency on subsidies, very low contribution of the community towards the rehabilitation of remote areas, lack of service orientation of line departments and a lack of qualified supporting NGOs. In addition to these bottlenecks, social constraints such as labour shortages, heavy workload of women and individualistic behaviour of villages, necessitated a paradigm shift from existing project approaches.

The Indo-German Changar Eco-Development Project (IGCEDP) was initiated in early 1993 in the Changar region. The project covered a population of 1.3 lakh in 578 villages. The average size of a land holding was less than one hectare (Table 3.1).

The villages consist of three types of households:

- Resource-poor farm households, owning only a small patch of land, who depend largely on the common property resources and on income from wage labour.
- Marginal farm households, that depend on the forests and common property resources to a large extent.
- Small farm households, that get highest remittances while meeting most of their requirements (food, fuel wood and fodder) from their own farm.

Objectives

- To empower people in the project area to manage their natural resources for the improvement of their livelihood options with the help of HPEDS and other institutions.
- To enable, motivate and mobilise other institutions working in the field of eco-development to adopt a people-oriented approach.

The project thus had two goals—a project goal, which was reduction of ecological degradation in the Changar area, and a development goal, which was improvement of natural resource management that would lead to better living conditions in the project area. HPEDS and other cooperative agencies have been the catalysts of development in the region. These societies have empowered the community towards realising the following objectives:

- Promoting self-help groups (SHG) amongst the villagers.
- Raising awareness of rights and duties in the community.
- Giving advice on sustainable management of natural resources.

- Imparting and rooting technical know-how in villages.
- Ensuring access of villagers to available services.

Salient features

The potential for development in the region centred around the existence of large tracts of degraded communal and forest lands available for developmental activities, improvement of land management, high potential for horticulture, diversification in farm management, small timber production along *nalas* (ditches) and eco-income generation activities (Box 3.1).

Box 3.1 **Supporting framework conditions**

Political will, conducive economic policies and an enabling legal and institutional framework are key contributors to the sustainability of development projects. In 1991, Himachal Pradesh introduced the new policy of joint forest management and planning. It assures local communities a fixed proportion of 25 per cent of the net timber sales from plantation areas and secures their rights in using the forest for fodder and fuel wood collection. This policy is a major step in granting more rights to people and creating a secure environment for the sustainable use of natural resources. It is viewed as a positive indicator of the overall trend of decentralisation in India.

Source: Indo-German Changar Eco-Development Project, November 1996

Project set-up

The project set-up consists of the villagers, their community-based organisations, Panchayati Raj Institutions (PRIs), non-government organisations (NGOs) and researchers from various research & development (R&D) organisations.

Joint forest management (JFM) schemes of the Forest Department were initially developed through the introduction of community forest management plans. These were jointly prepared and implemented by the villagers and the project/Forest Department and incorporated into the departmental forest management plans. Consolidation of joint forest management beyond the project period was thus achieved. The project ensured technical back-stopping and protection of plantations by supporting the efforts of the villagers to obtain rights to use the final product. Thus the project has ensured sustainability by involving the villagers in the management and protection of the forest cover surrounding their areas.

Implementation

- The implementation of the Changar project was based on the concept of the Integrated Resource Management Plan (IRMP). This plan followed the principles of watershed management while reflecting the natural resource development (NRD) priorities of the villagers. The role of women and marginalised groups was specially taken into consideration, and responsibilities and time frames for implementation were delineated. Thus, the IRMP reflected the contributions of all the groups involved in the project. It empowered resource users towards decision-making, implementation, as well as monitoring and evaluation, and imparted a sense of ownership of the project to the villagers.

- Villagers are often unable to access services provided by government organisations and R&D institutions. Simultaneously, these institutions lack adequate linkages to rural areas and are thus often unable to address 'real' grassroots problems. The project strategy focused on increasing the villagers' livelihood options through improved accessibility to and management of natural resources. This was facilitated by developing linkages between villagers, government organisations, NGOs, and R & D institutions (Fig. 3.1).
- The project applies the principles of watershed management in the village. The main tenets of these principles are: (a) village institution development mechanisms, e.g. village development committee (VDC), user groups; (b) development of technical support and local expertise at village level; and (c) strengthening of HPEDS, NGOs and line departments.

Strategies

Planning and implementation sequence

The planning and implementation of the project has a particular sequence. The first stage involves a situation analysis (Appendix 3.1). This involves six steps, viz., (1) awareness meetings and hamlet discussions, (2) participatory social appraisal, which provides 'livelihood information', (3) cross visits for institutional and technical know-how, (4) participatory rural appraisal, to prepare a draft village action plan, (5) village meetings for VDC and village maintenance and development fund (VMDDF) formation and (6) implementation of one need-based 'eco-logic' activity. The outcome of the situation analysis indicates whether the VDC is ready for cooperation. The situation analysis also depends on whether the VDC is ready for cooperation.

Once the VDC agrees, the second stage of the Integrated Rural Management Plan is strategised. This includes two steps: (1) updating of base map by applying the PRA results and (2) preliminary technical feasibility survey. These steps influence the issue-based workshops at village level and the general house meeting, which approves the IRMP. This is followed by the annual work plan as per IRMP, which prepares the techno-designs. The designs form a support for the implementation, the participatory monitoring and evaluation and updating of the future IRMP. The updating of the IRMP also depends on the annual plan that has been formulated. However, if the VDC is not ready for cooperation then it puts an end to the involvement of the IGCEDP in the village. Thus, the VDC plays a very important role both at the planning and implementation stage.

Implementation of natural resource management – I

- Rehabilitation of degraded areas: tree nurseries and community plantations.
- Improvement of productivity of farming systems: soil and water-conservation measures, fodder production, private lands and homestead horticulture.

Implementation of natural resource management – II

- Water resource development: repair and construction of perennial water sources.
- Eco-income generation: marketing support to village groups.
- Innovative activities: silage making and off-season quality fodder production.

Fig. 3.1 **Institutional structure**

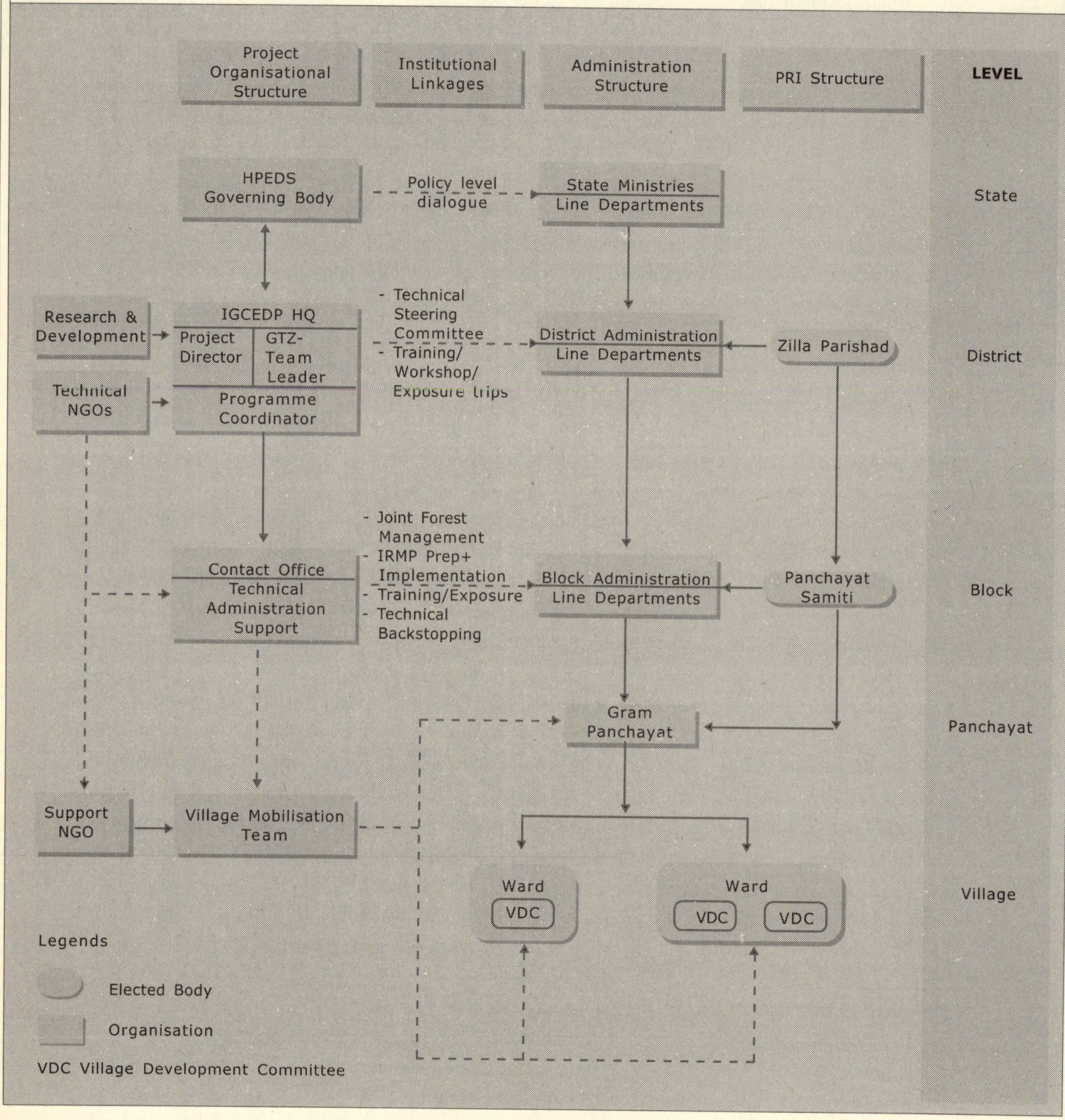

Samridhi initiative

Samridhi is a federation of village-based women's production groups (WPGs) registered as a cooperative, which aims towards capacity building and empowerment of women. Female producers gather fresh and graded handpicked wild fruits and undertake initial processing in their production centre in the village. These are conducted under strict quality control norms and are sent to the apex unit at Thakurdwara for finishing. This initiative involves the maximum of manual labour and uses the traditional skills of sun drying and natural preservation to produce nutritious and healthy foods. These are then tested for quality on the standards set by the FPO and PFA. The products are marketed under the brand name 'Changar', which is receiving a good response from consumers.

In 1995-96, Samridhi operated in a single cluster with just two WPGs and 16 women members. By 2000-01, this increased to three clusters, 15 WPGs and 182 members. Further, the wages earned by members have increased from Rs. 6250 to Rs. 43,5103. The Samridhi initiative ensures wages to all women producers, and the final profits are also used for the common good. They are also developing income-generating activities into sustainable round-the-year livelihood options, setting up literacy centres for illiterate women, implementing savings and credit schemes and providing social security through insurance cover.

Impact

The impact of the Changar project can be assessed from both socio-economic and ecological perspectives. At the macro level, the project has also effected policy-level and structural changes in the management of natural resources at the grassroots.

Socio-economic impact

Livestock management has become an integral part of the farming system, which is important not only for economic reasons (e.g. manure, agriculture) but also for socio-religious ones. Eco-development in Changar has been adapted to individual village-based NRD programmes, which are selected and implemented by applying watershed management principles. This allows for focused and need-based development at the village level and generates sustained community interest. It also takes into consideration the potential of the villagers for implementation, financial contributions and readiness to take over responsibility for management of the programmes.

The implementation of the NRD programmes has led to:

- Augmentation of drinking water and increase in grass production, which in turn has led to cohesion in communities and improved eco-awareness.
- Substantial increment in grass production, after early years of plantation enclosures, has in many villages motivated user groups to further strengthen their local management mechanisms (equitable grass distribution, bye-laws, etc.).
- A positive economic impact for progressive and interested farmers who have benefited directly from various NRD-related activities (e.g. individual tanks), has led to the refinement of IRMP preparation procedures.

However, large plantation enclosures and cut-and-carry practices from remote plantations have been to the disadvantage of the resource-poor and added to the workload of women. Similarly,

Box 3.2 **Community land management in Jikhla Behru**

Jikhla Behru is a small village in the heart of the project area. Women head most of its 32 families. Fifty-four per cent (45 ha) of the total 83 ha village land is community-owned. These commons are heavily degraded due to open grazing, and the effects of gully erosion are visible on different sites.

Jagdish Chand is one villager who was concerned about the deteriorating community lands. He realised that the annual decrease in the village water table was largely due to the vanishing vegetation on the commons. Chand saw a chance for betterment when IGCEDP offered its support in 1994. He convinced the villagers to close 10 ha of common land and plant local fodder tree species, including bamboo, to check soil erosion.

It has been noticed that as more and more people in Jikhla Behru are switching to a cut-and-carry system, fodder supply has increased significantly. Women, who were initially skeptical because of the reduced grazing grounds for cattle, now see the advantage of the new land management system in their village. Instead of walking long distances to their remote private pastures, they can cut fodder from nearby community land and keep the animals at home.

Source: Indo-German Changar Eco-Development Project, November 1996

individual activities benefiting only select groups (e.g., cattle shed renovation, stall-feeding) have sometimes affected the cohesion of the community and have ultimately led to waning interest in the project concept. This has led to the refinement of IRMP preparation procedures and consequently in the incorporation of user groups (Box 3.2).

Ecological impact

- Plantation, soil and water conservation activities have reduced and delayed surface runoff. While the impact of these activities in recovering degraded soils is typically intangible, studies have revealed that the carbon content of soil has increased in some sites from "poor" to "medium/ high" (about one per cent of weight) and that water availability in some villages has gone up.
- The impact of afforestation on degraded and eroded hillsides of the Changar watershed has resulted in tangible benefits for farmers and long-term benefits towards diversified natural re-growth. Forestry in the region concentrates on increasing the infiltration capacities and moisture content of the soil. Multi-purpose indigenous broadleaf species like *Grevia optiva* and *Bauhinia* have restored degraded lands and contributed towards the increase of fodder output in the region.
- The reduced nutrient input in plantations (no manure through grazing, continuous biomass removal in the shape of fuel wood, fodder, etc.) have been upgraded by adapted management systems.

Policy impact

- Participatory planning has proved effective in mobilising the village communities, in instances where the planning was process-oriented and where the community's NRD-priorities were met.

- Direct access of project experiences and findings to the government through the project governing body has proved effective in supporting policy-making.
- Village groups/organisations have been supported to plan and implement activities for the sustainable use of their natural resources.
- Locally adapted, sustainable NRD programmes have been developed for rehabilitation of degraded areas, improvement of productivity of the existing farming systems, water resource development and eco-income generation.
- The technical and social expertise of resource users in the sustainable use of natural resources and their corresponding linkages with the government and NGOs have been strengthened.
- Professional capacity of staff and other functionaries of HPEDS have been strengthened, and organisational structure and procedures of HPEDS have been developed.

Long-term impact

- IGCEDP is likely to increase the command of villagers due to certain features like full responsibility for planning, implementation and monitoring and evaluation.
- Development and improvement of NRD programmes.
- Technical know-how will be rooted in the villages through training of grassroots technical animators (village para-professionals).
- Expansion of village maintenance and development fund to include a savings and credit component.
- Linkages and cooperation with other sector departments, R&D agencies and NGOs.
- Further development and promotion of the joint forest management schemes.

Summary

The Indo-German Changar Eco-Development Project was introduced in early 1993 in the Changar region of Kangra district. The project covered a population of 1.3 lakh in 578 villages. It was formulated with an objective to empower the people in the project area to manage their natural resources for the improvement of their livelihood options with the help of HPEDS and other institutions. It was jointly financed by the Government of Himachal Pradesh and the Government of the Federal Republic of Germany.

The potential for development in the Changar region was around the existence of large tracts of degraded communal and forest lands available for developmental activities, improvement of land management, high potential for horticulture, diversification in farm management, small timber production along *nalas (*ditches) and eco-income generation activities. The Integrated Resource Management Plan (IRMP) followed the principles of watershed management while reflecting the natural resource development priorities of the villagers. The role of women and marginalised groups was specially taken into consideration, and responsibilities and time frames for implementation were delineated. The project strategy focused on increasing the villagers' livelihood options through improved accessibility to and management of natural resources. This was facilitated by developing linkages between various groups like the villagers, government organisations, NGOs, and R&D institutions.

The Samridhi initiative ensures wages to all women producers and the final profits are also used for the common good. They are also developing income-generating activities into sustainable round-the-year livelihood options, setting-up literacy centres for illiterate women, implementing savings and credit schemes and providing social security through insurance cover. The project, on the whole, has empowered resource users towards decision-making, implementation, as well as monitoring and evaluation, and imparted a sense of ownership of the project to the villagers.

Replicability

Eco-development is a long-term effort, which must be integrated into mainstream development activities. It necessitates the support of governmental and non-governmental actors. The project was tested across different institutional arrangements, from direct implementation in a somewhat parallel structure to full integration with PRIs. Thus, institutional development was process-oriented. The willingness of the community to participate in the schemes was also gauged.

It was also noted that the improvement of existing systems rather than introducing new systems, had a better chance for long-term survival. Empowerment of the villagers through institutional capacity building at village level (village development committees, user groups) and rooting of technical know-how at village level (village technicians/animators) were at the core of the programme.

The key to the success of the project lay in holding the attention of the villagers by addressing their priorities, without losing focus of the long-term goal of sustainable development. Economic upliftment is the biggest incentive for marginal groups to participate in eco-development activities. The programme's focus on eco-income generation activities has ensured sustainability and replicability of its schemes.

Contact

Dr. Silvio Decurtins, Indo-German Changar Eco-Development Project
P.O. Box 25, Palampur 176 061, India
Telephone: 91-1896-30567
Fax: 91-1896-30567
E-mail: decurtins@gtzindia.com
Website: www.gtz-asia-online.org

Appendix 3.1 **Planning and implementation sequence**

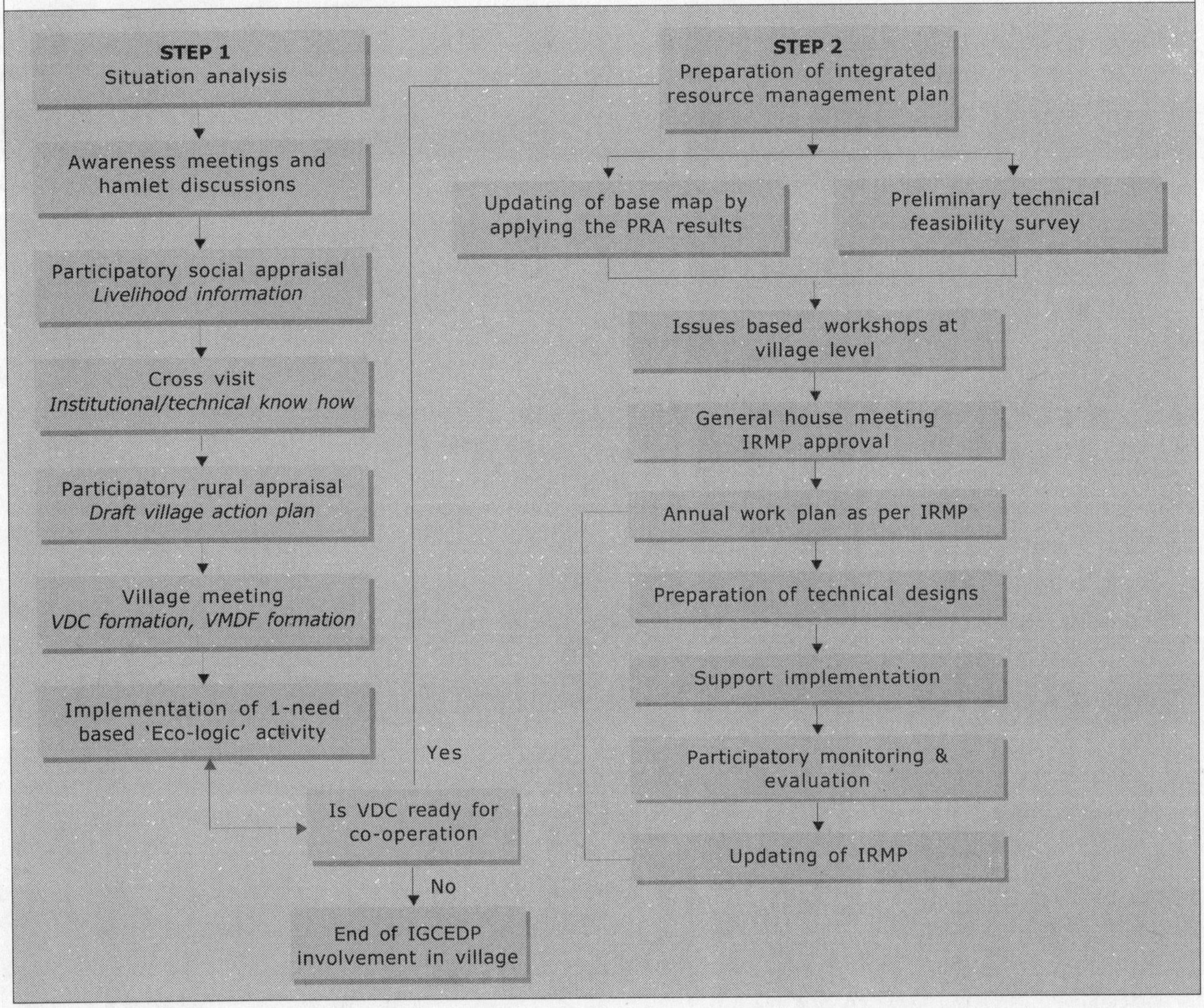

CHAPTER 4

Success with Shallow Tube Wells

Samridha Krishak Yojana, Assam

Introduction

As per the Basic Agricultural Statistics, 1997-98, the annual foodgrain production in Assam was about 36 lakh metric tonnes (LMT) against the requirement of about 44 LMT. There was a shortfall in productivity despite the fact that the net crop area of the state was 25.4 lakh hectares (ha) and the gross cropped area was 36.94 lakh ha, with cropping intensity being 145 per cent. The area under rice cultivation accounts for 68 per cent of the gross cropped area. The state required an additional production of 9.56 LMT to meet its annual requirement of rice. The low productivity was primarily due to annual floods, inadequate irrigation facilities and lack of research support.

To increase production at the state level, it was found necessary to give an impetus to production of summer rice in terms of both area and productivity and to ensure additional irrigation facilities, especially during the *rabi* (winter) season. The available irrigation facility in the state during the *rabi* season was only 2.73 lakh ha, which was far lower than the required level. The Samridha Krishak Yojna (SKY) was conceptualised to improve agricultural productivity, provide employment opportunities to the workforce in the rural areas and raise the income levels of the farmers.

Background

Being a predominantly rural economy, economic policies in India have focused on boosting agricultural output through various methods. In Assam, over 90 per cent of the populace lives outside the towns and due to lack of urban employment opportunities, there was an urgent need to use agriculture as the engine to boost real incomes. Samridha Krishak Yojana (which means 'plan for making the farmers prosperous') is one such scheme that showcases Assam's success in improving agricultural practices via administrative initiative along with people's involvement.

Launched in October 1999, SKY was meant to cover 18 districts with the installation of one lakh shallow tube wells (STWs) by March 2001. The primary objective of the scheme was to boost agricultural production, especially during the *rabi* season and thereby create additional employment opportunities and promote income generation in the agricultural sector. While the technical rationale was to increase irrigation resources to enhance farm output, the method adopted was popular participation through cost sharing between the state and the beneficiaries on a 2:1 ratio. The farmers who used to cultivate barely one crop a year, after the initiation of the SKY project, have willingly shifted to multiple cropping patterns, as they have been assured of regular irrigation facilities.

Objectives

The primary objectives of SKY are to improve agricultural production, especially during the *rabi* season, and at the same time create additional job opportunities and income generation in the agricultural sector. The strategy adopted is providing additional irrigation facilities through installation of STWs since irrigation facilities in the pre-project situation (as stated above) were grossly inadequate. STWs were seen as appropriate and cost-effective methods of minor irrigation in the region, which has relatively high ground-water levels.

Some of the targets listed in the project report prepared by the Department of Agriculture are as follows:

- One lakh STWs would be installed in the state, covering 18 districts.
- All the activities of the project would start from October 1999 and be completed by end-March 2000. Later, the target date of completion was modified from 31 March 2000 to 31 March 2001.
- The total cost of the project was estimated at Rs. 230 crore. The project would contain a beneficiary share of one-third of the total project cost, i.e., Rs. 76.67 crore. The balance amount of Rs. 153.33 crore would be shared by National Bank for Agricultural and Rural Development (NABARD) loan [under Rural Infrastructure Development Fund (RIDF-V)] and the Government of India through the non-lapsable central pool of resources. The unit cost of installation of an STW is Rs. 23,000 and the command area is 2 ha.
- After completion of the project, an additional area of 2,00,000 ha would be brought under assured irrigation facilities with an expansion in area under *rabi* crops in the state.
- Cropping intensity was projected at 200 per cent for flood-affected areas and at 300 per cent for flood-free areas for this project.

Salient features

Project set-up

The SKY project was based on the project report of the Chief Engineer, Department of Agriculture, as the Nodal Officer, during the implementation of the STW programme under the Assam Rural Infrastructure and Agricultural Services Project (ARIASP) assisted by The World Bank and the Central Ground Water Board's recommendations that about 9.63 lakh ha area of the state is feasible to be exploited by STWs. The report highlighted issues such as installation of the STWs and other engineering-related issues. However, there was no mention of the arrangements such as availability of input materials, storing, transportation, marketing, remunerative prices for the agricultural produce, etc.

The Agricultural Extension Officer (AEO) collects applications from the intending Field Management Committee (FMC). The Assistant Executive Engineer (Agri/Executive Engineer) selects the FMC. The FMCs that are able to deposit the farmers' share of funds for the STWs are automatically selected. The FMCs install the STWs and the record is maintained by the secretary of the FMC.

Administrative set-up

To overcome the deficit in production of rice and other food-grains in the state, the Department of Agriculture, Government of Assam, started the SKY scheme with assistance from NABARD for installation of one lakh STWs under the RIDF during the year 1999-2000. To formulate and implement the scheme, the Chief Engineer (Agriculture) under the Department of Agriculture is the state-level nodal officer and the Executive Engineers (Agriculture) of the implementing districts are the district-level nodal officers.

Funding

The FMC as the lowest unit of implementation, is required to submit an application to the Executive Engineer or Assistant Executive Engineer, along with the amount of farmers' share for sanction of STWs. The government's share is released both in cash and kind to the FMCs for installation of STWs. The beneficiary farmer, NABARD, and the government contribute equal proportions, viz. one-third of the total amount to finance the project. The government's share includes contribution from the state and the central governments. Of the total estimated expenditure of Rs. 230 crore, the farmers' share and loans from NABARD were Rs. 76.66 crore each, while the balance government share included Rs.30 crore from the central government. The contribution from the farmers is released for the purchase of materials and installation of the STWs. The government's share and the NABARD contribution is released by the Department of Finance to the Department of Agriculture of the state.

Impact

An evaluation of the scheme was done by the Evaluation and Monitoring Division, under the Planning and Development Department, Government of Assam in January 2001 at the instance of the Planning Commission, Government of India. A total of 99 beneficiary farmers, 33 FMCs and 12 districts were selected for the study. The study concluded that irrigation coverage had increased leading to (1) a boost in farm output and (2) an increase in job opportunities.

Physical impact

- From November 1999 to January 2001, the physical achievement of the project was 82,666 against a targeted 1 lakh STWs in less than 14 months, indicating an achievement of 82.67 per cent (Table 4.1). There have certain inter-district variations in the progress of installation of STWs (Box. 4.1).
- The total gross area under crops was 16.32 lakh ha and the total irrigated area was 3.34 lakh ha. Thus, the percentage of area under irrigation from STWs was 20.45 per cent. Increase in gross production due to irrigation from STWs was 5.35 lakh MT approximately 9.61 per cent of the production level. The cropping intensity achievement was 144.09 per cent–though short of the project target of 200 per cent for flood-affected and 300 per cent for flood-free areas (Table 4.2).
- Additional area under irrigation contributed by the installation of STWs under this scheme rose by more than 20 per cent (Table 4.2). The estimated additional production due to irrigation by STWs towards paddy, *rabi* crops, and all crops was 4.23 lakh MT, 3.81 lakh MT, and 8.03 lakh MT respectively.

Box 4.1 District-wise installation of shallow tube wells

The Evaluation and Monitoring Division examined the monthly progress of the installation of STWs in the sample districts. Among the 18 districts, the lowest achievement of 66.71 per cent was made by Nabari district, while 100 per cent achievement was recorded by Barpeta and North Lakhimpura districts. Other districts had achieved 71–90 per cent of the targets.

The month-wise installations in the sample districts indicated a total achievement of 73.59 per cent during the period November 1999–June 2000, while the remaining targets were achieved between July 2000–January 2001. The reason for the slow percentage of installation has been attributed to the monsoon season and floods in several parts of the state between July–September. Other constraints also included inadequate groundwater within the admissible limits and non-conducive surface soil, as in case of Jorhat district. These factors increased the costs of providing STWs and hence the scheme was found to be technically infeasible and economically non-viable.

Hence, the Division recommended suitable modifications of the scheme within and around the unit cost of STWs that would also adhere to conditions in the local areas.

Source: Government of Assam, 2001, Evaluation Study on Samridha Krishak Yojana, Report No. 187, Evaluation and Monitoring Division, Planning and Development

Employment generation

Direct employment generation

Agricultural production in Assam is relatively non-mechanised, hence various stages of production like ploughing, weeding, harvesting and threshing are accomplished by employing additional manual labour. With the introduction of the SKY project, farmers engaged additional labour on daily wages and even leased out a share of the land to cultivators and landless farmers on a contract basis. The project has also assured landless farmers full-time and part-time employment during the *rabi* season in nearby areas.

The district-wise estimates of such direct employment generation is estimated to be 10,000 and at the state level total it is 1,80,000. Further, 50 landless cultivators and agricultural labourers were employed in one FMC where irrigation facilities were available through STWs.

Indirect employment generation

The scope for indirect employment generation was created by the scheme through dealership of seeds, fertilisers, pesticides, spare parts of pumps and diesel for pump sets. Additional indirect employment was also generated in transportation and marketing of agricultural produce like the 'lawala', bullock cart operators, engine boat operators in river and 'char' areas and small traders of agricultural goods and commodities. As the persons falling under indirect employment group covered more than one FMC and operated their business activities from the bazaar and towns, an assessment was required to be made on the district basis. On an average, 500 persons were estimated to be indirectly employed in a district and the indirect employment generation in the state totalled 9000. Overall, SKY generated additional employment for 1,89,000 persons in the agricultural sector of Assam.

Table 4.1 **Gross area under crops production and cropping intensity achieved in sample districts**

District	Crops	Area under crops (Hectares)	Area irrigated by shallow tube well (Hectares)	Total production (Metric tonnes)	Additional production due to shallow tube well (Metric tonnes)	Cropping intensity (percentage)
Kokrajhar	Paddy	58255	3980	129144	10225	148
	Rabi	NA	NA	NA	NA	
Dhubri	Paddy	123170	66550	309805	61060	146
	Rabi	53813	20380	201364	15885	
	Paddy	69618	6532	4035	2330	157
	Rabi	21732	7432	100000	18000	
	Paddy	159081	76877	166844	51206	NA
	Rabi	51697	10750	27185	2703	
	Paddy	163991	50682	310000	13500	170
	Rabi	50074	9100	73600	3120	
	Paddy	120978	2523	356209	6252	129
	Rabi	24237	3110	50035	20802	
	Paddy	74500	500	106440	781	139
	Rabi	18100	620	41750	6732	
	Paddy	124000	10000	131440	23374	207
	Rabi	46778	10803	59361	10945	
Dibrugarh	Paddy	79956	13411	197617	29588	139
	Rabi	17892	5996	197617	29588	
Nagaon	Paddy	257822	11255	629227	53772	187
	Rabi	69296	12481	415332	109244	
Sibsagar	Paddy	3891	2515	11758	8550	162
	Rabi	5889	5562	261602	9640	
Jorhat	Paddy	11051	1567	84804	10452	147
	Rabi	26187	1080	139667	17308	
Total of all sample	Paddy	1246313	246390	2437283	281088	
districts	Rabi	385695	87310	3664355	284091	
	All crops	1632008	333700	6101638	535179	
Total of all sample	Paddy	103859	20532	203107	23424	
districts	Rabi	32141	7276	305363	21174	
	All crops	136000	27808	508470	44598	
Total of all sample	Paddy	100	19.77	100	11.53	144.09
districts	Rabi	100	22.64	100	6.93	
	All crops	100	20.45	100	9.61	

NA = Not Available

Source: Government of Assam, 2001, Evaluation Study on Samridha Krishak Yojana, Report No. 187, Evaluation and Monitoring Division, Planning and Development

Table 4.2 **Sample district-wise gross area cultivated, gross production received, and average income generated by sample beneficiary farmers**

Sample District	No. of selected	Gross area cultivated by a farmer (Hectares)		Gross production received by a farmer (Metric tonnes)		Average value of production (Rs. in '000)		Total income generated by a farmer (Rs. in '000 pa)
		Paddy	Rabi	Paddy	Rabi	Paddy	Rabi	
Darrang	9	1.55	0.65	8.60	3.20	34.00	12.8	46.8
Dhemaji	6	2.82	2.27	13.47	15.82	67.34	47.46	114.78
Dibrugarh	9	1.15	1.15	4.35	5.18	21.78	15.52	37.31
Dhubri	9	2.18	0.65	7.39	5.67	36.94	28.33	65.28
Jorhat	9	3.73	0.84	16.97	3.82	84.83	18.89	103.72
Kokrajhar	9	3.75	0.44	19.10	1.84	95.5	5.33	101.03
N. Lakhimpur	6	2.53	2.68	12.17	15.63	60.83	78.17	139.00
Morigaon	9	2.55	0.59	15.71	5.53	78.55	16.60	95.15
Nagaon	9	4.80	0.71	20.44	3.18	102.22	16.91	119.13
Sibsagar	9	1.21	0.29	6.55	0.15	29.50	0.31	29.81
Sonitpur	9	0.83	0.81	4.69	2.35	18.09	9.42	27.61
Tinsukia	6	1.62	1.18	5.30	8.03	22.70	37.27	59.97
TOTAL	99	2.40	0.93	11.31	5.23	54.73	21.17	75.90

Source: Government of Assam, 2001, Evaluation Study on Samridha Krishak Yojana, Report No. 187, Evaluation and Monitoring Division, Planning and Development

Fund flow and utilisation

About 88.37 per cent of the total amount required as the government's share was released to the FMCs. Of this, 87.26 per cent was utilised (Table 4.3). Again, 99.88 per cent of the farmers' share was released and 100 per cent utilisation of this release was achieved.

Income impact

The total income generated by beneficiary farmers from agricultural production was Rs. 75,900 which included cost of cultivation and expenditure on family consumption. At the district level, income generated by a farmer in Sonitpur district was Rs. 27,510, the highest being in north Lakhimpur district at Rs. 1,39,000.

Lessons for the future

Weighing all aspects of the programme, it may be said that the outcome of the scheme can be called a success that is worth replicating in predominantly agricultural situations, if the lessons drawn from this experience are selectively utilised. In a state where there are a high number of registered educated unemployed, and the per capita income is very low, the SKY scheme has brought in new hope. Therefore, it is worth assessing the basic achievements of what is essentially 'a success story', and simultaneously seeing what lessons can be derived to make the Samridha Krishak Yojana a replicable programme in the rest of Assam.

However, the project could be improved further in the following manner:

- The uni-polar emphasis on civil construction should be expanded to cover both backward and forward linkages. For example, arrangements should be made for input materials, storage, transportation, marketing and remunerative prices fixed for the agriculture produce. Only then will there be a sustainable increase in the farmer's income.
- Ancillary agro-based industries should be identified to create additional demand for agricultural commodities.
- Different types of appropriate cropping programmes can be worked out to help farmers to go in for economically and commercially gainful crops.
- All farmers with cultivable lands within an FMC should be persuaded to contribute towards the farmers' share but in proportion to their land holdings so that the entire process – from installation of STWs, their utilisation as well as operational maintenance – becomes the joint and common responsibility of all the farmers, not just a few.
- There could be an in-built system of project monitoring, both through desk reviews at the state level as well as field inspections at district and village levels.

The Evaluation and Monitoring Division has recommended a focused and packaged approach for future planning and implementation that not only stresses the construction side of installing 1 lakh STWs, but also the overall development through increased incomes.

Summary

Assam has been dependent on the vagaries of the monsoons and the floods that ravage the state. In contrast, there are many rural areas where people have waited for months for the monsoon to break. It is against this background that SKY was conceptualised. The SKY project showcases Assam's success in improving agricultural practices via administrative initiative along with people's involvement. The primary objective of the scheme was to boost agricultural production especially during the *rabi* season and thereby create additional employment opportunities and promote income generation in the agriculture sector.

The farmers, NABARD and the state/central governments finance the SKY project. This unique scheme has led to an increase in the gross cultivable area as well as the irrigated area. The introduction of the STW scheme has enhanced the involvement of farmers in financing of irrigation facilities in the state. As overall agricultural productivity has increased, it has generated direct and indirect employment opportunities in the sample districts studied. Further, there has been a substantial improvement in the income of the beneficiary farmers.

Replicability

The recommendations made by the evaluation study team have helped replicate the scheme in all districts of Assam and in other states as well. This calls for an extension approach, which is multi-faceted, and if done institutionally through the Panchayati Raj system, will get organically integrated at the district level with all departments. Such a convergence of all agencies will add to mutual synergy and more successful implementation.

The scheme has ensured the participation of the people in the form of one-third contribution to the total cost. This feature provides a sense of responsibility and ownership to the people. With

Table 4.3 Average depth of boring distance between shallow tube wells and percentage distribution of installation of shallow tube wells according to period of months in sample beneficiary Field Management Committees

Sample District	No. of beneficiaries FMCs (No.)	Average depth of boring of STWs (Metres)	Average distance between STWs (Metres)	Percentage of STWs installed during		
				Nov. 1999 to April 2000 (%)	May 2000 to Oct. 2000 (%)	Nov. 2000 to Jan. 2001 (%)
Darrang	3	22.35	200	100.00	0.00	0.00
Dhemaji	2	22.82	295	100.00	0.00	0.00
Dibrugarh	3	28.70	260	100.00	0.00	0.00
Dhubri	3	25.00	350	100.00	0.00	0.00
Jorhat	3	27.94	234	69.23	24.62	6.15
Kokrajhar	3	30.00	100	100.00	0.00	0.00
N. Lakhimpur	2	21.32	350	15.91	0.00	84.09
Morigaon	3	22.00	130	100.00	0.00	0.00
Nagaon	3	27.10	200	80.00	8.57	11.43
Sibsagar	3	28.00	250	10.13	50.63	39.24
Sonitpur	3	30.28	288	100.00	0.00	0.00
Tinsukia	2	28.75	200	100.00	0.00	0.00
Total	33	.26.19	238	68.21	10.91	20.88

Source: Government of Assam, 2001, Evaluation Study on Samridha Krishak Yojana, Report No. 187, Evaluation and Monitoring Division, Planning and Development

marginally stronger monitoring and control mechanism in place, the scheme would be ideal for adoption in other states.

SKY has been a success in terms of its physical achievements—added irrigation, increased farm output, and higher income for farmers—and efficiency of financial utilisation. It shows the way forward for better utilisation of groundwater resources for increasing agricultural productivity in a participatory and cost-effective manner in regions where there is a high water table. Such a scheme has potential for application in large parts of eastern India, including eastern Uttar Pradesh, Bihar, and West Bengal.

Contact

Mr. S.C. Das, Commissioner and Secretary
Government of Assam
Planning and Development Department
Dispur-781 006, Guwahati
Tel. No. : 0361-226 1321
Fax No. : 0361-226 6967/2260900
Website: www.assam.org

CHAPTER 5

Canal Systems for Arid Areas

The Bundi Project, Rajasthan

Introduction

Capricious monsoons and drought are endemic in Rajasthan, a state that has faced drought for 44 of the last 50 years. The geographical location of the state is a major cause for scanty rainfall. Around 60 per cent of the country's 'arid zone', i.e. 3.2 million sq. km, is found in the 12 districts of western Rajasthan. About two-thirds of this desert area has aeolian sands with little clay or silt to support agriculture. This area is also subject to high wind erosion and sand deposition. Overexploitation of water resources and increasing human and livestock population, have also had a significant impact on agricultural production in the state. These have drastically changed the drought profile of the region. The Central Arid Zone Research Institute (CAZRI), Jodhpur[1], noted the following in a perspective plan in 1997:

- The human population in the arid zone of Rajasthan, which was 17.44 million in 1991, is projected to reach 28.45 million in 2020.
- The water table is depleting rapidly in 75 per cent of the area. If present water consumption trends continue, the Thar desert will not have any economically viable water resources by 2020.
- Over-cropping in the arid zone has increased.

To rejuvenate Bundi, it was planned to distribute water through the minor and major irrigation facilities in the district.

Background

Bundi is a small district in south-east Rajasthan with an area of around 5,000 sq. km and population of 9,61,269 persons as per the 2001 census. The district is characteristically agrarian in nature and nearly 61.7 per cent of the workforce is engaged in agriculture and allied activities. As per the 2001 census, the distribution of workers into main workers, marginal workers and non-workers indicates that the percentage share of workers in total population is less than 50 per cent, particularly in the urban areas where it is considerably low at 30 per cent (Table 5.1).

[1] http://www.managedisasters.org

In Bundi district, out a of total area under cultivation (3,82,081 ha) about 2,30,478 ha is irrigated. The district is known for production of sugarcane and 'basmati' rice. However, there has been an increase in area sown under paddy from 80,000 ha at the expense of area under sugarcane. Other major crops are wheat, mustard and soyabean. Currently, about 86 per cent of land irrigated in the Bundi district is through traditional sources (Fig.5.1).

Table 5.1 Composition of workforce in Bundi district: 2001

(percentage)

Category	Total	Rural	Urban
a) Total population			
Total workers	47.56	51.52	30.28
Main workers	31.82	33.12	26.13
Marginal workers	15.74	18.39	4.15
b) Total workers			
Main workers/ total workers	66.90	64.29	86.28
Marginal workers/ total workers	33.10	35.71	13.72
Non-workers/ total population	52.44	48.48	69.72

Source: Registrar General of India, 2002, Population Census 2001, html version

The remaining land is irrigated through major and minor irrigation projects (Box 5.1). The total area under cultivation in Chambal command area in Bundi district is 1.02 lakh ha. The area under cultivation in medium and minor irrigation projects is 0.41 lakh ha and the area where traditional sources of irrigation are being used is 0.87 lakh ha. This area is not only crucial for people in the command area but also for the rest of the district. The economies of the thriving *Krishi Upaj Mandis* (agriculture produce markets) of Bundi and Keshoraipatan are largely dependent on the produce of this area. There are 32 rice mills and three rice based export units based in Bundi town itself. Thus the command area of the left main canal of Chambal is very crucial for the livelihood of people and the economy of the whole district.

Against this background, the canal area of Bundi presents a peculiar paradox in that water for irrigation purposes is not available to tail areas of the canal even though the total availability of water is sufficient to meet the irrigation needs of the entire region. This problem is prominent in Ajeta, Hanotia, Rihana, Deikhera, Laban, Ghat Ka Barana, Badakhera and Papadi. Besides these villages, the tail areas of individual minors, which are at the head of distributaries, also face problems

Fig 5.1 Area under irrigation in Bundi

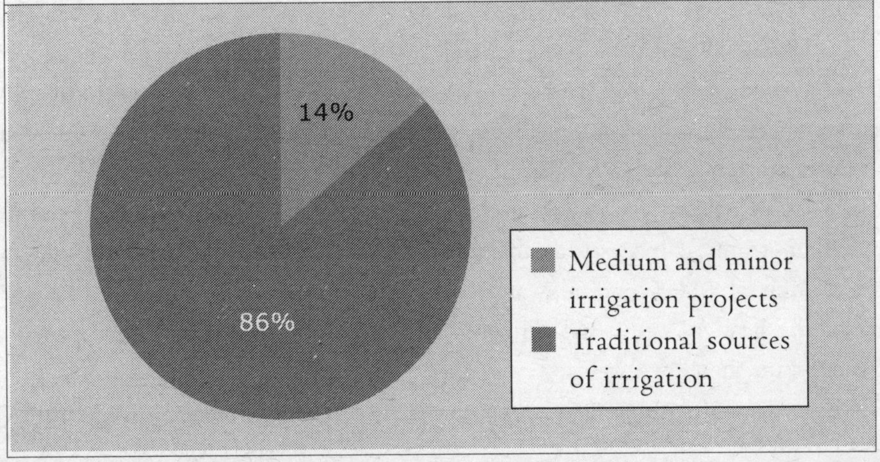

Box 5.1 Major sources of irrigation in Bundi district

There are four sources for irrigation:

- Chambal Canal System, called the Left Main canal of Chambal, is a major irrigation system in the district.
- Gudha Irrigation Project is a medium irrigation canal.
- Minor irrigation projects such as Gothara, Paibalapura, Burdha, Motipura, Batawadi, Dugari, Basoli, Inderani, Narayanpura, Poor ka Kheda, Mardia, Dabi, Roonija, Mendi, etc. are other important sources of irrigation.
- Traditional sources such as village wells, tanks, anticuts etc., are also used in command and non-command areas.

of chronic dearth of irrigation water. This has often led to law and order being disrupted by angry farmers demanding their fair share of water for the irrigation of their fields.

Objectives

The objectives of the Bundi canal project are as follows:

- To monitor and supervise water distribution arrangements.
- To ensure sufficient irrigation water in the tail areas of major and minor distributaries in the command areas.

Existing canal system in Bundi district

The left main canal of Chambal is the lifeline for most agriculturists in the region. This region falls in the command area of Chambal and comprises 53.80 per cent area of Bundi district. It has three main distributaries—the Bundi branch, the Patan branch and the Kapren branch. Each distributary has a number of minors that flow through a number of villages. The flow of water in minors is regulated by the opening and closing of mechanical gates at the head of the minor. The area closest to a distributary is known as the head area of the minor and the farthest area is known as the tail area of minor. Similarly, the area closest to the end of the distributary is known as the tail area of the command system. The tail areas have problem of insufficient or non-availability of irrigation water.

The problem

There are many villages with no water supply despite being in the command area. The reasons for insufficient availability of irrigation water in the tail areas are as follows:

- The canal system is very old and the canals are kutcha. The Common Area Development Department (CADD) could not take up the maintenance of these canals on a large scale for many years due to paucity of funds.
- There is a lot of vegetative growth in canals, which causes obstruction in the flow of canal water. This not only damages the canal but also results in the deposition of silt, which affects the smooth flow of water. The rainwater also brings a lot of silt into the canal. Moreover, the farmers at the head of the canal put obstructions in the canal system (known as *oddas*) to divert water into their own fields.
- There is no system of regulation of water as per rotation or Barabandi programme in the whole

command area. Therefore, even if water runs at full capacity, it does not reach the tail areas of the main distributaries and the tail areas of the minors situated at the heads of the distributaries. Moreover, the engineer in charge of the head area tends to be less interested in the regulation of water in an equitable manner compared to the engineer in charge of tail areas. Junior engineers at the head of the canal would satisfy farmers in the areas of operation by providing maximum water to the farmers at the head of the canal, without bothering about consequences for the farmers of tail areas.

- Large farmers, who are highly influential, tend to put obstructions in the canal and junior officials feel helpless in taking action against such offenders of the law.

Salient features

Project set-up

The CADD is headed by the Commissioner, Command Area (Divisional Commissioner, Kota, is the ex-officio Commissioner of Command Area Development, Kota) and is responsible for providing irrigation facilities in this area. CADD has different wings such as the irrigation wing, the agriculture wing, etc. The irrigation wing comprises engineers and work-charge employees called Beldars and Mats. At the district level, the Executive Engineer heads the irrigation wing.

Project activities

Teams were constituted with the Executive Magistrates, the CAD Engineer in charge of the area and police officers to monitor and supervise water distribution arrangements. They were asked to remove all obstructions put up by the farmers. Action was also taken against some of the influential farmers who did not respect the law. These teams functioned in a coordinated manner and effective vigil was maintained, at night time as well. They established direct rapport with farmers of the region. A sensitive feedback system from various functionaries of the project started yielding results for better regulation of irrigation water. Direct contact with the villagers resulted in motivating the villagers to take up works such as removal of obstructions and cleaning of the canal themselves.

The local Member of Parliament recommended Rs. 54 lakh under MPLADS (Member of Parliament Local Area Development Scheme) for restoration of the canal in tail areas. These works were taken up on a priority basis and yielded good results. They created a momentum, which generated the need for formulating a rotation programme for the equitable and just distribution of water.

Rotation programme

The rotation programme was framed after consulting farmers of the region and was executed under the active leadership of the district administration. This rotation programme had a two-fold advantage. Firstly, even when discharge of water in the canal was low, since it was directed to a particular part of the system, that part could be fed completely and then another part of the canal could be taken up for irrigation.

Secondly, when water is released in a particular part of the canal several times, there is a problem of growth of weeds in the canal, which causes obstruction in the flow of water. Thus, a rotational system of feeding some minors completely and then taking up other minors for irrigation has also helped in lowering growth of weeds and allowing the smooth flow of water.

Orders were issued whereby the engineer in charge of the head was also put in charge of the tail area by rationalising areas under control of each engineer. The temporary headquarters of engineers and all officers dealing with CADD were shifted to the field. All the local Magistrates and command area officials were given maps of the entire command area to better understand the system, which helped in the proper supervision and regulation of water wherever necessary. The communication system was made more effective and wireless services of the police department were used for effective and speedy communication of problems noticed in the command area.

Having identified the problems, the CADD in the Department of Irrigation, Government of Rajasthan, formed place teams (including Executive Magistrates and CADD Engineers) in charge of the Bundi area as well as a police task force to monitor and supervise water distribution arrangements. Community participation, a major tenet in the irrigation policy of the state, was ensured through consultations with villagers in the formulation of irrigation and canal project plans. Thus in a systematic manner, measures were taken up to ensure sufficient irrigation water in the tail areas of main distributaries and also in the tail areas of all minors situated in the command area. A follow-up system has also been formulated for continuing some of the activities on a regular basis for which action has already been initiated. These include the following:

- Desiltation of canals by voluntary action of local people and governmental funds.
- Cutting of vegetation along the banks of the canal so that it does not cause obstructions. (Groups of *Beldars* have been formed to work at this. Being a group activity, it also ensures that other members report absenteeism.)
- Chemical treatment to check growth of *aakaras* (weeds), which grow back in a period of three to four months.
- Education of farmers about maintenance of canals through literacy programmes.
- Establishment of societies to take up the work of maintenance of canals. (In Bundi command area, over 100 societies have already been formed. These societies have been given funds for cleaning and maintenance work of canals. These societies are also responsible for recovery of irrigation dues from individual farmers.)

- Formation of a rotation system for control and regulation of flow of water in canals on the basis of the experience of the year 1999-2000.

Summary

The Bundi Project was initiated as a public intervention to monitor and supervise the distribution of water through the major and minor irrigation facilities developed in the district of Bundi. The CADD in the Department of Irrigation, formed teams which included Executive Magistrates and CAD Engineers in charge of the Bundi area and also a police task force to monitor and supervise water distribution arrangements. Community participation, a major tenet in the irrigation policy of the state, was ensured through consultations with villagers in the formulation of irrigation and canal project plans. Thus in a systematic manner, measures were taken up to ensure sufficient irrigation water in the tail areas of main distributaries and also in the tail areas of all minors situated in the command area.

One of the main features of the rotation programme was that it was framed after consulting farmers of the region and was executed under the active leadership of the district administration. This helped target specific canals and tackle the problem of weeds and smoothen the flow of water.

Replicability

Since 1999-2000, the supply of water reaches most places in the command areas. In certain areas such as Hanotia, Rihana, Badakhera and Papri, irrigation water has become available after a gap of 20 years. There have been no agitations on this issue in the whole district since December 1999. Efforts at better management of water for irrigation have been replicated in other medium and minor irrigation systems of the district. These measures have resulted in bumper crops in the region so much so that the *Krishi Mandis*, where farmers sell their produce, did not have enough storage facilities at Bundi and Patan.

The canal system shows how community involvement and social awareness can lead to better utilisation of scarce resources for all. The canal system in Bundi district has demonstrated the following:

- Regular extension activities and maintenance of canals can help in ensuring water for irrigation in the whole command area.
- Better use of water by farmers and monitoring by local water management committees enhance availability of water for irrigation in future years.
- A rotation programme for irrigation, even when discharge of water in the canal is low, can be directed to reach all if managed in consultation with the people.

Contact

Chief Engineer, Common Area Development
Sinchai Bhawan, JLN Marg
Jaipur – 302017, India
Tel.: +91-141-702 673
Fax: +91-141-702 207
E-mail: cecad@rajirrigation.com
Website: http://www.rajirrigation.com

CHAPTER 6

Success in Rubber Block Plantation
A Case Study from Tripura

Introduction

Growth of natural rubber plantations has been one of the important success stories of Tripura. Rubber has been identified as one of the thrust areas in Tripura, in view of its suitability to the terrain and the acceptability amongst the people. In terms of area under rubber cultivation, estimated to be about 23,500 hectares (ha) it ranks second at the all-India level after Kerala.

In common practice, individuals, groups and institutions plant rubber. The Block Plantation Approach (BPA) introduced in Tripura has emerged as a good example of an initiative where the cohesive development of the rubber sector has resulted in the empowerment of tribal communities to manage and sustain cultivation of the crop. The availability of large quantities of high-quality rubber offers ample scope for setting up rubber-based industries in the state.

There is a history of *jhum* (roving) cultivation by tribal farmers in certain areas of the state, a practice that is ecologically unsustainable. Rubber plantation in Tripura is generally taken up on *tilla* (uplands) lands. These lands are unutilised and fallow in nature and are ideally suited for rubber plantation. The BPA has brought these unutilised lands into productive use, thus contributing to the economic well-being of small and marginal farmers and *jhumia* tribal families.

Evolution of the rubber industry in the state

The first rubber plantation was undertaken by the forest department in 1963. Thereafter, in 1976, the Tripura Forest Development Plantation Corporation (TFDPC) took over the responsibility. Currently, rubber cultivation is one of the principal sources of occupation for the tribal population, which views it as an important means of economic development. The Rubber Board began functioning in 1967 and it was subsequently upgraded into a regional office in 1979 and into a zonal office in 1984.

Several state-level studies indicated the possibility of increasing the area under rubber plantation to about 1,00,000 ha in the state. Hence the Government of Tripura initiated an ambitious programme to increase the area under rubber plantations by about 20,000 metric tonnes (MT) by the end of the Ninth Plan i.e., by 2001-02. This programme was implemented with assistance from the Central Government, the Rubber Board and The World Bank. It is expected that the programme would improve the total rubber production from the current level of about 5,000 MT per annum to about 20,000 MT. Simultaneously, the state government is also keen to promote processing of rubber and setting-up rubber-based industries. The TFDPC aims to improve the existing capacity of the centrifugal latex processing factory from 5.76 MT per day to 13.44 MT per day. The Government of Tripura is planning to set-up a process-cum-product development centre at a cost of Rs. 1.20 crore, with a view to creating basic infrastructure for promotion of rubber-based industries.

Objectives

The Tripura Block Plantation Project is a joint venture between the Government of Tripura and the Rubber Board. The principle objective of the project is the economic upliftment of the tribal *jhumia* families engaged in rubber plantation on allotted lands, through an integrated approach. The participation in rubber plantation would enable the farmers to shift from *jhum* cultivation to a more settled form of livelihood and would also promote an eco-friendly method of cultivation. By 2001, the project is targeted to cover an area of 2,500 ha.

The Rubber Board also has various incentive schemes for the development of the rubber industry, such as:

- Planting material subsidy.
- Fencing subsidy.
- Planting grant.
- Smoke house subsidy.
- Sheeting rollers subsidy.

Salient features

Organisation and structure

- The Block Plantation Officer (BPO), appointed by the Rubber Board, ensures that all inputs required for plantation of rubber are readily available, and facilitates coordination with local authorities of the state government.
- The BPO is the focal point for all services at the block plantation level. Several ongoing state government schemes like immunisation drives, health camps, and animal husbandry camps are organised for the families in the block plantation.
- The Rubber Board and the Government of Tripura share 80 per cent of the cost and the beneficiaries contribute 20 per cent through their own labour.

Implementation

The project involves taking up of block plantation of rubber in a specific area with about 40–50 ha. The implementation includes simultaneous development of the plantation areas as well as various services including village roads, *balwadis*, health care centres, and drinking water schemes. Community participation is ensured through empowerment groups comprising Rubber Producers' Societies (RPSs) and Women Thrift Groups (WTGs). Each BPA has one Rubber Board Officer incharge of this operation. Plantation is taken up on individual lands that are owned by the beneficiaries who work on their plantations. Each beneficiary is paid wages. Such a method creates a sense of ownership and attachment to the plantation among the beneficiaries. One of the main objectives is to provide wage employment opportunities to the tribal communities. The BPA has involved community-level institutions as important participants in rubber-related aspects and socio-economic development of the region.

Strategies

- Each male member of the family is inducted into the RPS, which formulates several strategies for cultural operations, protects the rubber plantation, takes up income-generating activities and acts as a forum for dissemination of knowledge and transfer of technology. It holds regular monthly meetings to discuss issues related to rubber and other associated aspects. It is organised on the concept of self-help groups (SHGs). The RPS is involved in all operations of rubber production, including latex collection, processing, marketing and distribution of sales proceeds.
- The RPSs and WTGs monitor working of schools, Integrated Child Development Scheme centres and *balwadis* in their areas to ensure their proper functioning. They encourage families to send their children to school on a regular basis. Small village roads connecting plantations and habitations have been developed and drinking water sources have been created in the block plantation areas with the help of the rural development department.
- The WTGs play a vital role both in empowerment of women and generating additional income for families working in block plantations. The WTGs are formed with a single woman member of each rubber-growing family. The motto of the WTGs is 'Save, Borrow, Repay'. They encourage individuals/group to take up income-generating activities. This strategy has improved the confidence of women participants to deal with political functionaries and administrative staff. Additionally, the participation of women in rubber plantation activities has ensured the involvement of the entire family, thus, making BPA a family-based involvement.
- In order to sustain the families when the rubber plantation is relatively immature, especially during the first three years, the RPS and the WTG have been encouraged to generate additional income through non-rubber economic activities like piggeries, fisheries, weaving and other farm activities.

Impact

The block plantation method has paved the way for numerous tangible benefits, including wage employment opportunities to backward communities and sustainable means of livelihood for the community (Table 6.1):

- The BPA project provides farm as well as non-farm wage employment opportunities until the rubber plantation is mature. From the first to sixth year, the total employment generated per ha was 1,068 person-days.
- Rubber processing has contributed significantly to the success of block plantations. Income generated from latex has increased by about 30–40 per cent. Each BPA unit has been provided a processing facility at a cost of Rs. 5 lakh. This has reduced the dependency of rubber growers on dealers and also augmented their income. The cost of the processing facility is shared by the RPSS (Rs. 80,000), the Rubber Board (Rs.1,20,000) and the Government of Tripura (Rs. 3 lakh). A subsidiary of Rubber Board, M/s Manimaliyar Rubber Pvt. Ltd, is incharge of marketing of rubber.

Table 6.1 **Rubber production under TFDPDC Limited, Agartala, over the period 1997-1998**

District	No. of rubber holdings	Area under production (ha)	Average Yield (kg/ha)	Annual production (qty in '000 kgs)		
				Rubber sheet	Latex	Scrape
West Tripura	15	1049	970	873.4	...	42.3
North Tripura	11	636	765	404.5	...	82.5
South Tripura	16	1479	740	427.6	426	242.8
Dhalai	1	26	1065	22.2	...	5.5

Source: TFDPDC Limited, Agartala

- By adopting an integrated approach, the block plantation project has succeeded in converging various services at village level; created community-level institutions; empowered women; provided continuous wage employment; ensured a regular source of income; utilised fallow *tilla* lands productively; and established the community processing facility at the village level.
- 1,947 families have benefited from rubber plantation; of these, 150 belong to the Scheduled Castes and the rest are tribals.
- 41 block plantation units have been taken up. Tapping has started in four units and, in the first year, 214 families earned Rs. 16.73 lakh.
- Against the target of 2500 ha, the area planted till 2001 was 2,563.12 ha, with a financial outlay of Rs. 16.56 crore.
- By promoting a family-oriented approach, it has provided a profitable and viable means of livelihood for the community.

Summary

The BPA was initiated by the Government of Tripura to develop the rubber sector and empower tribal communities to manage and sustain cultivation of the crop. The availability of substantial quantity of high-quality rubber has offered ample scope for setting up of rubber-based industries in the State. It was implemented with assistance from the Central Government, the Rubber Board and The World Bank.

One of the main objectives is to provide wage employment opportunities to the tribal communities. The BPA has involved community-level institutions as an important participant in rubber-related aspects and socio-economic development of the region. The WTGs play a vital role both in empowerment of women and generating additional income for families working in block plantations. This strategy has improved the confidence of women participants in dealing with political functionaries and administrative staff. The total employment generated per ha was 1,068 person-days.

Rubber processing has contributed significantly to the success of the block plantation. Income generated from latex has increased by about 30–40 per cent. Of the 1,947 families that have benefited from rubber plantation, 150 belong to Scheduled Castes and the rest are tribals.

Replicability

The block plantation method of rubber production has been considered as an important success story of the Rubber Board as well as of the Government of Tripura. The reasons for its success are as follows:

- The method adopted in block plantation in a contiguous area as against scattered individual cultivation has resulted in several economies of scale. This has received acclaim from all quarters.
- Compared to other forms of rubber plantation, the block plantation mortality rate is very low.
- Block plantation ensures full participation by the stakeholders both in maintenance as well as in protection of the plantation.
- Community processing established at the block plantation level helps generate additional income.
- The concept of SHGs has had tremendous appeal amongst the tribal population.
- As opposed to schemes where a single beneficiary is considered a target, in block plantation the entire family including children and other members are considered equal stakeholders. All the members of a family participate in this enterprise, which generates a sense of belonging and responsibility.
- Rubber plantation has been accepted by the tribals as a culturally compatible and sustainable means of livelihood.
- The experiment has helped the tribals shift from the environmentally unfriendly *jhum* cultivation to settled rubber plantation.

The success of block plantation in Tripura has encouraged the state to pursue a similar model in the Tenth Five-Year Plan. The project has given a fillip to small and marginal farmers and has encouraged them to undertake the cultivation of rubber as a viable, self-employment activity. As per a study conducted by the National Land Use and Soil Survey Bureau (Nagpur), Tripura has the capacity to plant up to 1 lakh ha of rubber. The state proposes to platform rubber as a growth engine for development and the rehabilitation of tribal *jhumia* families as well as the development of downstream industries.

Contact

Director
Rubber Board Zonal Office
Chandamari, Kunjaban
Agartala – 799006, India
Tel.: +91-381-225 143
Website: www.tripurainfo.com/rubberproject

CHAPTER 7

Involvement of Women in Agriculture

TANWA, Tamil Nadu

Introduction

Rural agricultural households are characteristically dependent on the income of the male members. Women were rarely involved in decision-making regarding the crops to be grown or the agricultural techniques to be adopted. A striking feature of the Tamil Nadu Women in Agriculture (TANWA) project initiated in Tamil Nadu since 1986, is that it is aimed at training women in latest agricultural techniques. It is an innovative scheme which aims at improving the living standards of small and marginal farm households and inducing women in such households to play an active part in agriculture thereby raising agricultural productivity and family income. It is a project wherein both the trainer and trainee are women and it relies on its multiplier effect.

Objectives

The objectives of the project are as follows:

- To introduce the farm women to a package of 10–12 skills of relevance to them in crop production and related activities and to enable them to choose and adopt relevant agricultural practices.
- To spread agricultural knowledge and skills from TANWA trainees to non-trained fellow farm women.
- To improve access to existing agricultural extension services for women belonging to small and marginal holdings.

The long-term objective of the project is to increase the productivity of small and marginal holdings and to ensure full utilisation of the potential of farm women.

Salient features

Target group

Small and marginal farm women owning a minimum size of land holding (2.5 acres of irrigated land or five acres of unirrigated land or less) and engaged in cultivating their land, form the first stage target group of the project. The trainees are selected on the basis of a set of criteria specified for the purpose:

- Wife of small or marginal farmer cultivating own land.
- Female head of small or marginal holdings.
- Women in the age group of 20 to 45 years.
- Women possessing leadership qualities.
- Women interested in improving agricultural practices.

The women are imparted training in 10–12 skills relevant to a few important crops. Each TANWA trainee is expected to select at least 10 non-trained fellow farm women from her village and form a farm women's group. This group constitutes the second stage target group of the project. The TANWA trainee is also expected to explain at least two to four skills, in the presence of agricultural officers, to the women in the group.

Organisational set-up

The first phase of the project (TANWA-I) covered six districts—Chengalpattu, South Arcot, Thanjavur, Pudukottai, Tirunelveli and Sivagangai—over a period of seven years ending in 1993. The second phase (TANWA-II) has been designed in the light of the experience gained during TANWA-I. The Department of Agriculture (DoA) was the agency implementing the project. The Director of Agriculture is the apex authority for project implementation. The district Joint Director of Agriculture (JDA) monitors the implementation of TANWA-II activities at the district level. A TANWA Cell is established in each district to assist the Joint Director in supervising and monitoring the project activities. The members of the TANWA Cell are the Deputy Director of Agriculture and the Agricultural Officer (Farm Women Coordination). There is a taluk team consisting of three women Agricultural Officers (AOs) who implement the scheme. The Assistant Director of Agriculture (ADA) in the taluk provides necessary guidance and support to the team.

Programme implementation

Farm women were not given any skill training till TANWA was implemented. Training was given to women engaged in agriculture and allied activities like dairying, fish culture, etc., which helped them earn off-farm income. Women Agricultural Officers (WAOs) provided skill training to the 25 selected women farmers in a group. The follow-up action was undertaken in the fields of the farm women. Such measures helped increase the yield level. The farm women formed a TANWA Farm Women's Group (or self-help group) and shared the knowledge of technology will other women farmers. The TANWA Farm Women's Group (FWG) acts as a Village Focal Resource Centre (VFRC) creating technical, economical and social empowerment (Table 7.1).

Training activities

Training of small and marginal farm women and follow-up visits to the trainees are the two strategies under the project. They are carried out by a team of women AOs positioned at the taluk level in the office of the ADA. The training given to farm women is village-based and location-specific. The contents of the training vary with the location and cropping pattern of that location.

Village-based training (VBT) is a skill training exercise imparted over a period of five days to small and marginal farm women through a package of skills and information on the latest agricultural

Table 7.1 **TANWA second phase: 1994–2001 (in number of women)**

Year	VBT		Farm women conference		Follow-up		Special training		TANWA network conference		No. of farm women trained		No. of SC/ST trained
	T	A	T	A	T	A	T	A	T	A	T	A	A
1994-2001	2748	2599	116	110	13626	12088	171*	159*	27*	27*	68750	64968	16952
2001-02	370	339	NA	NA	370	313	NA	NA	56	55	9250	8475	2061
Total	**3118**	**2938**	**728**	**691**	**13996**	**12401**	**760**	**714**	**137**	**136**	**78000**	**73443**	**19013**
2002-03	370	131	NA	NA	310	2	NA	NA	56	NA	9250	3275	655

Notes: a) * data pertains to 1999-2000
b) T: target
c) A: achievement
d) VBT: village-based training

Source: Commissioner of Agriculture, Government of Tamil Nadu, Chennai

practices. A total of 225 farm women are trained in a taluk, and of them 60 are selected and given special training in agriculture and allied activities such as animal husbandry, agro-forestry and sericulture, lasting for six days. It is organised in consultation with the respective departments. A Farm Women Conference (FWC) is conducted twice a year and all the trained farm women can attend. The conference provides opportunities for sharing experiences and problems on the adoption of techniques learned.

On completion of training, the farm women have follow-up visits by the AOs who trained them. The follow-up visits are undertaken with a view to inducing the farm women to adopt the skills learned by them.

Funding

Financing of the TANWA project is based on assistance provided by the Danish International Development Agency (DANIDA). During the first phase, 14,000 farm women were trained at a total cost of Rs. 4.13 crore. The second phase of the project was developed at a total cost of Rs. 28.73 crore and commenced in the remaining districts in 1994. The project will close at the end of March 2003 and is expected to train 6 lakh farm women. However, as per the recommendation of the External Review Mission, the project fund has been revised to Rs. 33.92 crore up to March 2003 due to cost escalation.

Impact

A study of 530 sample trainees for the reference years 1994-1995 under TANWA I, made by the State Directorate of Evaluation and Research (DEAR), revealed the following results:

- Selection of farmers for the programme: Wives of small/marginal farmers constituted 95.3 per cent (505) of the sample trainees.
- Ownership of land: About 87 per cent of trainees (462 women) were engaged in own cultivation and 7.7 per cent (41 women) in tenant cultivation, in addition to own cultivation.

- Leadership qualities of the trainees exhibited during their participation in community activities: 46.0 per cent (244 women) actively participated in community activities.
- Interest in improving agricultural practices: The adoption rate of improved agricultural practices by the trainees after the completion of TANWA training would broadly indicate the extent of keenness shown by the trainees in improving agricultural practices. 94.5 per cent (501 women) trainees adopted one or more of the skills in their farming operations and a small percentage (5.5 per cent) did not adopt any skill.
- Ability and commitment to share knowledge with other farm women: The DEAR study indicated that 98.3 per cent (521) had contacted other farm women at the rate of 10 per trainee and conveyed TANWA messages.
- Educational status of the trainees: The DEAR study showed that 9.8 per cent (52 women) were illiterate, 30.2 per cent (160 women) had studied up to Class V and 60.0 per cent (318 women) had studied up to Class X and above.
- Community status: A vast majority of trainees in the project belonged to backward and most backward classes (82.3 per cent) followed by scheduled castes (16.4 per cent).

Adoption of skills versus decision-making in family.

Decision-making in each family, with regard to farming activities, was studied to ascertain the level of importance given to the farm women in their families. The DEAR study showed that 50 per cent of the targeted women were in a position to take decisions on their own. Further, about 18 per cent were also part of the collective decision of the family (Table 7.2). Thus, TANWA improved the status of women at the household level by enhancing her contribution to the decision making of the household and increased involvement of women in farming activities.

Table 7.2 Decision-making in the family relating to farm activities

Decision-maker	Number	Percentage
Trainee	264	49.8
Trainee's husband	158	29.8
Elders	13	2.5
Family as a collective	95	17.9
Total	530	100

Source: Field study, Director of Evaluation and Applied Research, Chennai

Response from beneficiaries, local body and the people

Presently, TANWA-II has trained nearly 5.5 lakh farm women (1994–2002) both by direct and indirect methods. The farm women who were very reluctant to join the training in the initial stages have responded very positively as the project advanced. The farm women now demand services from extension functionaries especially through their FWGs.

Group formation

Over the reference period (1 April–30 September, 1997), about 73 per cent of TANWA farm women organised groups immediately after training and, in their groups, discussed technical messages, conducted demonstrations motivating the other farm women to adopt technologies, and encouraged small savings. About 99 per cent of non-TANWA farm women conveyed that they needed TANWA training. The FWGs also discuss technical details amongst themselves and have been taking adequate help from sister departments in various programmes, thus demanding extension services (Government of Tamil Nadu, 2002).

Yield details

The yield difference obtained before and after TANWA training over the reference period is shown in Table 7.3. A perusal of this table indicates that pulses production increased by 60 per cent and paddy yield increased by 28 per cent. Yield of oilseeds, such as groundnut and gingelly, varied between 16 per cent and 20 per cent, while cotton yield increased by 16 per cent. The increase in yield is substantial and shows the extent to which TANWA women have benefited (Boxes 7.1 and 7.2) from the training and utilised the technologies learned during training for increasing the yield of their holdings.

Table 7.3 **Yield obtained (kg/ha) by TANWA women**

Crop	Before training	After training	% increase
Paddy	3807	4859	28
Groundnut	1002	1162	16
Pulses	336	536	60
Cotton	1006	1170	16
Gingelly	488	585	20
Cholam	965	1051	9
Maize	2470	2677	8
Turmeric	3642	3800	4
Sugarcane	113000	123000	9
Potato	174000	180000	4
Carrot	163000	165000	1

Source: 18th Monitoring and Evaluation Report No. 166, Commissioner of Agriculture, Chennai 1998

Box 7.1 **TANWA success stories**

- A Farm Women's Group in Trichy run by Anthoniammal (a trained farm woman) is successfully making and selling vermicompost and earning money from this venture.
- A farm woman, who has come to be known as the Jhansi Rani of Mesiapuram (Tirunelveli District) has bagged the Rs. 1 lakh award from the Aspee foundation for her exemplary work in dairy farming in her group.
- Menaka of Tiruvarur and Kannagi of Cuddalore have become famous for promoting mushroom cultivation in their groups.
- Many other Farm Women's Groups are creating savings in their group by functioning like mini banks through a micro-credit system. With the savings earned, they promote small-scale household activities like soap manufacture, doll making or other income-generating activities.

Source: Collector, Tirunelveli District, Tamil Nadu

Box 7.2 TANWA farm women groups take up dairy farming

The active participation of TANWA-trained farm women in Virudhunagar district has helped form 93 FWGs. The members were given special training in agriculture and allied activities. In another instance, 20 trained farm women joined to start an SHG on 4 August 1998 in Ramasamiapuram of Srivilliputhur taluk.

The members of the group individually save Rs. 50 per month. They started a bank account at Pandian Grama Bank, Koomapatty. They received a revolving fund of Rs. 20,000 from the District Rural Development Agency, Virudhunagar. They also got the Best TANWA Group Prize of Rs. 5,000 for the year 1998-99 from the DoA.

Financial assistance to the tune of Rs. 2,65,000 was sanctioned under the Swarna Jayanthi Scheme, with the initial release of Rs. 1,32,000. The groups opted for dairy farming on an individual basis and coordinating activities through their SHG, based on the analysis of local resources, marketability of milk, and other infrastructure facilities.

Eleven milch animals were purchased at a cost of Rs. 1,32,000 during the month of September 2000. The animals were reared by the members of the SHG and the bank loan remitted back at the rate of Rs. 250 per week per member. The group has remitted Rs. 34,000 to the bank for the said loan and the balance amount will be remitted in due course. The milk yield per milch animal ranges from 10 to 12 litres per day and each member gets a net profit of Rs. 25 to Rs. 40 per day by marketing the milk through a cooperative society.

The group has taken one acre of land on lease for the cultivation of paddy during the first and second seasons. The paddy yields from the land were 1,610 kg and 1,660 kg respectively. Within eight months, they earned a net profit of Rs. 2,300 besides getting fodder for their milch animals and finding profitable employment for themselves and their family members.

Thus for rural farm women, dairying and crop cultivation through SHGs can become sustainable and profitable ventures and serve as models for new groups to emulate.

Source: Collector, Virudhunagar, Tamil Nadu

Scope for improvement

The TANWA project has contributed a great deal to the involvement of womenfolk in agriculture in Tamil Nadu making them aware of the importance of using modern agricultural techniques. But there are still some areas that offer scope for improvement:

- The department could take steps to help the training teams function in full strength so as to avoid overburdening the co-team worker for a longer period and in order to make the activities of the team more effective.
- The increase in the yield obtained by the TANWA-trained farm women after training shows the success of the scheme. The success could be further highlighted to the farming community through effective publicity. The media could play a leading role in raising awareness and motivation among other farm women and could lead to greater replication and sustainability of schemes.
- Special efforts should be taken to increase the adoption of technology learned to 100 per cent from the present level of 30–60 per cent, in different districts in a phased manner.

- The study reveals that training in skills relevant to paddy, sugarcane and groundnut could be extended to the co-farm women. Other crops such as pulses and cotton may also be covered.
- Besides skills in seed selection and treatment, proper application of chemical fertilisers, and pest management techniques, the women need training in additional farm operations like preparation of soil, weeding, husking and sorting and storing of grains as these operations are exclusively performed by them. The project should focus on enhancing these skills of farm women.

Summary

TANWA is a DANIDA assisted project that has been in operation in Tamil Nadu since 1986. It aims to improve the living standards of small and marginal farm households by imparting training to farm women on the latest agricultural techniques and inducing them to take active part in agriculture thereby raising their agricultural productivity and family income. The target group of the project are small and marginal farm women who own a minimum size of land holding viz., 2.5 acres of irrigated land or 5 acres of unirrigated land or less. Engaged in cultivating their land, these women form the first stage target group of the project.

The trainer is a woman AO from the DoA. The follow-up action is undertaken in the fields of the farm women. Such a measure has also helped increase the yield levels. The farm women formed a TANWA FWG (or SHG) and shared the knowledge of technology with other farmers. The TANWA FWG acts as a VFRC creating technical, economical and social empowerment. This project relies on the multiplier effect. The trainee is incharge of providing training to a new group of 25 women farmers.

Replicability

- The project stresses the upliftment of farm women from small and marginal farm households, which, according to the Agricultural Census, 1990-91, account for 93 per cent of total holdings and 59 per cent of total operated area.
- The training strategy has been devised to suit the needs of the farm women in different agro-climatic conditions. It comprises imparting agricultural skills, demonstrating skills and encouraging the trainees to practise the skills on their own. In each VBT session, the trainees are exposed to a combination of about 10 skills relevant to three or more crops, depending upon the location and cropping pattern. The package of skills includes a wide spectrum of activities such as seed selection, seed treatment, nursery management, planting, application of fertilisers, pest management etc., that lends itself to replication in other states and to other crops as well. The list of skills and demonstrations related to the major crops given in the VBT are given in Annexure 7.I.
- Being a women-to-women programme, there is no restriction on learning and follow-up; gender bias is ruled out. The women farmers adapt into their existing farming methodology the skills imparted to them. This results in increased productivity of different crops due to improved technology.
- The success of the programme can be assessed from various surveys and evaluation reports. The Monitoring and Evaluation Unit of the State Directorate of Agriculture has periodically brought out study reports on the impact of training and skill demonstration given to farm women on technology adoption, skill acquisition, development of communication skills, increase

in yield of crops etc. As per the 14th Monitoring and Evaluation Report of the Directorate of Agriculture (April 1999), the adoption of technology exceeds 50 per cent in almost all districts and there is a productivity increase in paddy, cholam, ragi and groundnut. The 18th Monitoring and Evaluation done by the Directorate of Agriculture (April 2000) made a very critical assessment of the impact of the project. Among other achievements, it highlighted the significant increase in the total farm women trained under the project (from 5,350 women in 1998-1999 to 7,775 in 1999-2000) and the increase in plan allocation from Rs. 507 lakh in 1998-1999 to Rs. 626 lakh in 1999-2000.

Contact

Mr. Mahendra Pal
Programme Officer (Agriculture)
Farm Women Extension Programme
Livestock Development Department
Royal Danish Embassy
11 Aurangzeb Road, New Delhi 110011, India
Tel.: +91-11-2301 0900
Fax: +91-11-2379 2019
E-mail: mahpal@um.dk
Website: www.denmarkindia.com/danida/agricul.htm
www.tn.gov.in/policy/agri

Annexure 7.I **Skills and Demonstrations imparted in the village-based training over the period 1996-1997**

Crop		Agricultural skills	Demonstration (in the class room - 1 in the field - 2)
Paddy	i.	Good seed selection	1
	ii.	Seed treatment with fungicide	1
	iii.	Seed treatment with bio-fertiliser	1
	iv.	Planting and maintaining optimum plant population	2
	v.	Application of zinc sulphate to main field (basal)	2
	vi.	Top dressing with neem-cake blended urea	2
	vii.	Application of weedicide	2
	viii.	Integrated pest management	1
Groundnut	i.	Seed treatment with rhizobium	1
	ii.	Application of gypsum	1
	iii.	Preparation and application of enriched farmyard manure	1
Sugarcane	i.	Sett treatment with fungicide	1
	ii.	Single budded poly bag nursery	1
Pulses	i.	Seed treatment with rhizobium	1
	ii.	DAP spray	2
Cotton	i.	Acid de-linting	1
	ii.	Seed treatment with bio fertiliser	1
	iii.	Application of micro-nutrients	2
	iv.	Integrated pest management	1

Source: Director of Evaluation and Applied Research, Chennai, 1997

CHAPTER 8

Participatory Poverty Reduction

From Malappuram to Kudumbashree, Kerala

Introduction

Anti-poverty programmes undertaken by the Government of Kerala have led to a reduction in poverty levels but persistent backwardness in certain locations and among particular groups of people worries the policy-makers. It is widely recognised that a top-down approach to poverty reduction that depended on isolated schemes delivered separately to individual families or groups of families had failed to yield desired results.

Kerala started a pilot project of participatory poverty alleviation initially in Allapuzha municipal area with the support of the UNICEF as part of the centrally-sponsored Urban Basic Services Programme (UBSP). Based on the lessons from the pilot phase, the model was extended to all the municipalities in 1995, which included the rural areas of Malappuram district covering 96 panchayats. Thus, the Kudumbashree (prosperity for the family) project evolved after intense experimentation in diverse conditions into the participatory strategy for taking power to the people and especially the poorest and weakest women.

Background

Kudumbashree is a women-oriented community-based poverty reduction programme being implemented in Kerala by the state government, with the active support of the Government of India, National Bank for Agricultural and Rural Development (NABARD), and UNICEF. Two bank-linked self- employment programmes of the Swarna Jayanti Shahari Rozgar Yojana (SJSRY), namely Development of Women and Children in Urban Areas (DWCUA) and Urban Self Employment Programme (USEP), provide Kudumbashree with nominal financial resources to encourage beneficiaries of the project to set up micro-enterprises. More than 10,600 USEP micro-enterprises and 685 DWCUA micro-enterprises have already been generated in Kerala and the Kudumbashree project is gaining international recognition as well. It has been awarded the coveted Commonwealth Association for Public Administration and Management (CAPAM) gold medal for the year 2000, for best practice in public management. The community marketing network concept of Kudumbashree is fast developing as a field-level reality.

Kudumbashree is an outstanding example of a successful government organised non-governmental organisation (GONGO).

Objectives

The mission statement of the Kudumbashree project is 'to eradicate absolute poverty in 10 years through concerted community action under the leadership of local governments, by facilitating organisation for the poor for combining self-help with demand-led convergence of available services and resources to tackle the multiple dimensions and manifestations of poverty holistically'.

The specific objectives of the project are as follows:

- Facilitating self-determination of the poor families through a transparent risk index composed of socially accepted indicators of poverty through a participatory survey.
- Empowering the women among the poor to improve their individual and collective capabilities by organising them into neighbourhood groups (NHGs) at the local level, area development societies (ADSs) at the ward level and community development societies (CDSs) at the local government level.
- Encouraging thrift and investment through credit by developing CDSs to work as informal banks for the poor.
- Improving incomes of the poor through upgradation of vocational and managerial skills and creation of opportunities for self-employment and wage employment.
- Ensuring better health and nutrition for all poor families.
- Ensuring access to basic amenities like safe drinking water, sanitary latrines, improved shelter and healthy living environment.
- Ensuring zero drop-out in schools for all children belonging to the poor families.
- Promoting functional literacy among the poor and supporting continuing education.
- Enabling the poor to participate in the decentralisation process through the CDSs as sub-systems of the local government.
- Helping the poor fight social evils like alcoholism, smoking and drug abuse, dowry, discrimination based on gender, religion, caste, etc.
- Providing a mechanism for convergence of all resources and services meant for alleviation of poverty in the state.
- Collaborating with government and non-government institutions and agencies in all activities related to improving the quality of life of the poor.

Salient Features

The Malappuram model

Malappuram has been identified as one of the most backward districts in India. The district has the highest fertility and infant mortality rates in Kerala. The Union Ministry of Health has enlisted Malappuram as one of the 90 problem districts in India. The percentage share of families below poverty line in the district was as high as 45 per cent.

A fact sheet of the district is given in Table 8.1

Table 8.1	Profile of Malappuram district	
Area	3548 sq. km	
Population: 2001 Census		
Male	17,59,479	
Female	18,70,161	
Total	36,29,640	
Socially disadvantaged groups*	2,55,731	
Social indicators vis-à-vis state average	**District Average**	**State Average**
Decadal growth rate (1991–2001)	17.22%	9.42%
Infant mortality rate*	22	13
Women literacy	85.96%	87.86%
Average family size*	6.49	5.3
Families below poverty line *	45%	26%
Note: * data pertains to 1991 Census		

Source: Census of India (2001) Provisional Population Tables

Identification of the poor

The methodology used to identify the poor suffered from two basic deficiencies. First, since it is based on income, there was substantial under-reporting and the officials conducting the survey had to exercise a great deal of discretion in the absence of verifiable data. Second, the identification was used only to provide direct assistance under a single programme, the Integrated Rural Development Programme (IRDP). It was felt that a layman-friendly index based on a non-monetary set of indicators to determine poverty would be more reliable and acceptable. Based on a system of trial and error in Allapuzha municipality of Kerala, a nine-point risk index was developed consisting of the following elements:

- Poor quality of house i.e. *kutcha* house.
- Lack of access to safe drinking water.
- Lack of access to sanitary latrines.
- Number of illiterate adults in the family.
- Single income households.
- Number of individuals getting barely two meals a day or less.
- Number of children below the age of five in the family.
- Number of cases of alcoholism or drug addiction in the family.
- Scheduled caste or scheduled tribe family (i.e., belonging to socially disadvantaged groups).

The households with four out of nine factors were classified as poor. Thus a community-based transparent identification system of the poor was attempted. This index represented significant innovation and a fundamental departure from existing norms.

Organisation of the poor

Hitherto, poverty alleviation programmes in India, by design or default, have focused on equipping the male head of a household with skill or wage employment that the family could rise above the poverty line. Programmes have been delivered without any lateral linkages or follow up appraisals. No attempt has been made to view the target groups as cohesive units and provide a suitable basket of services and schemes. A conscious attempt was made to get over these problems in the Malappuram project.

At the local level, the identified families were organised into NHGs of 20 to 30 families. Each family in the NHG was represented by a woman. These NHGs of women were networked into ADSs at the level of the Ward or electoral constituency. These ADSs were then federated into a CDS at the village panchayat or municipality level. There were also higher levels of networking at the level of the intermediate local government tier, viz., the block panchayat at the district level.

Organisation set-up

- NHG: Each NHG prepares a development micro-plan based on the needs of the members as identified through surveys and discussions. The basic building block of the community-based organisation is the NHG. This grassroots level body democratically elects five volunteers from its members who function as *barefoot experts* performing the following functions:
  - The President presides over the weekly meetings and imparts necessary leadership and guidance to the group members.
  - The Secretary records the details of the proceedings of the meeting and is responsible for necessary follow-up including motivation and team building.
  - The Community Health Volunteer looks after various health related issues of the group members, particularly among children, women and the aged, and is responsible for the convergence of various programmes undertaken by the health and social welfare departments.
  - The Volunteer for Income Generation Activities looks after the collection, consolidation and maintenance of books, accounts and registers in connection with thrift mobilization. Necessary training is imparted by NABARD towards capacity building of the volunteers (Table 8.2).
  - The Volunteer for Physical Amenities acts as a catalyst for local development by identifying gaps in the availability of critical physical amenities; trying to integrate the resources of various government programmes; and liaising with local government organs for the follow up of programmes.
- ADS: This is formed at the ward level of the village panchayat or municipality by networking NHGs, normally 8 to 10 in number. The ADS functions through three distinct bodies:
  - The General Body consists of all presidents and secretaries of federated NHGs along with the representatives of resource persons selected from that area.
  - The Governing Body is constituted by electing a president, secretary and five-member committee from the members in the general body. It oversees the functioning of the general body.
  - A Monitoring and Advisory Committee is formed under the chairmanship of the elected member of the village panchayat or municipality representing that ward. Since the ward is the basic unit for laying down priorities for local development, the ADS acts as a lobby of the poor in the preparation of development plans by local governments. The ADS puts together the micro-plans of the NHGs into what is called a *mini plan*.

Table 8.2 Training by National Bank for Agriculture and Rural Development (NABARD)

Period	Category of training/trainees	No. of training's	Topics
1995	CDS presidents	3	Thrift and credit operation
	ADS chairpersons	8	Community financial management,
	Resource persons	3	Micro-credit mechanism
	Associated panchayat Co-ordinators	5	- - -
	Community organisers	5	- - -
	Community volunteers	2	- - -
1996	CDS Presidents	11	Community financial management, auditing, evaluation
	ADS chairpersons	11	- - -
	Resource persons	1	- - -
	Community volunteers	9	- - -
1997	CDS presidents	9	- - -
	ADS chairpersons	9	- - -
	Community volunteers	9	- - -

Source: www.kudumbashree.org

- CDS: CDS is a registered non-government organisation (NGO) formed at the level of the village panchayat or municipality and comprising of a federation of ADSs. Like the ADS, it has also three sub-systems:
  - The General Body consists of all ADS chairpersons and ADS governing body members along with representatives of resource persons, officers of the local government who are involved in implementing various poverty alleviation and women empowerment programmes.
  - The Governing Body consists of a president, member secretary and five selected committee members. The president is the elected representative whereas the member secretary is the local officer in charge of anti-poverty programmes. Other government officials and representatives of resources persons are nominated to the Governing Body.
  - Monitoring and Advisory Committee: The municipal chairperson/president of the panchayat is the chairman of the Monitoring and Advisory Committee which is convened by the municipal secretary/panchayat secretary.

The CDS is co-terminous with the village panchayat or municipality and prepares development plans at the local government level by consolidating the plans prepared by the ADSs. The CDS is recognised as an agency to which local governments can entrust the execution of small public works through the process of community contracting. The participation and representation of the women of the community, who constitute the core of the NHG model, imparts a gender dimension to the programme and ensures that the voice of the disadvantaged is heeded. There are CDSs at the block level and district level, which serve to coordinate as well as provide feedback and take up higher order development activities. Regular weekly meetings are held and the discussions and decisions are recorded. These meetings serve as forum for the dissemination of information, development of consensus on collective requirements, and the discussion of possibilities of cohesive action.

Key features

- The programme covers every family below the poverty line.
- Each poor family is represented by a woman, a paradigm shift from the a priori male-centric model of poverty alleviation programmes. Women have imparted a new dimension to the project in terms of feedback on poverty indicators, sensitivity to problems of the poor, commitment to poverty alleviation, and special attention to gender concerns.
- The whole system is democratic and encourages full participation through periodic discussions and rotation of volunteers every two years.
- The volunteers have ample opportunity to hone their leadership qualities through regular capacity building initiatives.
- The democratic hierarchy of the organisation facilitates interventions at different stages of the local development planning process.
- The representative character of the organisation enables it to be a powerful interest group representing 30–35 per cent of the population.
- Since decisions are taken based on analysis of the field situation and through the medium of regular discussions, the plans represent the felt needs and priorities of the community.
- The hierarchical organisation with the higher levels 'nesting the representatives of the lower level' affords good channels for quick and effective communication.

Strategies

Informal bank for the poor

A major function of the organisation is to act as an informal bank for the poor (Box 8.1). Women pool their savings at the weekly NHG meetings. The ADS is authorised to open accounts in banks to deposit the savings. So far in Malappuram Rs. 2.67 crore has been collected out of which Rs. 2.06 crore has been circulated as loans among the members mainly for immediate needs like medical treatment, educational expenses and repayment of old debts. About 70 per cent of the disbursements are used for consumption purposes or to ward off indebtedness. The remaining disbursements are for economic development activities either for the strengthening

Box 8.1 **The poor women's bank**

In 1995, a thrift and credit society was started as a small savings scheme for poor women with an objective to encourage the poor to save and widen their resource base. The women contribute small sums at group meetings. This money is entrusted to the Commanding Officer who then deposits it in the nearest bank. Each member is given an individual pass book, which ensures transparency in the maintenance of accounts. Members are given loans from the thrift society to meet their immediate needs like medical treatment, purchase of school books and uniforms for children etc. Each request for a loan is discussed in the NHG meeting.

The thrift and credit society has made astounding progress. In a span of one-and-a-half years, the women could mobilise Rs. one crore as thrift savings. These societies have been acclaimed as the largest informal bank in Asia, in terms of participation and savings mobilised. As on 31 October 1998, the thrift savings were Rs. 1.50 crore.

Source: www.kudumbashree.org

of existing activities or for taking up new activities. Since the whole process, and in particular the financial component of the project is transparent, there has been 100 per cent repayment of loans. As on 31 March 2002, the number of NHGs was 4,645, with a total thrift of Rs. 5,36,30,006 and total thrift loan of Rs. 5,51,38,883.

To ensure accountability, a simple community financial management system has been designed and is operated by the secretary of the ADS. This ensures regular monitoring of loan repayment as well as close scrutiny in the accounting and audit of balance sheets.

The main objective is to go beyond mobilising thrift from members towards attracting credit from commercial banks. It is expected that with the strengthening of the system the banks would lend nine times the savings without any guarantee. NABARD has already provided credit to 808 NHGs. The loan repayment is 99.98 per cent as against 51 per cent for the traditional anti-poverty programmes.

Role of government

The government acts as a proactive facilitator of the programme. At the district level, there is a full-time coordinator for the programme, appointed by the government, who acts as a catalyst without infringing upon the autonomy of the CDS system.

A massive capacity building exercise has been undertaken within the CDS matrix. Experts as well as key resource persons selected from amongst the community imparted the training. There has been a significant effect of the training programme[1]:

- In 1994, nearly 13,000 volunteers were trained in identification of risk families.
- Between the period 1994–98, 1,06,000 community volunteers were trained on concept, strategy and operations of the project.
- During 1995–98, about 4,645 volunteers were trained in community health management.
- 2,000 training courses were conducted on community finance management by the CDS in 1995-96 and by NABARD in 1995-97.
- About 20,000 volunteers were trained in preparation of development plans in 1995-96, in implementation in 1996-97 and monitoring in 1996-97.
- In 1998, about 3,000 volunteers were trained in Participatory Learning and Action (PLA) techniques.
- In 1995 and 1996, 850 volunteers were trained in micro-enterprise development.
- In 1995, 99 awareness camps against alcoholism were conducted.
- During 1995–97, 1700 training camps on immunization were held.

[1] Dr. Ommen, M.A., 1999, *Impact of CDS in Kerala*, Report submitted to the Government of Kerala, Indian Institute of Social Science, New Delhi.

Achievements

The CDS system has translated into several impressive achievements that have been delineated below:

Environmental sanitation and drinking water

The programme has facilitated the construction and capacity building of several sanitation and drinking water initiatives. It has provided:

- 5,600 sanitary latrines with the support of the government and local bodies.
- 20 bore wells under the Drought Relief Scheme of the government.
- 10 open wells under the Drought Relief Scheme of the government.
- 53 toilets in schools.
- Rural Sanitary Marts in 14 blocks.

It has also introduced rainwater harvesting techniques in the district and trained and equipped 200 women masons.

Education

The programme has also led to the following tangible benefits in the field of education:

- Additional facilities created in pre-primary and primary schools.
- Formation of Mother Teacher Associations (MTAs) in primary schools.
- Reduction in drop-out rate. (According to volunteers/activists actively involved in the CDS programme, the drop out rates which were 35 per cent in 1991 declined to 11–12 per cent. Further, the teachers involved in the programme state that there has been an increase in the number of girl students in 5th to 8th standards, from 10–15 per cent to 30–35 per cent, respectively.)
- Remedial education for under-performing students from poor families.
- DPEP has been extended to marginalised groups.

Community Health

Improvements in the collective health of the community have been a palpable plus point of the CDS system. This has been due to the following achievements in the sphere of community health:

- Improved use of medical facilities.
- Convergence of health programmes.
- Universal coverage in immunization against polio.
- Reduced incidence of diseases of poverty such as cholera, typhoid, malaria and diarrhoea.
- Better outreach of reproductive and child health (RCH) programmes.
- Participatory implementation of AIDS control programme.
- Opening of Rural Health Depots for First Aid and Oral Rehydration Salt.

Development of micro-enterprises

The CDS system has enabled the development of several sustainable micro-enterprises:

- 12,322 micro-enterprises set up and assisted through revolving funds.
- Direct marketing groups selling consumer goods set up.
- Festival markets organised through group action.

- Micro-enterprise consultants trained to form a support network.
- Variety of initiatives ranging from solid waste management to computer centres implemented (Box 8.2).

Box 8.2 Micro-enterprise development by Kudumbashree

Kudumbashree promotes micro-enterprises for women below poverty line. These enterprises include catering, soap making, goat rearing, rice cultivation, bookbinding, copra production, spice/coffee packaging and managing computer booths. Till 2002, 35,196 women have been engaged in micro-enterprise and 26,505 units have been created. The total investment in micro-enterprises in Kerala, as on 30 April 2002, has been Rs. 64 crore.

Source: Royal Netherlands Embassy Appraisal Mission, 2002

Lessons learned

The first five years of the Malappuram experience yielded several lessons that are of relevance to the alleviation of poverty:

- Community-based involvement of the poor through simple transparent criteria has resulted in better identification of the poor. Since the criteria are in tune with the perceptions of the public, there is greater objectivity and reduced patronage in classifying the poor families for various benefits.
- The organisation of the poor has provided a powerful social safety net against vulnerability. The poor now have a well-defined role in public life, particularly in the development process right from the planning stage. The internal dynamics of the system often helps it to develop organically with cohesion and purpose. The highly democratic and participatory structure of the system has helped it to be recognised as a true representative of the poor. There has been a gradual but perceptible improvement in the confidence levels of the poor and they have begun articulating their demands. From expressing their 'voice', they have to be enabled to use their power of 'choice'. Their 'freedoms' have been enlarged and 'capabilities' enhanced in small but significant degrees.
- The Malappuram experience represents the conscious empowerment of the poor through a gender-sensitive process. It has imparted a new dimension to the role of the state. By actively promoting awareness amongst the public, capacity building of the community and the design of self-management systems, it has proved that the state can play a crucial role in the empowerment of poor communities through consistent policy efforts. The community development system has been authorised to select and identify the beneficiaries of various developmental programmes of the poor sponsored by the state as well as local governments. Also, it is encouraged to take up implementation of public works through community contracting.
- By focusing on the social dynamics of the organisation and by encouraging thrift, the culture of Self-help (Box 8.3) has been inculcated. This is in sharp contrast to the earlier practice of providing subsidies, doles and 'freebees' to the poor to enable them to rise above the poverty line.
- The quality of interventions for reducing poverty as enunciated in the mission statement has improved through the participatory planning undertaken by the system. Rapid gathering of

Box 8.3 **From dependence to self-help**

With the formation of Thrift Societies, there has been a visible change in the attitudes of women. In the initial stages of the programme, projects like the Community Based Nutrition Programme and the Poverty Alleviation Programme (PAP) were considered as just additional channels for providing latrines. However, the real concept of the programmes is gradually catching on. With the formation of self-help groups, women have come to realise that the fundamental cause of their poverty is very low levels of income and unless they are able to earn some extra money, their condition will not improve. As a result of this, their demands for starting income-generating activities increased exponentially.

In 1998, UNICEF provided Rs. 7 lakh for initiating activities that contributed to supplementing family incomes in all the panchayats in the district. These funds have been used by women to purchase goats and cows, to initiate mushroom cultivation and even to set up tea shops and garment manufacturing units. NABARD is also supporting the programme under its self-help group scheme and two banks viz., Canara Bank and South Malabar Gramin Bank, have sanctioned Rs 18.5 lakh to the district community development system for lending to the women without any collateral security.

Source: www.kudumbashree.org

essential data, interactive prioritisation of developmental needs and collective identification of economic development opportunities have contributed to the preparation and implementation of improved poverty reduction schemes at the local level.

- The transparent functioning of the system has promoted trust amongst the poor and has enabled them to identify persons most needy of assistance. This has contributed towards preventing ungainly jockeying for benefits and crude dependence-inducing patronage systems among the population.
- The experiment has contributed to bringing about more responsive governance through:
  - Improved outreach of developmental software.
  - Better access and utilisation as well as reduction of costs of public services.
  - Improved accountability, transparency and targeting in developmental systems as well as greater convergence of Governmental resources.
  - More efficient management of public assets such as water supply systems.

In short, the Malappuram experience shows that empowerment of the poor is an unfolding process with clearly discernible phases having sequential progression. Based on the evidence, the stages in the empowerment process are depicted in Fig. 8.1.

The above sequence holds true in a majority of cases though it is possible to leave out or combine some of the stages. For such a scheme to be a success there is undoubtedly a need for cooperation and coordination by the community at every stage, as well as facilitation and commitment from the state government.

Fig. 8.1 **Stages in the empowerment process**

1. Better awareness of government programmes & services for the poor
2. Improved access and utilisation of such facilities and programmes
3. Generation of savings and lending them for consumption purposes and emergencies
4. Lending for improving existing self-employment ventures
5. Micro-level planning for minimum basic needs
6. Micro-level planning for social infrastructure
7. Micro-level planning for economic development through income-generation activities
8. Seeking and availing of bank credit for individual and group micro-enterprises
9. Demand for improvement in public services especially those relating to primary health, and reproductive and child health, pre-primary and school education, welfare entitlements related to food security and social security
10. Readiness to manage public assets like water supply systems
11. Public action against social evils like alcoholism, which mainly affects women
12. Public action to facilitate the creation of a political space to influence policy-making

Replicability

The Malappuram example has shown that empowered poor women are important catalysts in the fight against poverty. This example has highlighted the need for co-ordinated efforts and convergence of resources to achieve basic human needs such as drinking water, primary health care and education. It has shown that the strengthening and expansion of women oriented participatory approach is a viable alternative for monitoring poverty alleviation programmes. The CDS system has a critical role in the conceptualisation and implementation of anti-poverty programmes, in the identification and selection of beneficiaries of such programmes and in performing social audit functions, as a watchdog of the public.

Malappuram CDS is the largest NGO of women in the whole of Asia. It has internationalised a dynamic system whereby 1.66 lakh women network through about 5,000 NHGs every week to facilitate overall individual and community development. The twin concepts of convergent community action and self-help have ushered in a new paradigm in community development.

The Malappuram experience has revealed that novel methods for tackling various dimensions of poverty, both causative and symptomatic. The Government of Kerala has decided to replicate this all over the state through the Kudumbashree programme. For this purpose, a State Poverty Eradication Mission has been created specially maintained by officers selected from various development departments on the basis of proven capability and commitment, at the state and district levels.

Contact

Kudumbashree State Poverty Eradication Mission
State Municipal House
Vazhuthacaud
P.O. Sasthamangalam
Thiruvananthapuram
Kerala 695 010, India
Tel: +91-471-724 205, 728 320
Fax: +91-471-724 205
E-mail: spem@asianetindia.com
Website: www.kudumbashree.org

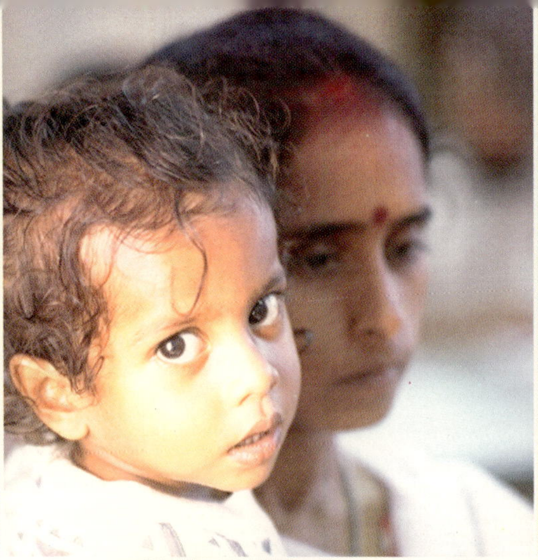
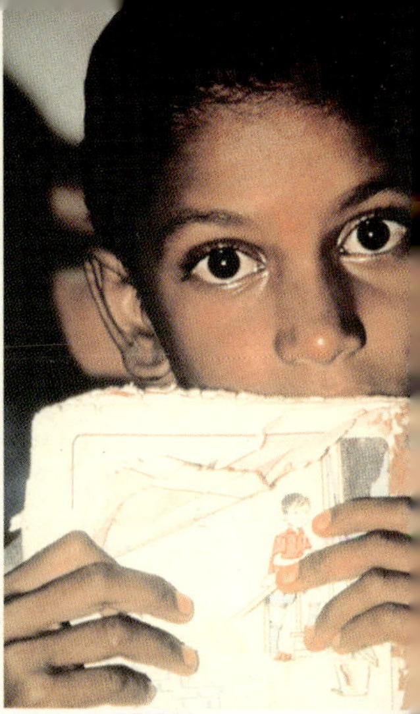

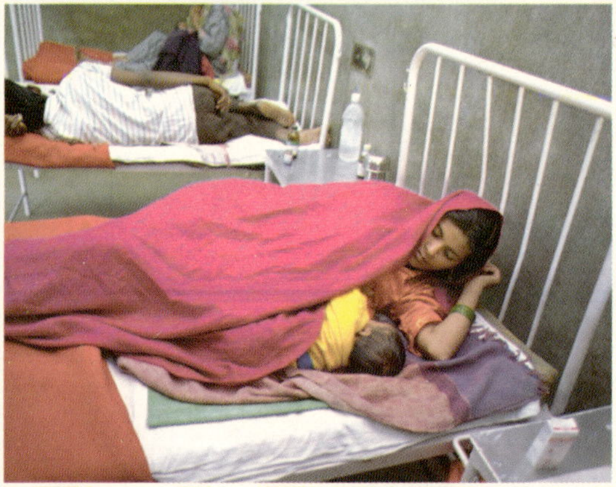

Section II

Human Development and Social Services

Introduction

Education is a basic building block of human development. It is an enabling tool in expanding the range of opportunities, choices and capabilities of an individual for sustained improvement in well-being. Improvements in educational attainments translate into increased productivity and hence increased economic growth. In that sense, education is both the means to and the end of human development. The Human Development Report 2002 states that although worldwide primary school enrolments rose from 80 per cent in 1990 to 84 per cent in 1998, 113 million school-age children (97 per cent from developing countries) are not in school.

The 1990s witnessed significant improvements in the educational attainments of people across the country. According to the 2001 Census, the all-India literacy rate is 65.37 per cent, approximately 12 percentage points higher than the 1991 Census rate of 52.21 per cent. Though gender inequality, an inherent feature of Indian society, is reflected in the wide disparity between male and female literacy ratios, it is encouraging to see states that were previously considered educationally backward making significant progress in their literacy levels. The progress of these states along with improved literacy and enrolment figures throughout the country seem to suggest that inspite of the absence of a 'single model' of education, there has been a commonality of approach that has ensured the sustainability of education-related schemes in India.

Nevertheless, inspite of concerted policy focus and public intervention in the provision of education-related services, nearly one-third of the population in the age group of seven years and above is not yet literate according to the National Human Development Report 2001. While government expenditure on education (both centre and states) was about 4.5 per cent of the gross domestic product (GDP) in 1998-99 (UNDP, 1999), it falls short of the Ramamoorthy Committee

(Government of India, 1991) recommendation that at least six per cent of GDP should be spent on the education sector by the government. The launch of the Sarva Shiksha Abhiyan hopefully portends a change in this situation.

Given their importance in the human development context, this section discusses a number of education initiatives from Himachal Pradesh, Madhya Pradesh, Maharashtra, Rajasthan, and West Bengal. All these initiatives were fraught with similar challenges including inadequate outreach of educational facilities especially in rural and tribal areas, insufficient support to academic processes and a delivery hierarchy that did not factor in the perceptions of its large user community. These initiatives have been successful in improving the accessibility of children to schools, creating a positive environment for education, increasing enrolment ratios and improving the quality of teaching-learning processes to promote retention (i.e., decreased drop-out rates) and learner achievement levels. They are testimony to the fact that partnerships between the government, non-governmental organisations and the community can achieve tangible results.

The Education Guarantee Scheme from Madhya Pradesh with its concept of 'a school for the asking' has universalised access to primary education in an extremely cost-effective and time-bound manner without compromising on quality of delivery. The Shiksha Karmi and Lok Jumbish initiatives from Rajasthan have tackled the problem of teacher absenteeism by substituting each absentee professional teacher with a team of two local staff members. These programmes are grounded in the recognition that improvements in the quality of education are inextricably linked to improvements in teachers' abilities and attitudes.

The Shishu Shiksha Karmasuchi example from West Bengal is a system of alternative education that operates through effective partnerships between organs of local self-government and the community. It is a novel effort at a participatory approach to education that is both rights-based as well as demand-driven. The Himachal Pradesh model of primary education has served to teach several lessons. The deployment of the Department of Primary Education officials to recruit and train teachers, the transfer of responsibility for the appointment of para teachers to gram panchayats, and the institution of statutory committees to monitor school-related schemes have broken new ground in tackling the problem of teacher absenteeism. The experience has been that decentralisation of responsibilities and participation by the community leads to greater efficiency in management of schooling systems. The Aamchi Shala initiative in Maharashtra is one example of how a state-government-led intervention, with support from UNDP and other UN agencies, can better prepare communities for larger school education projects.

The issue of health, especially in the Indian context, is important for more than one reason. From a purely economic point of view, the nexus between poverty, undernutrition, morbidity, and fertility implies low productivity of the country's human resources. Public spending on health (both revenue and capital) in India began decelerating since 1983-84 and the deceleration was more pronounced since 1990-91. To address the situation, various experiments like levying user charges and decentralising public sector expenditure are being implemented in different parts of the country. The Rogi Kalyan Samiti (Patient Welfare Committee) from Madhya Pradesh is one such interesting example of how participatory management has led to the resuscitation of the ailing health delivery mechanism in the state. It signifies a paradigm shift from the 'top down' approach of the delivery of social services in the country. It has been successful in bringing together members of hospitals along with user communities, through a process of mutual understanding and problem sharing, for the common goal of improving local health service systems. Much more clearly needs to be done in working out innovative approaches to address the implementation difficulties in this sector.

Women tend to bear the brunt of a region's poverty. In many parts of the country, gender discrimination hinders access to education. Women tend to have relatively low access to basic health facilities, resulting in high maternal and infant mortality rates. Similarly, low priority accorded to destitute women and children means that benefits to these sections of the population under various government schemes are under-utilised. Further, this destitute population remains largely unaware of its entitlements from the government. The efforts of the district administration in the Nilgiris district of Tamil Nadu, in endeavouring to identify and delineate the women-related profile of the district, has been a signal attempt in making a start towards redressing the inequities in gender-related development in the country.

CHAPTER 9

An Innovative Approach to Universalise Education

The Education Guarantee Scheme, Madhya Pradesh

Introduction

Traditionally, the delivery of education in India has been perceived as a supply-driven model with the responsibility for the coordination of education resting solely with the state government. Although planning for education has invoked considerable government action, these programmes have been highly centralised in character and tightly controlled by the bureaucracy. Moreover, the system has been long characterised by a lack of evaluation and assessment, and does not adequately reflect the aspirations of people.

Madhya Pradesh is one of India's poorer states. According to the 1991 census, about 44 per cent of its population was illiterate, far below India's average of 52 per cent. District Jhabua in western Madhya Pradesh had the lowest rate of total literacy in the country at 19.01 per cent. An urgent need was felt to take concerted action in favour of the disadvantaged and the disempowered, to redefine education priorities in the state and to enable the use of education as an effective implement to redress and reduce social inequities. This resulted in a social revolution in January 1997, in the form of the Education Guarantee Scheme (EGS) in Madhya Pradesh. Thousands of villagers across the state are now taking up the government on its unprecedented offer of a 'school for the asking'.

The results of the EGS revolution bear testimony to the success of the endeavour in Madhya Pradesh. The 2001 Census of India revealed that the literacy percentages of men and women in the state were 76.74 per cent and 50.29 per cent respectively as compared to 58.4 per cent and 28.9 per cent in 1991. The total literacy rate of the state thus improved its average to 64.09 per cent. Jhabua recorded a literacy level of 36.87 per cent, an attainment level higher than 14 districts in the state. It was no longer the district with the lowest average literacy in the country.

Background

The EGS is a single significant expression of an innovative paradigm evolved by the Rajiv Gandhi Prathmik Shiksha Mission. The mission was set up as an autonomous registered society headed by the Chief Minister of Madhya Pradesh to supplement the state government's efforts to universalise primary education. The primary deterrents to the effective delivery of education remained inadequate outreach of educational facilities, especially in interior, rural and tribal areas; marginalisation of economically or socially deprived children; insufficient support to academic processes; and above all, a delivery hierarchy that did not factor in the perceptions of its large user community. Additionally, the government realised that intermediaries were appropriating a large quantum of state funds and several well-intentioned projects were starved of resources. Government figures suggested that a high 86 per cent of the state's children in the age group 5–14 years were enrolled in primary school but that less than 30 per cent was literate. This suggested that nearly 60 per cent of the children dropped out of school.

In order to verify the official figures, the Mission undertook a door-to-door survey and mobilisation campaign, designated as the Lok Sampark Abhiyan (LSA), in July–August 1996, covering 55,295 villages in 34 District Primary Education Project (DPEP) districts. The campaign contacted about 1.01 crore children in the age group of 5–14 years. The LSA formulated an alternative peoples' information system on the status of primary schooling in these districts, exposing the 'veracity' of the official figures. The LSA found out that the actual enrolment figure was 73 per cent, far below official numbers. A little less than five per cent of the children and not 60 per cent as government numbers claimed, actually dropped out. Moreover many children classified as drop-outs had in fact, never been to schools in their lives. Funds had been allocated for many years to pay for non-existent schools and fictitious teachers.

LSA indicated that the topmost priority of the government should be to make schooling reach isolated groups, especially those areas populated with socio-economically deprived groups. The mission responded to this challenge by formulating the EGS.

The EGS represents a partnership, based on the principles of decentralised management between the government and the community, in universalising access to primary education. Introduced on 1 January 1997 to bring education to remote villages, the scheme has resulted in the creation of over 21,000 learning centres at a pace of about 20 schools a day. Approximately 87,000 children (more than three per cent the number enrolled in normal schools) attend these centres and nearly 47 per cent of EGS students are girls.

Objectives

The EGS is a novel effort at a community-centred approach to education that is both rights-based as well as demand-driven. By operating on a decentralised basis through effective partnerships between the government, the panchayat and the community, it has served to address problems arising out of skewed planning in education across Madhya Pradesh.

The objectives of the mission were as follows:

- Create a positive environment for education.
- Increase enrolment of children in schools.
- Improve the quality of teaching-learning processes so as to enhance retention and achievement levels.

Salient features

Project set-up

The EGS is a pioneering initiative in the country, which not only acknowledges a child's right to primary education but also guarantees it. Under the programme, the government gives a guarantee to provide a primary school facility to the children in a habitation (where there is no such facility within a kilometre) within a period of 90 days of receiving a demand for such a facility by the local community.

Under the EGS, any community having a group of 25 children from a tribal area or 40 children from a non-tribal area, without access to a school within a radius of a kilometre, can ask for a school. The government on its part, has to respond with Rs. 8,500 delivered to the village heads. This sum pays for the services of a teacher (Rs. 500 per month), covers the cost of books and provides for contingent and administrative expenses. The community plays an active role throughout the process, ensuring the selection of competent teachers as well as overseeing the day-to-day management of the school.

Implementation

Working through village representatives and using flexible, fast-track procedures, the Mission has been able to address salient educational issues with urgency and establish an effective model of decentralised educational management. The Mission devolves 85 per cent of its funds to panchayats of which 57 per cent goes to gram panchayats, investing them with critical powers of recruitment, construction and procurement. The Mission has paved the way for institutional restructuring of primary education enabling the community to become more involved in the management and functioning of the local schools.

The Mission views the responsibility for providing education under the EGS as a three-way partnership to be undertaken by the community, the local government, and the state government.

Community

The community plays a vital role in collaborating and contributing towards the EGS initiative. It is the community that first raises the demand for a school to be instituted under the EGS scheme. The community then identifies a local resident to be a *guruji* (teacher). The decision to appoint or discharge a teacher is made by the community. It is mandatory that the *guruji* belongs to the particular village community. This ensures better rapport between the teacher and the members of the village and increases accountability towards the community. The space for learning is provided by the community. Members of the village, through the village representatives, are also responsible for ensuring the smooth functioning of the EGS schools.

Till 2001, 2,632 school buildings had been constructed and 3,379 more are under construction. 198 Block Resource Centres (BRCs) have also been constructed in 19 DPEP districts while 171 BRCs are under construction in 15 DPEP districts, to facilitate teachers training at the block level. 5,221 additional rooms are also being constructed in EGS schools over the state.

Local government (panchayat)

The panchayats discharge the vital role of overseeing school functioning as well as tackling contingent issues that may arise in the day-to-day functioning of the school. Primary amongst their responsibilities is tackling the issues of teacher absenteeism and school drop-outs. The panchayat is also responsible for appointing a teacher on behalf of the community.

State government

Giving children a school on demand is the primary responsibility of the state government. The government also arranges training of teachers, supports schools through grants for the teacher's salary and administrative expenditure as well as provides teacher-learning material. The government also conducts regular academic supervision of EGS schools and provides periodic inputs for improving the quality and delivery of education.

Strategies

The provision

EGS perceives this guarantee as immediate action for creating opportunities of education rather than as a legal decree. It views the market and especially the community as an indispensable factor for the operationalisation of education systems. There are certain key factors that govern the provision of facility:

- Any community without a primary schooling facility within 1 km, and with 25 children in tribal areas and 40 children in non-tribal areas, can make a representation to the gram panchayat for a school.
- The panchayat forwards the demand for an EGS school to the block panchayat or the janpad. After making the necessary inquiries, this body has to make a decision regarding the demand within a week.
- If the habitation is in need of a teacher, he/she is chosen from within the community (should have passed standard XII) and is then trained by the government. The teacher is appointed or discharged from service by the community and is fully accountable to the community.
- The space for learning is provided by the community, which also proposes the *Guruji's* nomination; it is mandatory that the *guruji* belongs to the particular village community (Box 9.1).

Box 9.1 **Motivation to learn**

In Ganeshpura village, Ram Swaroop Manderia, a 22-year-old farmer with XII grade education has become *guruji* (teacher). When his fellow villagers demanded a school, they inducted him as the village school master. He earns Rs. 1,100 a month. Parents who send their children to school in Ganeshpura are nearly all illiterate, but are grateful to Manderia for their children's minimal education, which has helped them at home in many ways. The children read government notices and wedding invitations to the parents and do basic mathematics so that merchants can't cheat their families.

In Fakibiza, a remote village in Madhya Pradesh inhabited by the indigenous Baiga tribe, none of the adult women can read. But in a one-room school, begun two years ago under the EGS, girls outnumber boys 23 to 11. Dev Lal, a father of two young girls believes that it is more important for girls to be educated than boys. When his daughters get married and leave home, Lal says, "If the family tries to exploit one of my daughters, their ability to cope will be strengthened by education."

- A special curriculum is followed where relevant.
- The government guarantees to provide the EGS school within 90 days of people petitioning for it.

Teaching-learning material (TLM)

The Mission has brought the issue of the quality of learning to the forefront. In a pioneering attempt by the state, teaching-learning material (TLM) for primary classes was developed on a field trial basis involving teachers, NGOs, academicians and knowledgeable people from the village.

The novel TLM designated as the *Sikhna Sikhana* (teaching-learning) package is intended to facilitate competency-based learning. Its impact, contrasted with the a priori highly centralised approach, is presented below:

- There has been a quantum jump in training of teachers in the state. Prior to the Mission, an average of 12,500 teachers were trained in a year. As a result of the Mission's academic interventions, an average of 1 lakh teachers are trained every year for a period of 12 days.
- Prior to the Mission, institutional academic support was centralised, inadequate and far removed from the schools. The Mission filled in this major gap in the academic system by setting up 369 BRC and 6,296 Cluster Resource Centres (CRCs). Such academic decentralisation has created regular academic support and supervision system for schools, hitherto missing.
- Above all, it has inverted the hierarchical structure of academic support and brought the school teacher into focus. The teachers' community has developed about 15,000 teachers as master trainers and academic coordinators, thereby creating an ownership of schooling tasks.

Other related initiatives

Related initiatives, such as alternative schooling, Shishu Shiksha Kendra and Mahila Shiksha Abhiyan, have also been formulated under the EGS.

Alternative schooling

Alternative approaches to the curriculum have been initiated through the Alternative Schooling (AS) Programme (Box 9.2), which investigates the possibility of non-graded contextualised learning to motivate children, particularly those from marginalised groups, to participate in schooling. The main features of the AS approach are as follows:

- Flexibility in matters of enrolment.
- Self-paced, non-graded and group-centric nature of classroom learning.
- Integration of fun and learning.

By encouraging child-to-child learning, removing the stigma of examination failure, and laying greater focus on the early years of schooling, the AS package, even under less than ideal classroom situations, results in moderate to impressive gains in student achievement and confidence. The initiative has also been able to arouse considerable community participation in contributing resources to constructing durable attractive shelters and buildings for schools. About 3,366 ASs have been opened in 34 districts across the state.

Box 9.2 ***Agrasar* (Headstart scheme): an example of alternative schooling**

- *Agrasar* (Headstart) was started to introduce computer-enabled education at the primary level in rural areas. In each district, 18 computers have been provided for selected sectors. Computer training for teachers and cluster coordinators is organised by the DPEP. Approximately 18 lessons covering each subject have been prepared by the state and learning material compiled on compact discs (CDs) are provided to the teachers. Two primary school students are taught how to operate the computer in a week. It is intended to provide more computers for the district clusters to cover more schools and the project is being considered for replication in other states.
- One school for every 8–10 villages will be equipped with a computer and other facilities for imparting education through computers and CDs to children in middle schools (or Jan Shiksha Kendras).
- *Padhna-Badhna Andolan*, a programme of literacy and capacity building is being implemented under which committees of unlettered persons choose their teachers. The Mission has provided training to the teachers and learning materials to the members of committees. For every successful learner, the teacher will be entitled to Rs. 100, to be given by the government. *Padhna-Badhna Andolan* aimed at achieving 70 per cent literacy before the 2001 Census. The committees of learners will be transformed into self-help groups (SHGs). This will enable them to get assistance under various self-employment programmes of the government.
- A mission on food security is also being implemented in tribal districts of the state. In 366 villages in these districts, grain banks have been created. This enables the poor people to borrow grain during slack season and repay after harvesting.

The missions have brought to the forefront in the minds of people, representatives and the bureaucracy, the agenda for water and education. They have demonstrated that if government priorities are in consonance with people's needs and if communities are entrusted with planning, implementation and supervision, a programme can be a success even with limited resources.

Shishu Shiksha Kendra

For the first time in Madhya Pradesh, pre-primary education was introduced in rural schools through Shishu Shiksha Kendras (SSKs). These centres cater to children in the 3–5 years age group and are intended to foster a basic awareness in young children, through the medium of a schooling environment. SSKs also facilitate children, especially girls engaged in sibling care, to attend regular primary school. This pre-primary initiative lays the foundation for integrated future learning and inculcates the habit of attending school from a tender age. The number of SSKs that had been opened till 2001 across Madhya Pradesh were 4,025.

Mahila Shiksha Abhiyan

Innovations in the sphere of education have succeeded in creating increased opportunities for girls' education, making schooling more flexible and locally proximate. In 1997, the Mahila Shiksha Abhiyan was undertaken as an initiative to increase the number of girls enrolled in schools across the state. This initiative succeeded in enrolling seven lakh additional girls in schools. The programme accords special emphasis on girls belonging to Scheduled Castes and Tribes. The programme has also been able to mobilise community attention pertaining to women's education rights. The idea of using the Mahila Shiksha Abhiyan's premises as training centres to improve the presence of women in the teaching cadre is being explored.

Impact

A backlog of 30,000 accessless habitations could be eliminated in two years through the implementation of the EGS. Every habitation in the state has a schooling facility within one kilometre. By 1998, the EGS has been able to achieve universalisation of access to primary schooling facilities in Madhya Pradesh in an extremely cost-effective and time-bound manner without compromising on the quality of delivery. As a contrast to the formal system that provided 80,000 primary schools in 50 years, the EGS scheme in a span of four years (1997–2001) has provided 26,331 schools in 30,274 habitations, indicating a dramatic acceleration in the rate of growth of school services. These facilities are dominantly in remote, deprived habitations, indicating the targeting of school services towards the more needy groups. The scheme is especially sensitive to the habitation pattern in the tribal areas of the state. Out of this total, DPEPs have managed 10,985 entities in 34 districts and a startling 19,289 have been introduced through the EGS within one-and-a-half years. In 2002, an estimated 12.21 lakh children in the age group of 6–14 years were studying in EGS schools of which 47 per cent viz., 5.7 lakh are girls. Similarly, nearly 5.44 lakh tribal children are presently studying in EGS schools. Thus, the EGS has been able to reach even the remote areas of the state and has also been able to extend the services to the marginalised communities of the population.

Funding

The project originally provided for Rs. 50,000 for each school and a teacher's salary of Rs. 8,500 for one year, which is deposited with the gram panchayat. An additional Rs. 850 is given to each school towards acquiring books and stationery. It is the responsibility of the community to manage the school and provide the space. So far 20,000 such schools have been formed in Madhya Pradesh catering to nine lakh students. EGS schools offer education up to Class V.

As a novel method of resource mobilisation, the Madhya Pradesh government has hosted a web site, on behalf of 26,000 EGS schools: www.fundaschool.org. The web site provides an interface for forging community-to-community partnerships for the education of children. Under this scheme, any person or organisation can own any EGS school for a year by contributing Rs. 16,000. This is an innovative idea to raise funds from people who are looking for opportunities to educate poor children. The site was set up at a modest cost of Rs. 83,000 and so far has yielded more than Rs. 200 lakh for the schools. As the programme qualifies for 100 per cent income tax exemption, it is likely to attract corporate donors and individuals looking for a tax break.

Summary

The EGS has become a national model for community-based primary education in India. Madhya Pradesh's EGS, involving universalising primary education in the state, was given the annual Gold Award under the 'International Innovations Award Programme' of the Biennial Conference of the

CAPAM at Kuala Lumpur, in 1998. EGS was chosen to be awarded from among 121 submissions from 24 countries and shared the honours with a Canadian innovative programme called 'Ontario Delivers'.

Jyotsna Jha in *Evaluation of Community-Based Initiatives in Primary Education, Madhya Pradesh Education Guarantee Scheme and Alternative Schooling* states, "These initiatives have also given a new meaning to decentralisation and community involvement by rising above the tokenism and transferring the initiatives in their hands". Ranjana Srivastava, in the same document concludes, "The state and the districts have succeeded in providing the critical immediate inputs that contribute to universal primary schooling."

The EGS has contributed greatly in providing access to disadvantaged and marginalised groups. As Mr. Gopalkrishnan (the Mission coordinator) has stated "...people are not seen as a problem, but as a solution". Through the EGS, the Government of Madhya Pradesh has enlisted community support and panchayat participation and has effectively integrated structures for literacy and school education at the local level. According to a National Sample Survey Organisation report, the state of Madhya Pradesh has registered an over 12 per cent growth in literacy between 1993 and 1997.

Village schools in Madhya Pradesh have spread rapidly and have had such an impact that two other states have decided to send an identical message to their illiterate villagers: Demand a school and we'll give you one. Rajasthan has created 11,000 makeshift schools under the EGS and Uttar Pradesh with a population of 140 million is just getting started.

Replicability

A review of the *Sikhna Sikhana* package and the Eklavya package in the formal primary schools of Shahpur Block (Betul) and the AS package for the alternative and EGS schools, by Indian Institute of Management (Ahmedabad), highlights the following main features of the AS package that may be considered as best practices:

- Flexibility in matters of enrolment.
- Self-paced, non-graded, and group-based nature of classroom learning.
- Integration of fun and learning.

These aspects can be applied to the larger schooling system as it exists today. The positive results that can be derived from these features are apparent in terms of matching what children are taught with what they know, encouraging child-to-child learning, removing the stigma of examination failure, and a greater focus on the early years of schooling. These features of the AS package, even under less than ideal classroom situations result in moderate to impressive gains in student achievement and confidence.

The non-graded model at the lower levels can also be tried out in formal primary schools in order to take advantage of the primary strength of the AS package, in building a strong foundation in basic competencies. Another feature that can be expanded in scope is the integration of fun and learning, including child-peer group learning that is found in the Eklavya AS schools. This feature is best integrated into the training that is offered for transaction of the curriculum in the classroom. In order to overcome one of the problems observed in the AS package, namely, difficulty in grouping children according to their ability levels subject-wise, a closer exploration of current practices concerning grouping and monitoring of children is necessary. Another idea that can be examined is the feasibility of *Mahila* Training Centres to improve the presence of women in the teaching cadre.

Contact

Amita Sharma
Mission Director, Rajiv Gandhi Shiksha Mission
Rajya Shiksha Kendra
B-Wing, Pustak Bhawan, Arera Hills
Bhopal – 462 011, India
Fax: +91-755-272 644, 271 268
E-mail: mdrgpsm@sancharnet.in
Website: www.fundaschool.org

CHAPTER 10

Partnerships in Education

Shiksha Karmi and Lok Jumbish, Rajasthan

Introduction

According to the *Human Development Report 1990*, literacy is a person's first step in learning and knowledge building and hence, literacy indicators are essential to gauge human development (UNDP, 1990). Education attainments in Rajasthan have been among the lowest in India even till the 1990s. During the period 1991–2001, however, there has been a substantial improvement in the literacy rates from 38.6 per cent to 61 per cent (Government of Rajasthan, 2002). As per the 2001 Population Census, about 44 per cent women were literate while the literacy rate among males was over 75 per cent. Despite such improvements, the enrolment rate in the state was as low as 60 per cent. The proportionate share of girls in total enrolment in the pre-primary and primary level education has been as low as 36.8 per cent even in 1995-96. Another fact is the high of drop-out rate of girl children even without completing primary education.

Several measures have been implemented in recent years to improve formal education system, and/or to facilitate access to education. Among these, the Government of Rajasthan initiated two ambitious and innovative education programmes—the Shiksha Karmi Project in 1987 and The Lok Jumbish project in 1992. These projects have developed novel responses to deep-rooted problems of education and have transformed the delivery of education in the state. Both Shiksha Karmi and the Lok Jumbish were initiated as micro-level initiatives and later integrated into state-wide strategies to meet the educational needs of deprived rural communities. By doing so, they have avoided problems associated with parallel systems, which operate alongside the mainstream structure, for the delivery of education in the state. These programmes have been financed as joint ventures with the Swedish International Development Agency (SIDA) and the Government of India.

Shiksha Karmi Project

The Shiksha Karmi Project (SKP) literally means 'education worker' and is being in implemented Rajasthan since 1987. The project aims to transform dysfunctional schools into more efficient ones through the provision of quality education with the help of locally available youth albeit with lower qualification.

The programme was formulated on the basis of a successful project of a non-government organisation (NGO) called the Social Work and Research Centre (SWRC) at Tilonia in Rajasthan. During a pilot project in 1984-86, the SWRC ran three experimental primary schools using local teachers and providing continual in-service training. The curriculum and textbook design related directly to life in a rural environment, and the education outcomes were impressive. When the project was evaluated, these schools compared very favourably with government primary schools. The Government of Rajasthan in cooperation with SWRC, extended the project to 13 more villages where teacher absenteeism was particularly high. This project is implemented by an autonomous body called the Shiksha Karmi Board (SKB) at the state level. It is presently in the third phase (1999–2003), and is financed by the Department for International Development (DFID), UK.

NGOs along with the community play a pivotal role in the implementation of the SKP. Village education committees (VECs), constituted for the purpose of monitoring schools, have contributed to the improvement of the school environment, augmentation of infrastructure and facilities, and increased enrolment of children through school mapping and micro-planning in Shiksha Karmi schools.

Objectives

Some of the objectives of the SK Project were to achieve the following:

- Universalisation of primary education in remote, socio-economically backward villages in those blocks of Rajasthan where the existing primary schools have been dysfunctional.
- A qualitative improvement of primary education in such villages by adapting the form and content of education to local needs and conditions.
- Improvement in enrolment of all boys and girls in the age group 6–14 years.
- Building of a level of learning equivalent to the norms of Class V.

The project also strives to bring about a qualitative improvements in the delivery of education in the state.

The project identified teacher absenteeism as a major obstacle in achieving the goal of Universalisation of Elementary Education (UEE). It realised that a primary school in a remote village that has a non-village-resident teacher tends to become dysfunctional, and parents as well as children fail to relate to such an institution, leading to high drop-out rates. The basic strategy developed by the Shiksha Karmi Project, involved substituting each of these absentee professional teachers with a team of two local staff members. The premise of the SKP was that a change agent, especially in the field of education, can work effectively if he/she belongs to the same locality. Hence, greater preference is given to his/her willingness and ability to function as a social worker rather than only to educational qualifications.

Under the SKP, teachers with records of absenteeism are being replaced by local teachers who are less qualified but are specially trained to teach primary school children. The Shiksha Karmi (SK) is a resident of the village who has to satisfy the minimum educational requirement of Class VIII for men and Class V for women. To overcome the basic lack of qualification, SKs are given intensive training through an induction programme as well as periodic refresher courses.

Enrolment of girls and their attendance and retention in primary schools is one of the serious challenges in achieving UEE in Rajasthan. The SKP aims at addressing these through decentralised initiatives involving the community. At the grassroots level, panchayat samitis (block-level administration), Shiksha Karmi Sahyogis, subject specialists of NGOs, SKs and the village community constantly interact with each other to achieve the aims of the project.

Salient features

Project set-up

The SKP is initiated by identification of a remote and backward village where a government primary school is dysfunctional. The criteria to verify the targeted village includes factors like, extremely low enrolment, low attendance of children, low retention of boys and girls, low academic attainment among children, pattern of irregular attendance, and absenteeism of teacher resulting in frequent closure of school. The villagers and the SKB, collectively decide on the appointment of a SK teacher for the school.

Implementation

The SKP has reached its present level of expansion through high level of local participation, allied to strong logistical support. Villages are selected on the basis of requests from the panchayat samiti. Candidates for teacher's training have to qualify through a written and an oral test and must possess knowledge of numbers and basic teaching and learning processes and awareness of hygiene and environment. The selection board comprises representatives from SKB, a local NGO, the Pradhans (members from the local self-government), and the Block Officer of the Government of Rajasthan. The process also involves intensive discussions with local households that at times stretches over several weeks. Although the selection procedure has been one of the main bottlenecks during efforts to expand the project, the success of the programme can be attributed to its concerted efforts to find the right candidates.

There is also an in-built monitoring process at the village, block, headquarter and state levels. There is a provision of joint biannual reviews by SIDA, the Government of India and the government of Rajasthan and of independent evaluation by teams consisting of national and international experts. Review and planning meetings are held regularly as support interventions to the SKs at the block level, while at the village level, support is provided by the VEC with respect to monitoring enrolment and attendance rates as well as school mapping and micro-planning exercises. An elaborate monitoring structure is built into this programme on a monthly basis by the SKs themselves and on quarterly basis by the VECs. In addition, monitoring activities are carried out at the regional level by the resource unit and the members of the SKB and at the state level by the executive committee of the SKB. The regional activities are monitored by the SKB and the state level by the executive committee of the SKB. The Executive Council chaired by the state Education Secretary takes decisions on issues pertaining to management and funding, support to NGOs and expenditure. The SKB is guided by a Governing Council chaired by the Education Minister of Rajasthan. The council annually reviews the progress of the project and provides policy guidelines.

Note that the structure of the programme is relatively de-bureaucratised, as SKs are not permanent government employees. The participation of the community and people working in the sphere of education outside the framework of the government are other factors contributing to the elimination of red-tapism in the system. However, many problems remain to be addressed. Because of traditional society's attitude towards working women, it has proven difficult to recruit female teachers, who still account for only 27 per cent (1999-2000) of total teachers in the state. One consequence is that while overall enrolment levels have increased markedly, the gender gap in enrolment has not closed significantly. While, enrolment of boys has increased from 50 per cent to 88 per cent; girls' enrolment has risen from 21 per cent to 65 per cent. Participatory assessments involving the community have identified a range of measures to address these problems. The target now is to have at least one female SK teacher in each school, to develop girls-only courtyard schools, and to provide escorts for girls who have to walk large distances to school.

Finance and cost

During the first phase of the SKP (1987–1994), Rs. 21.12 crore expenditure was incurred which was shared between SIDA and the Government of Rajasthan on a 90:10 basis. In the second phase of the SKP (July 1994–June 1998), a total expenditure of Rs. 72.21 crore was incurred on the project which was shared between SIDA and the government on a 50:50 basis. DFID UK has agreed to share the cost of Phase III (1998–2003) of the project on a 50:50 basis with the government of Rajasthan. Phase III will continue till March 2003, and has an expenditure budget of Rs. 240 crore. By the end of Phase III, the project expects to cover 4,100 villages/day schools, 7,335 Prehar Pathshalas and 21 upper primary schools, covering all districts in Rajasthan, with an expected enrolment of 3,24,345 students.

The SKB prepares an annual indicative budget based on the financial plan and the existing status of implementation, individually for each block. The financial resources are kept in the Government of Rajasthan account at the Block Development Office. In 2000, the per child cost under the SKP was as low as Rs. 1,065 per annum as against Rs. 2170 per annum in a government school. About 25 per cent of the resources are allocated on items such as training and teaching-learning materials.

Strategies

Training of Shiksha Karmis

Since the SKs have modest educational qualification and no professional qualification, they are initially trained in a 37-day residential course by an NGO called Sandhan, which has developed specialised courses tailored to the needs of rural Rajasthan. SKs are trained with teaching abilities that helps them handle multi-grade and multi-level teaching, develop appropriate teaching material and provide special training to encourage girls' education and completion of at least primary education. This is supplemented by refresher courses and regular in-school training, aggregating 54 days a year. The government pays stipends to the teachers, but their management and supervision is delegated to local communities and non-government organisations.

Gender issues in SKP

To attract more girl children to education, the SKP programme involved women SKs as well. Initially, there was a shortage of village women with the required qualification and self-confidence to become an SK. Special residential women's training centres known as Mahila Prashikshan Kendras (MPKs) have been established across the state by NGOs, to train young women imbibe the basic education required to become an SK. Most women SK are mothers of young children. To facilitate their training, the centres also have crèches and child care units with a women helper. In 2000, an estimated 14 MPKs were spread over 13 districts, providing training to nearly 345 women SKs.

Further, to improve enrolment of girl children looking after siblings at home, the MPKs also provide *Mahila Sahayogi* (female escorts) who are local women, appointed to collect children from their homes, escort them to schools and take care of the younger siblings during school hours. Such an initiative has contributed significantly in enabling girls to attend SK schools.

The concept of *Aangan Pathshalas* (courtyard schools) was introduced in 1992-93 to provide effective contextual intervention to encourage sustained participation of girls in primary education. A rural woman, with a minimum education qualification of Class V and willingness to teach girls, is engaged to teach a group of at least 15 girls in the age group of 6–14 years in her neighbourhood.

Prehar Pathshalas

Prehar Pathshalas (PPs) or schools with convenient timings provide educational programmes for out-of-school children who cannot attend regular school due to preoccupation at home. In PPs, a condensed formal school curriculum and simplified learning materials are followed. Angan Pathshalas have proved effective in attracting girls to primary schools. Mahila Sahyogis have confirmed their utility in motivating girls to attend PPs in remote areas. Integration of children with partial disabilities into day schools and PPs has been conducted on a pilot basis. Shiksha Karmi Sahyogi (One supervisor) is appointed for every 15 SKP schools, to provide support and monitor the performance of Shiksha Karmis. Every SK is expected to teach in a PP. Each PP centre caters to a minimum of 25 learners in the age group of 6–14 years (Fig. 10.1).

Figure 10.1
Integration of Shiksha Karmi Project into formal education

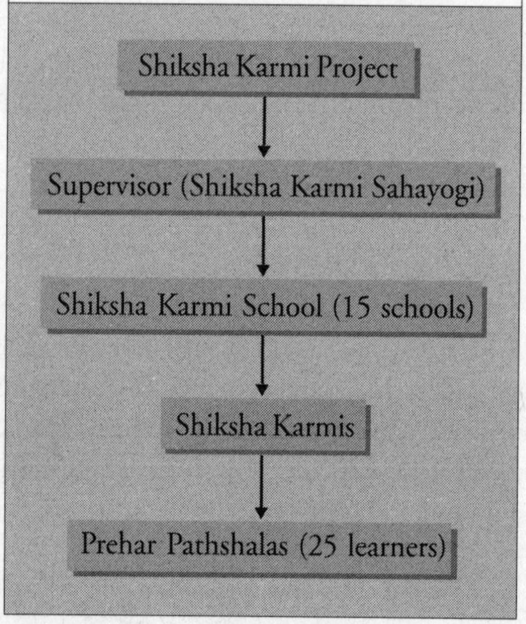

Achievements

The SKP has been responsible for several tangible achievements. The project was extended in two phases to cover 300 villages by 1991 and 2,000 remote villages in 140 blocks by 1995. The project now covers 2,715 villages in 146 blocks of 32 districts of Rajasthan and 6,285 SKs provide primary education to 2.16 lakh children in day schools. There are 2,715 day schools and 4,829 PPs. According to The Progress Report 1998-1999 of the Department of Elementary and Secondary Education, Government of Rajasthan:

- In 1998-99, the SKP was functional in 146 out of a total 237 blocks in 32 districts of Rajasthan.
- The state runs 2,600 day schools, 48,229 PPs and 97 Anganshalas. In these schools, 6,213 SKs serve 2.16 lakh children, 40 per cent of which are girls.
- Although retention rates are still low, at 50 per cent between Class I and V, it is an improvement over the 30 per cent retention rate in 1989. Over 40 per cent of the children successfully complete Class V.
- There has been a six-fold increase in the enrolment of children in the age group of 6-14 years (from 37 per cent to 83 per cent) in Shiksha Karmi Schools and Prehar Pathshalas.
- Retention of children in schools increased from an average of about 19 per cent to 65 per cent.
- Monthly attendance of children in SKP schools has improved from 58 per cent to 84 per cent.
- Nearly 67 per cent of the children belong to disadvantaged social groups.
- An outstanding achievement is 100 per cent enrolment of children in the age group of 6–14 years in 576 villages, i.e. more than one-fourth of the project villages.
- The SKP has constituted 2,600 VECs to promote community involvement in primary education and encourage village-level planning, supervision and management in improving effectiveness of schools.
- PPs have enabled out-of-school children, especially girls in the remote areas, to avail of opportunities for primary schooling at their own pace and with sufficient flexibility. At present 22,138 girls (who constitute 68 per cent of learners in PPs) are benefiting from this facility.
- Angan Pathshalas (APs) have been set up for young children, particularly girls who cannot travel long distances to attend schools. At present, 97 AP centres are in operation with 4,023 children.
- In order to facilitate and increase the enrolment of girls in villages where literate women are not available to work as SKs, 14 *Mahila Prashikshan Kendras* (Women Training Centres) have been set up in interior rural areas where 334 women are being trained.

Lok Jumbish Pariyojana

The Lok Jumbish (People's Movement) programme is a joint initiative developed by the Government of Rajasthan in cooperation with local NGOs. The programme, which has been underway since 1992, is functioning in 13 districts of Rajasthan. It aims at providing elementary education by mobilising the community and soliciting its involvement in the running of local schools. The programme views education both as an end to and means of socio-economic change and transformation, especially with respect to gender equality. It is built around the core ideas of de-bureaucratisation and the decentralisation of decision-making in the sphere of primary education. It has created structures, forums and partnerships between people from the village-level community on one hand and educationists and NGOs on the other. SIDA agreed to provide the funds, with a funding pattern of SIDA, Government of India and Government of Rajasthan in the ratio of 3:2:1.

Objectives

The primary objective of the Lok Jumbish Project (LJP) is to achieve the universalisation of elementary education through mass mobilisation and the participation of people. It places special emphasis on the education of girls and disadvantaged sections of society and views education as a tool for empowerment. The project strives to bring about a qualitative improvement in formal schools and their social environment. It also endeavours to reduce construction costs of school buildings through utilisation of local materials and technologies.

Some of the main goals of the LJP are as follows:

- Providing access to primary education to all children between five and 14 years of age.
- Striving to enrol children in regular schools, as far as possible and in Sahaj Shiksha centres wherever necessary.
- Ensuring that all enrolled children regularly attend school Sahaj Shiksha centres and complete primary education.
- Improving quality of education by emphasising active learning, child-centred processes and achievement of at least minimum levels of learning by all children.
- Creating necessary structures and processes to empower women, making education an instrument of women's equality.
- Ensuring equity in education to all members of the society.
- Modifying, if necessary, the content and processes of education to better relate it to the environment, people's culture as well as their living and working conditions.
- Effectively involving people in the planning and management of education.

Salient features

Project set-up

The unit of decentralisation planning and administration in the LJP is the village and block respectively. The links between the village and the block are provided by a cluster of 25–35 villages with similar geographical and socio-economic conditions. Each development block is further divided into five to seven compact clusters. The role of the cluster personnel is to translate the ideas of the LJP into action in the villages. The responsibility at the cluster level rests on the Block Steering Group (BSG) or an established the NGO, wherever available.

Implementation

The LJP aims at establishing a decentralised education system, with VECs taking a central role. Each VEC comprises about eight members who are nominated by community assemblies. In addition to these village-level structures, LJP has established block-level committees, including government, NGO and VEC appointees. These committees, covering 100–150 villages, are vested with the power to open and upgrade schools and to appoint new teachers.

Members of the informal VECs manage the education system in their village. They provide a link between the larger village community and the LJP personnel, help in implementation of the programmes and also assess the requirements of the village and seek to fulfil them.

The next rung in the administrative ladder is the block. At this level there are two main LJP outposts—the BSG and the Block Education Management Committee (BEMC). The BEMC is a powerful decision-making body of the LJP. The BSG is constituted by representatives from the panchayat samitis (elected local self-governing bodies) and officers from the Department of Education, Government of Rajasthan.

The Lok Jumbish Parishad is the headquarters of the whole project. The Parishad is a society registered under the Rajasthan Societies Registration Act, 1958. It is the main coordinating and guiding agency of all the regional offices of LJP. All review and planning meetings at the state level are organised by the Lok Jumbish Parishad.

Strategies

School mapping

One of the most important Lok Jumbish innovations has been the village-mapping exercise. Over 4,000 villages have participated in developing 'maps', which go beyond identifying the location of schools and road, to establishing the social and cultural problems faced by local communities in accessing schools. Issues of elementary education quality, curriculum relevance, distance and teacher attitudes all figure prominently in this exercise. Women's groups were involved to identify the major deterrents to girls' education. All these exercises have helped to mould LJP responses. More importantly, they have provided an entry point for local people to participate, for the first time, in discussions over the bottlenecks in the current delivery of education and the requirements of the local community.

The processes evolved during Phase I of the LJP (1992–1994) and were stabilised and extended to new blocks during Phase II (1995–1999). After the successful completion of the first and second phases, the third phase with an outlay of Rs. 400 crore has now been launched. The school mapping activities till December 1999 were completed in 8,212 schools across 9,576 villages. About 8523 Prerak Dals or core teams comprising of 65,765 male and 42,181 female members were formed. It set up 6813 women groups with a total membership of 62,750. The BEMC had approved 529 primary schools, 268 primary schools that were upgraded to upper primary schools and 1,255 posts of teachers in primary and upper primary schools.

Micro planning

The micro-planning process is initiated after necessary education infrastructure is provided to the village. Micro-planning involves family-wise and child-wise monitoring by the teachers and VEC and occasionally by the cluster-level staff. The VEC identifies the child out of school and from the Village Education Register (VER), contacts the concerned families and undertakes relevant action to ensure regularity of attendance and retention of children in schools. The micro-planning process involves three instruments—(1) *Praveshotsav* (Festival of Entry), (2) Retention Register, and (3) Village Education Plan. The main objective of the Praveshotsav is to create a positive and creative environment for education among children and develop a sense of responsibility in the minds of the parents to send their child to school. The retention register was introduced to record the progress of children enrolled in school. Lastly, the Village Education Plan prepared by the core team and later pursued by the VEC is a means to review and improve the enrolment, retention and quality of education and provide suggestions for further improvement. This plan is then presented to the BEMC.

Focus on gender equality

The status of gender sensitivity and equity permeates all the programmes and processes in the LJP. Women workers at every level are considered indispensable and appointment of workers in specific proportion is considered mandatory. The state-level committee 'Samvadika' reviews LJ activities from a gender perspective and provides suggestions for women's development and to weave measures conducive to gender issues in to the content and process of education.

Special training programmes are organised for women workers at the grass roots.. The Women Teachers' Forum or the Adhyapika Manch was set up in 1994 in Pisangan block of the Ajmer District with the purpose of enhancing women teachers' participation in the residential teacher training camps to encourage them to develop themselves into trainers. Other initiatives includes formation of Women's Group and Field Centres, Women's Residential Institute for Training and Education and workshops for school-going boys and girls, a step towards gender sensitisation of school children. However, since 1998-99, the progress in the area of gender-related activities has slowed down due to paucity of funds and repatriation of project personnel.

Quality of education

The activities to improve the quality of education in LJP have been through the introduction of competency-based education or the Minimum Levels of Learning (MLL) scheme in 1992. The MLL to be achieved by children at various grade levels then forms the basis of the curriculum development and its implementation in the field. The MLL scheme started in 45 schools in Arain Block (Ajmer) covered 2,096 children. In 1998-99, the MLL scheme has been extended to 5,945 schools employing over 16,905 teachers and covered over 5.4 lakh children. The MLL programme includes a bench-mark component, development of teaching learning material, MLL-based teacher training, implementation and back-up support for MLL, pupil evaluation, post-test analysis and management information system for MLL (MIS-MLL). The 1997, benchmark and post-test studies based on scientific sample survey revealed that there was an annual seven per cent improvement in the learning levels of the children.

The LJP also developed an incentive programme for people in the desert and tribal belt. The main thrust of the scheme was enrolment followed by retention. The social, economic and educational deprivations were the main criteria for selection of the block. The four blocks covered under the scheme were, Phagi, Chohatan, Shahbad and Pratapgarh. Items provided as incentives towards education included provision of slate, pencil, scale, rubber, sharpener, wax crayons, exercise notebooks and drawing book. During 1998-99, about Rs. 3.04 million was spent on these items across a total of 88,150 children, comprising 60 per cent, boys and 40 per cent girls.

Non-formal education

LJP introduced a non-formal education programme: Sahaj Shiksha (SS) in 1993. It was later revamped in 1996 and was equivalent to formal system i.e., it was also linked to a competency-based curriculum and provided a certificate, built the teaching personnel from the community and provided teacher training, back-up support personnel for the teachers and structured the management as resource groups for the SS and formed cluster- level monitoring groups or the Sanchetan Dals. The SS programme extended from 6 blocks in 1993 with an enrolment of 8,336 to 42 blocks and 49,952 in 1999. An evaluation of the project by the Operations Research Group (ORG) in 1996, revealed that the programme continued to be successful in attracting the target segment of girls and children belonging to the socially disadvantaged sections of the population like the SC/ST. It also found that nearly 15 per cent children joined formal schools from the SS centres. There is scope to improve the existing scheme through (1) upgrading infrastructure facilities in the centres through bigger space and lighting; (2) institutionalising the system of learner evaluation; and (3) bettering remunerations for the instructors.

Achievements

Between 1992–98, the initiative had extended to 75 blocks, comprising nearly one-third of rural Rajasthan. About 1,000 elementary and 300 upper primary schools fall under its administration, along with over 1,000 non-formal education centres. The project has developed its own teacher training modules, through which over 2,300 teachers have benefited.

Over the first four years of the project (1992–1996), enrolment rates in Lok Jumbish villages increased by 24 per cent. Enrolment of girls increased faster than that of boys (from 29 per cent to 59 per cent) narrowing the gender gap, even though enrolment of girls continues to account only for about one-third of total enrolment.

One of the most important concerns identified by women in the mapping exercises was the shortage of female teachers. A Women's Teachers Forum has been established to attract new recruits. Considerable emphasis has also been given to teacher training. Two-week motivational courses are run every year and 900 master trainers provide constant in-service assistance.

Lok Jumbish has also contracted external agencies to help develop textbooks in language and mathematics for Class I and II. For the first time in India, prototypes were tested on parents and children, and amended in the light of their comments. Surveys show that children find these books more interesting and comprehensible than standard texts.

Summary

The Shiksha Karmi project was initiated in 1987, with the primary objective of universalising primary education in regions with dysfunctional government primary schools and in remote areas without the provisioning of education facilities. The SKP was initiated against the backdrop of high rates of teachers' absenteeism in government schools that also led to low attendance and retention rates in schools. The Government of Rajasthan along with the SIDA funded the SKP project. The project now covers 2,715 villages in 146 blocks of 32 districts of Rajasthan and 6,285 Shiksha Karmis provide primary education to 2.16 lakh children in day schools. The enrolment and attendance of girl children also has improved due to several innovative strategies like the Mahila Sahayogi and the Aangan Pathshalas.

The project has proved to be a good alternative system of education conceptualised and implemented by the Government of Rajasthan. There are certain facets which could have been given more attention like teachers, qualification and attention to the vision of education, and motivation to qualified graduates participation in the programme. This would have strengthened the objective of the programme into an ideal project.

The Lok Jumbish Prayojana—the Education for All project—was initiated in 1992 to universalise elementary education (Grade level I to VIII and age group 5–14 years). Besides universalising the access, the focus of the programme was also on retention and quality of elementary education of children in the age group of 5–14 years. There has been a conscious and concerted effort to achieve gender equity and social equality in the LJP by stressing on women's participation in all the schemes that have been formulated as well as designing specific programmes for the socially disadvantaged sections of the population. Presently, it is in Phase III through which the LJP aims to extend all the programmes initiated in the second phase despite paucity of funds. Despite certain drawbacks, the LJP has been one of the pioneering programmes to introduce competency-based curriculum and thus enhance the quality of education. It also introduced non-formal education system to increase the coverage of the services to the social disadvantaged sections of the population.

Replicability

The SKP and LJP initiatives have changed the mechanism of the delivery of education in the state. Their innovative community-centric approach has achieved tangible results making them worthy of replication across Indian states. Both projects have avoided the trap of donor dependence. From providing over 90 per cent of financing in the early stages, the share of state government funding has increased.

The programmes illustrate that concerted cooperative action between local communities, NGOs, government and international donors can achieve concrete results. The DPEP, a nationwide plan for achieving universal primary education, that became operational in Rajasthan in 1998, has integrated into its framework many of the Shiksha Karmi and Lok Jumbish blocks. The lessons from these micro-level projects are being replicated at the state level.

Another positive feature of the two projects has been the high standard of evaluation carried out by participants in Lok Jumbish and SIDA. These have helped to identify problems and shortcomings, notably in relation to achievement of gender equity in a non-partisan and bias–free way.

The two programmes demonstrate that successful approaches to partnerships between the government and local communities are based on cooperation, flexibility, and a willingness to learn in the pursuit of shared objectives rather than a one partner monopoly that develops plans for building partnerships by decree, with local communities used merely as vehicles for service delivery.

The approach has already been extended to other states through DPEP and through the Sarva Shiksha Abhiyan (SSA) which was launched in December 2000 and is to be implemented in all districts in the country.

Rajasthan has achieved remarkable success in improving its literacy rate in 2001 to 61 per cent from merely 38 per cent in 1991. By realising that the conventional 'top down' approach to education would not yield results given the specific social and cultural setting of Rajasthan, the Shiksha Karmi and the Lok Jumbish Projects have developed innovative ways of reaching the people. Such projects can be taken up in other parts of the country, using Participatory Rural Appraisal (PRA) exercises to understand the requirements of people in the context of their local environment and by putting in place robust monitoring and review mechanisms to make the projects sustainable.

Contact

Mr. V L Sharma
Chairman (Lok Jumbish)
B 10, Jhalana Institutional Area
Jaipur - 302004
Tel.: +91-141-707 350
E-mail: jumbish@satyam.net.in
Website: www.rajshiksha.net

CHAPTER 11

An Approach to Universal Elementary Education

Case Study from Himachal Pradesh

Introduction

Educational attainments in Himachal Pradesh were considerably lower than all-India in 1961, at 21 per cent for males and nine per cent for females. The state was classified as a 'backward' region of north India. The literacy rate improved steadily in Himachal Pradesh through the 1970s and 1980s to 75 per cent for males and 52.13 per cent for females in 1991[1]. As per the Census data for 2001, the literacy rates were at a creditable 86.02 per cent for males and 68.08 per cent for females.

The Public Report on Basic Education (PROBE) (1998) which examined the state of primary schooling in India has singled out Himachal Pradesh among the north Indian States for its remarkable progress towards achieving the goal of universal elementary education. The Report suggests that the state has done better than Kerala and Goa despite its low literacy levels.

Some of the noteworthy features of such rapid progress in the education sector are: the progress from mass illiteracy to near-universal primary education has been in a much shorter span; bulk of the education expansion has been in government schools as compared to private institutions; the topography of the state, characterised by scattered village settlements over large areas, with nearly one-third of the rural population residing in villages with less than 300 people, has been one of the major constraints and child workers have played an important role in the Himachal Pradesh economy, due to the dependence of many households on environmental resources and a high proportion of the adult women working outside the household.

The Report lists enabling circumstances for the success of the programme in the state. These include:

- High motivation levels of parents.
- Social consensus about the priority to be accorded to schooling.

[1] In 1991, literacy rates in the 10-14 age group were as high as 94 per cent for males and 86 per cent for girls.

- Low gender bias.
- Better maintained schools.
- Positive work culture and attitude towards education of school teachers.
- Board examinations at the end of Class V.

Salient features

Legislative framework

An outstanding feature of the primary education system in Himachal Pradesh is that no single 'scheme' or administrative modality has been responsible for the momentum gained by primary education in the state. Increased enrolment rates amongst primary school children can be attributed to the combined efforts of the state government and the community in ensuring that children go to school.

On 1 April 1997, the state enacted the Himachal Pradesh Compulsory Primary Education Act, a legislation that has given special impetus to the drive to achieve universal access to elementary education in the state. The Act makes it mandatory to constitute School Committees to propagate the spread of primary education, supervise implementation of mid-day meal schemes, report cases of absentee children as well as absentee teachers, impose a duty on parents to ensure that their children attend schools and extend support to government officials in discharging their functions. Fines are imposed on parents who do not comply with the Act. All services rendered by children during the hours they are required to be at school have been prohibited by the Act. The state government on its part, is obliged to provide for primary education in the state and the Act confers powers on the state government to make rules for the same.

The developments in the sphere of primary schooling for children in the state in recent years need to be viewed keeping in mind this favourable steadily rising trend of literacy.

Political commitment

The other relevant facet has been the development strategy pursued by the state. Public policy included a continued emphasis on the development of rural infrastructure which included development of roads as well as schools. Schools were made accessible in remotest villages. The political commitment towards education translated into relatively higher per capita expenditures on education, which was about twice the all-India average. The teacher-pupil ratio also was twice as high in Himachal Pradesh compared to India as a whole.

Further, public policy also aimed at reducing inter-regional disparities across all development indicators. Government expenditures in the remote tribal districts of Kinnaur, Lahul and Spiti were enhanced considerably. Several incentive schemes like provision of free textbooks up to class X for the socially disadvantaged pupils belonging to scheduled caste and scheduled tribe were introduced. The concerted effort to improve education management was noticed in case of the Operation Blackboard in reducing the number of single teacher schools. The proportion of single-teacher schools reduced sharply during the period 1986-95 from 28 per cent to two per cent of all schools.

Parental motivation

Effective utilisation of the expanded public provisioning has ensured due parental motivation to educate children to improve the prospect of better jobs, enhanced by the 'demonstration effect' of army recruits and other government recruits. The PROBE Report mentions that 'Himachal Pradesh has benefited from a virtuous cycle of active state intervention, high parental motivation and decent teaching standards' (p.124). Further, the social structures in terms of divisions of class, caste and gender are less pronounced, making villages more homogeneous. This factor has enabled the emergence of consensual social norms, such as education being an essential part of every child's upbringing. The sense of village community ownership fostered the notion that *the local school is everyone's school.* The community ensures that the local school does not become dysfunctional.

Implementation

The District Primary Education Programme (DPEP) focuses on decentralisation and participatory planning as well as civil works and infrastructure provisions at state/sub-district and school levels. Enhancing school effectiveness and ensuring equity in opportunity are also primary tenets of the programme. A separate society was registered as the implementing agency for DPEP with the resolve that this society, while working in four selected districts in Phase I, would also transfer efficiency of programme implementation to other districts.

The district has been conceived as the unit of local area planning with the active participation of the community in promoting enrolment and retention as critical to its success. The process of community participation has been institutionalised under DPEP through Village Education Committees (VECs) and bodies like Parent Teacher Associations (PTA). Academic resource institutions at block and cluster levels have been created to serve as an interface between the educational administrators at the district/block level and the schools. These institutions train teachers and provide supportive advice to them to adopt better teaching methods. Funds to the tune of 24 per cent are earmarked at district levels for the construction of schools, Block Resources Centres and State Councils of Educational Research and Training (SCERTs).

Strategies

Legislative framework

The Himachal Pradesh Compulsory Education Act, 1997, mandated that the provision of primary education is a fundamental duty of the state government. The Act makes it compulsory to constitute School Committees as a medium to propagate the spread of primary education, supervise implementation of mid-day meal schemes, report cases of absentee children as well as absentee teachers and support government officials in discharging their functions. The School Committee has been given powers to supersede the guardianship of errant parents and cause children to attend schools. Fines are to be imposed on parents for not complying with the Act. Services from children during the hours they are required to be at school have been prescribed by the Act. Similarly,

a notification of Himachal Pradesh Gram Vidya Upasak Yojana 2001 for recruitment of teachers by Gram Panchayats was also initiated.

Teachers' recruitment and training

Enhancement of school effectiveness has entailed deployment of additional teachers as well as the rationalisation of deployment of teachers in the whole state:

- In the four DPEP districts of Chamba, Kullu, Lahaul-Spiti and Sirmour, 1616 teachers were recruited. This had two effects:
  - The number of schools with at least 2 teachers increased to 52 per cent and the number with more than 2 teachers to 34 per cent, of all primary schools in these districts.
  - DPEP Himachal Pradesh, took up a rationalisation exercise for posting teachers in schools as per state norms. 1,175 teachers were shifted from teacher- surplus schools to teacher-deficient schools.
- Teacher training was taken up in right earnest under DPEP:
  - About 7,500 teachers in DPEP districts were provided a minimum of 15 days in-service training.
  - 1,414 Vidya Upasaks (288 from DPEP) districts were trained in a 21-day induction module developed by DPEP.
  - Master trainers for District Institutes of Education and Training (DIETs) were trained in teaching mathematics who in turn went on to train teachers for the entire state. Teacher guidebooks and enhanced learning materials were developed.

During the period 1995–1996 to 2000–2001, the recruitment of teachers and the rationalisation of their postings to address the problem of teacher absenteeism correlated positively with the increased enrolment figures for primary education in the state.

Para-teachers

Given the geographic and demographic reality in Himachal Pradesh, multi-grade and multi-level teaching continue to pose a challenge to the quality of learning. Therefore, a scheme to recruit para-teachers for remote and difficult rural areas has been introduced.

Para-teachers have been broadly classified as:

- Part-time teachers belonging to the local community and working with out-of-school children.
- Full-time teachers who are para professionals and are paid lower salaries than government teachers. These teachers work in regular schools run by state government or local village bodies. The state government recruits persons who qualify Class XII examinations with 50 per cent or above marks and deploy them in the local school for 10 months on an honorarium of Rs. 2,000 per month. The government also conducts a Special Teachers Training Qualifying Condensed Course during vacations in the DIETs. Teachers who qualify at this course are eligible for appointment as Gram Vidya Upasaks by the Gram Panchayats. Funds are granted to the Panchayats by the state government, to meet a minimum honorarium of Rs. 2,500 per month for the Vidya Upasaks. These para teachers are employees of the Gram Panchayat. The latter has the jurisdiction to increase the salaries or dispense with the services of the para teachers if they deem it fit.

Strategies

The progress in achieving the goal of universal elementary education in Himachal Pradesh has been catalysed by noteworthy state government initiatives. These include:

- Additional finances made available by government of Himachal Pradesh for rapid expansion in the number of schools and number of teachers.
- District Primary Education Programme (DPEP) funds used since 1995-96 as an addition to the funds used for education programmes in the state and not merely as a substitute.
- Himachal Pradesh Compulsory Primary Education Act, 1997 which came into force with effect from 1 April 1997.

The increase in the finances made available in the state for primary education is given in Table 11.1. A perusal of the table indicates that the central government grants amount to no more than Rs. 30 crore per annum, while contributions from DPEP amount to less than Rs. 22 crore per annum. It is the state government's own financial initiative that bears the brunt of resource requirements in the sphere of education in the state.

Table 11.1 Budget allocation for primary education in Himachal Pradesh

(in Rs. Lakh)

Year	1994-95	1995-96	1996-97	1997-98	1998-99	1999-00	2000-01
Plan	1,444.34	2,762.06	2,763.47	4,186.59	8,245.23	10,802.20	14,536.70
Non Plan	8,407.21	10,149.10	11,790.70	13,609.20	19,000.00	22,455.70	21,131.70
Total (GOI + HP)	9,851.55	12,911.20	14,554.20	17,795.80	27,245.20	33,257.90	35,668.40*
Additional funds from DPEP	nil	5.12	156.49	1,492.58	1,735.21	1,972.26	2,187.38

Note: * The contribution of the central government to the total budgetary allocation in the year 2000-01, was Rs. 3002.70 lakh

Despite limited financial resources at the disposal of the state government, education remains the top most priority. According to Selected Educational Statistics 1999-2000, in 1998-99 the per capita expenditure on education in Himachal Pradesh was Rs. 890.33 while that of Kerala was Rs. 866.44. comparatively, the all India average for expenditure in the sphere of education was Rs. 620.15.

Impact

Near universal access to primary schooling has been achieved in the state in recent years. From a meagre 261 primary schools in 1948, Himachal Pradesh has a network of 10,633 primary schools (year 2000 figures) catering to the needs of the children in every corner of this hill state. Enrolment in the primary schools has increased manifold, from 8,697 in 1948 to 664,528 in 2000 and the number of posts of school teachers increased from 278 to 31,952. Education of girls has been made free up to university level including technical education. In 1996, the percentage of distribution of children currently enrolled in the age group 6-14 years for boys was 97 per cent while for girls was 95 per cent and the dropout rate was as low as two per cent and three per cent respectively. In the year 1999-2000, the participation of children in primary schools in the state also registered a spectacular improvement. While the average school size is about 62 students per school, the teacher-student ratio is 1:22. The ratio of girls to total enrolment was reported to be 49.5 per cent in 1999-2000 and dropouts have declined to three per cent (Box 11.1).

Box 11.1 **A model school**

The school in the Ner village in the Mandi district had a total of three teachers on the pay roll. The understanding of child development helped the teachers in the school teach peacefully and affectionately. It helped achieve high achievements and generated enthusiasm for education in the minds of students.

A twelve-year old Om Prakash, a student from a poor dalit family struggling to make ends meet, was in class V. He stated that, *'School jane mein maja aata hai. Aur naukari ke liye padhna jaroori hai* (I enjoy going to school. And it is also necessary for me to study to get a job).' The child also represented the school in the district level games.

The atmosphere in the school was conducive to learning. What startled the investigators was that every time the school bell rang to signal the end of a class, the children were given five minutes to wander around—an innovative and child-friendly practice. The school had a number of story books in its small library that were frequently borrowed by the children.

The teachers felt that parents had a positive attitude towards the school and were mindful of their children's needs. The parents were full of appreciation for the teachers and for the school. Some of the remarks given were *'Adhyapika bachhon ka poora dhyan rakhti hain. Hamein koi shikayat nahin'* (The teachers takes full care of the children. We have no complaints).

The teacher-pupil relationship in the school helped build a environment conducive for education and schooling. Ner has a school of which not just Himachal Pradesh but the entire country can be proud.

Source: PROBE Report, 1998

DPEP has had an impact not just on the selected districts but also on the training of teachers in the state as a whole. However, while lauding the administrative efforts under DPEP, ORG-Marg Study in 2000 found many lacunae in the implementation and impact of DPEP in the programme districts:

- The survey conducted in Kullu and Sirmour, revealed that the Parent Teacher Association/ Mother Teacher Association (PTA/ MTA) existed in only about half the villages (57 per cent); the Village Education Committees (VECs) existed in even a lower proportion of villages (30 per cent); and Village Construction Committees (VCCs) that were to be constituted as a sub-committee of VEC were found to exist in less than one-fifth of the villages.
- A mere nine per cent of total children below six years in sample households were enrolled in Early Childhood Care and Education (ECCE) centres. Only about 20-34 per cent teachers trained could recall the key aspects covered in training's attended by them.

Additionally, aspects such as preparation of low-cost teaching/ learning aids, pupil evaluation, multi-grade teaching, remedial teaching were not adequately addressed during training. Teacher absenteeism, not the lack of demand for schools has been seen as the single-most important factor affecting primary education in the state of Himachal Pradesh.

Summary

The remarkable progress in achieving near universal primary education in Himachal Pradesh has highlighted the role of that state-community partnership can play. The strategy adopted in Himachal Pradesh has renewed debate on the role and effectiveness of government provision and public policy in attaining gender equity and social equality. The continued effort to achieve higher levels of education has been through the strengthening of the legislative framework and enhanced provisioning even in the remotest areas of the state. Unlike other states in the country, the role of parental motivation, monitoring by the community in ensuring that the school does not become dysfunctional have been some of the highlights of the success story in Himachal Pradesh. However, factors such as teachers' absenteeism, improvements in the system of pupil evaluation, introduction of effective teaching-learning aids needs to strengthened. There have also been suggestions in improving the involvement of community level institutions.

An independent analysis of the state initiative however, has pointed towards a couple of gaps. These include (1) inadequate coverage of community-based associations in the interior and remote areas of the state; and (2) extremely low enrolment rates of children below the six years age group. Although the teachers have been provided training only about one-third teachers could recall key aspects covered during the training.

Replicability

The success of the Himachal Pradesh model of primary education has served to teach several lessons. The deployment of DPEP to recruit and train teachers, the institution of statutory committees to supervise implementation of school related schemes such as mid-day meal schemes and the transfer of responsibility for the appointment of para teachers to gram panchayats, are path-breaking approaches to the problem of teacher absenteeism and are worthy of emulation across states.

The Himachal experience has demonstrated that the groundswell in the demand for primary education which has been gathering momentum in all states across the country needs to be met by state governments. The state governments, on their part, are crucial agents in the provision of primary education services designed on a normative basis. Such services can be channelised by the legislators and administrators in the states by means of projects based on critical activities that address the problem of making sure that an adequate number of trained teachers exist and are deployed rationally. The enthusiasm of parents has to be translated into mandated duties, child labour has to be discouraged and local supervision and vigilance must be integrated into primary education projects by means of statutes. By ensuring the appointment of para-teachers by Gram Panchayats, states can move towards a situation where the local community appoints all teachers.

Contact

The Technical Officer
Directorate of Education
Shimla - 171 001, India
Tel.: +91-177-253 922
Fax: +91-177-211 247
E-mail: nodal_ofr@educationhp.org
Website: www.educationhp.org

CHAPTER 12

Quality Education through Community Mobilisation

Aamchi Shala, Maharashtra

Introduction

With a population of 96.8 million Maharashtra is the second most populous state in India. The literacy rate in the state has improved significantly during the 1990s from 64.88 per cent in 1991 to 77.27 per cent in 2001. The rural-urban literacy gap narrowed considerably due to faster improvement in rural literacy rate from 55.52 per cent to 70.84 per cent, between 1991-2001.

Background

The Government of India and five UN agencies ILO, UNDP, UNESCO, UNFPA and UNICEF conceived the Janshala programme as a holistic education programme to empower communities in an effort to bring them closer to schools, and make the formal school system more responsive to their needs and aspirations. It is not merely for students but for the community as whole. The programme is implemented in the regions not covered by the District Primary Education Programme (DPEP). This programme is being implemented in nine major states of Andhra Pradesh, Jharkhand, Karnataka, Chhattisgarh, Madhya Pradesh, Maharashtra, Orissa, Rajasthan and Uttar Pradesh.

The Aamchi Shala or Asha was initiated, in 1998, by the government of Maharshtra in two districts viz., Thane and Nashik. While Aamchi Shala means 'our school', Asha refers to 'hope'. The overall goal of the programme is to universalise primary education by transforming all schools into Aamchi Shalas. This is envisaged through a process of community mobilisation, involvement of Village Education Committees (VECs), Panchayati Raj Institutions (PRIs), NGOs and educational administrators at all levels. The programme aims to transfer ownership of education to the community to achieve 'Education For All' (EFA) by empowering people.

Objectives

The broad objectives of the Aamchi Shala initiative are:

- To enhance and sustain community participation in effective school management and the protection of child rights.

- To improve performance of teachers in the use of interactive, child-centred and gender sensitive methods of teaching in multi-grade classrooms.
- To redress social constraints that affect attendance and performance of school-age children, mainly girls in select districts.

Approach

The project Aamchi Shala includes several innovative steps to provide quality education along with ensuring community participation. These include:

- Strengthening community-based mechanisms for school management and support. This will particularly involve establishment and training of VECs in micro planning exercise.
- Developing government schools into 'empowered community schools' through a process of change emanating from fostering ownership of the school by the community.
- Improving teaching methodology for multi grade classrooms through teacher-development programmes and establishment of institutions like Cluster Resource Centres (CRCs) and Block Resource Centres (BRCs) to make teaching-learning more interactive, child centred and gender sensitive.
- Facilitating information exchange on best classroom practices, policy and community participation.
- Applying an integrated social development approach, which converges educational and development activities and resource inputs by all agencies and ministries.

Salient features

The salient features of the programme are analysed through three major facets viz., the project set-up, the nature of implementation and the level of community participation.

Project set-up

Aamchi Shala is being implemented in two phases in Maharashtra. The criteria for selection of blocks in the first phase were low female literacy, large tribal population, high drop-out rate, large-scale child labour and migration. Although the Asha project was launched in 1998, the Baseline Assessment Survey (BAS) was carried out only in October 2000. The survey was conducted in five project blocks in Nashik and six in Thane. Five schools were randomly selected in each block. Thus, 30 schools in Thane district and 25 schools in Nashik district were selected for the programme. The project is not implemented in urban areas. The survey measured the average performance of students (class I-IV) in competency-based achievement tests in language and mathematics. Differences with regard to gender and social groups, as well as the effect of variables like home, school, teacher, classroom practices, incentive schemes etc., on students performance were also analysed. In the second phase, eight blocks in Nashik district and six blocks in Thane district were selected.

Implementation

Aamchi Shala is a block based programme that advocates strengthening of blocks as a unit of planning and decision making in primary education. The programme consists of several measures to decentralise and provide financial and administrative autonomy to personnel at the block level.

The Maharashtra Prathamik Shiksha Parishad (MPSP) is the nodal agency for implementation. The programme is being implemented at the district level by the District Education Officer (DEO) assisted by District Resource Persons (DRPs) and at the block level by the Block Education Officer (BEO) assisted by Block Resource Persons (BRPs). Each block is further divided into 'educational beats' comprising of several clusters. Each cluster consists of 10-12 schools. The Cluster Coordinators and Resource Persons (CRPs) administer activities in these clusters. DRPs, BRCs and CRCs are trained at Bal Bhawan (MPSP office), Mumbai.

Community mobilisation

The Aamchi Shala programme in Maharashtra focuses on community mobilisation, improvement of quality and access to primary education. In this regard, a rigorous survey of eligible children in the age group of 6-14 years was carried out and followed by mass movement and campaigns throughout the districts. Several community mobilising measures included *prabhat pheris* (home visits), parent-teacher melas and *mata-palak* (mother-child) programmes, welcoming of newcomers and special enrolment fortnight celebrations in each school.

Each village has a VEC that supports and participates in enrolment drives. The VEC is headed by the *Sarpanch* of the village. It monitors the attendance of children enrolled in schools and conducts workshops on educational needs and issues in village. Efforts have been made by the community in general, VECs/ parent-teacher association (PTAs) and schools to universalise enrolment rates, improve attendance and retention rates of children in primary schools. Other steps include a review of the attendance and retention of students through regular meetings and information from the school teachers and head master. Steps to identify out-of-school children were conducted in the second phase in the survey conducted in 2002-03, indicated that there are about 2,727 and 2,905 VECs in Nashik and Thane district, respectively.

Micro planning

In 1999, the first round of micro-planning was conducted in Nashik and Thane districts while the second round was carried out in new blocks of the two districts with the help of Nehru Yuva Kendra, Chandrapur and Yuva Ved Manch, Yavatmal. This included training programmes for all VECs on educational needs and issues in villages and the steps to overcome these problems. Thus, while the community participation focused mainly on development of education infrastructure development, such training programmes helped the VECs identify areas to improve quality of education for their students (Box 12.1).

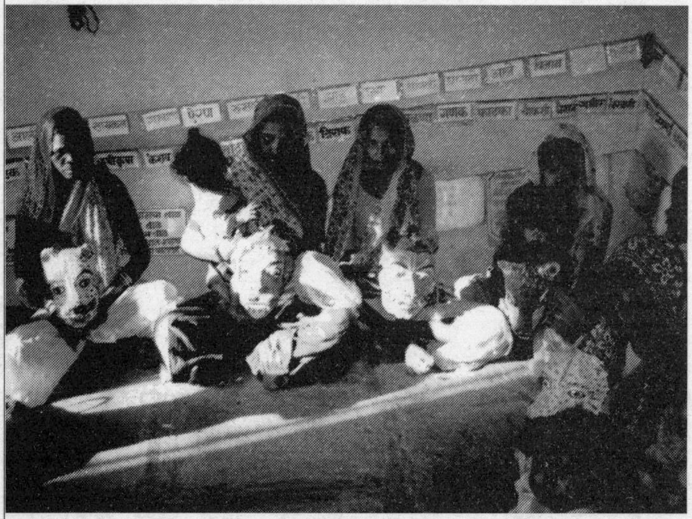

Habitations with no schooling facility within 1 km in rural areas or within reasonable distance in urban areas have been identified, micro planned and some form of community based schooling provided.

Box 12.1 **Micro planning for school education**

Vadkun Patilpada village, in Dahanu taluka of the Thane district, has a population of 2000 people. Most villagers were engaged in either making balloons or polishing spoons. The Zilla Parishad (ZP) School in the village provided education for classes I-IV and had a total enrolment of 269 children. Since there were only two classrooms, the school functioning was conducted in two shifts. The problem faced was that children in the morning shift used to come late and those in the afternoon shift used to come early, resulting in a loss of teaching time.

It was against this backdrop that the centre-in-charge held a meeting with parents, villagers and women on 12th December 1998. Over 150 villagers attended these meetings. A range of issues like the need for additional classrooms, enrolment and attendance of children, the quality of education, girls' education, and provision of physical infrastructure were discussed. Later on the 25th December 1998, the villagers, in another meeting, decided to build additional classrooms either by way of monetary contribution or in kind by manual work. Within a short time, a sum of Rs. 1,50,000 was collected, and a building with three classrooms was built within a month.

In another initiative, villagers in Thangaon, a small tribal village in Surgana Taluka of Nashik District, mobilised resources through monetary, material and manual contribution to build a stage, a compound and undertook repair work in the school. About 5 km from the village, at the Rakshas Bhuvan on the Maharashtra-Gujarat border, the villagers built a fence for the school. It was observed that parents often utilised the allowance given to students attending the school, and thus, the students attended without the school uniform. Villagers in a meeting of parents enforced the decision of utilising the allowances only for purchasing of school uniforms.

Thus, the initiatives of community in both the villages has improved the attendance and enforce a uniform dress code for children attending.

Source: Janshala (GOI-UN) Programme (2002)

An infrastructure grant of Rs. 2,000 per school was distributed in both districts, which was utilised to purchase blackboards, make minor repairs and develop self-learning material (SLM) based on the joint decision of the schoolteachers and the VEC members.

VECs in their regular meetings updated information about children who are out of school in *vastis* (hamlets). Vastishalas were provided if there were requisite number of 'out of school' children in far flung or inaccessible areas. The community through the panchayat or through other schemes provided space for the Vastishalas. There have been instances when individuals have provided land or a room for the Mahatma Phule Education Guarantee Scheme (MPEGS). In 2002-03, total number of Vastishalas in Nashik and Thane districts was 148 and 105, and total enrolment of children was 2,877 and 2,107, respectively.

Strategies

Several measures have been undertaken to improve the quality and accessibility of education at the school and extend services to the tribal sections of the population in the targeted areas.

Quality improvement in schools

Various initiatives have been undertaken so far to improve the quality of education being delivered at the Aamchi Shalas. These include several strategies towards capacity building of teachers, introducing multi-grade teaching and developing SLM, enrichment of school environment and monitoring the performance of the children enrolled in the programmes.

Capacity building of teachers: The onus to improve quality of education in the Asha Project has been through teacher training. Some of the initiatives include:

- Training programme at state and national level at Digantar, Jaipur, Shikshanchal, Alwar and Hyderabad.
- Special training for teachers teaching English in class I and IV for both districts for six days and a block level training programme of six days each.
- Training programmes for the resource persons in Vastishalas at Kosbad for four days and a second round training at the block level for over 20 days.
- Single day monthly meeting programme for teachers in Nashik.
- Training of 20 teachers through teleconferencing between March- November 2001. Other teachers were trained in subjects like art, music, dance etc.

Such training programmes helped teachers introduce new methods of teaching that attracted students towards education and instilled enthusiasm towards the otherwise neglected subjects of Mathematics and English (Box 12.2).

Box 12.2 **Encouraging innovations by teachers**

Programmes to improve the teaching-learning process, make it interesting and provide a forum to explore creative talents of students and teachers were implemented in the Dhasai Centre of Thane District. About 215 students and 24 teachers from centres like Zilla Parishad school in Dhasai, Ojiwane, Eklahare, Bangalpada and Dhasai Wadi participated in the programme. The programme included rangoli, essay writing, elocution, composition, poems, story-writing and drawing competitions for both students and teachers. The story telling and elocution competition helped students develop their talents for self-learning.

These programme also helped teachers adopt newer methods to teach languages to tribal children. For instance, a teacher from the Dhasai Wadi evolved a programme to teach language to tribal children who otherwise conversed only in their local dialect. The teacher was awarded the first prize for implementing an innovative project. Similarly, another teacher taught languages through drawing.

Thus, teachers training programmes helped the teachers and the students identify their talents and have also helped teachers to adopt innovative measures to attract tribal students towards education.

Source: Janshala (GOI-UN) Programme (2002)

Multi-grade teaching and SLM

Nearly 89 per cent schools in rural areas are functioning in multi-grade situations, where one or two teachers have to teach a number of classes simultaneously. For instance, the ZP school at Balegaon Umroli in Thane district had a total enrolment of 350 students. The ideal number of teachers was nine but the school has only six teachers. The teachers found it difficult to teach in multi-grade classes. Hence, the teachers and the centre-in-charge decided to encourage locally educated population to join the school.

Another measure to improve the quality of teaching 'Asha' has launched the SLM Pilot project in 26 schools of Surgana block, Nashik, with the help of an NGO Gram Mangal. Students were encouraged to develop SLM under the guidance of teachers. In March 2001, a special 10-day training programme was organised for teachers of all 26 schools at Aine taluka, Dahane. In this project, students were encouraged to develop SLM under the guidance of teachers. Effective utilisation of the SLM enabled children to participate actively in the teaching-learning process in peer groups. Later in June 2001, another two-day programme on multi-grade teaching and multi-class techniques was held in the two blocks. An estimated 213 and 183 volunteers from the Thane district and Nashik District have completed their 20-day training.

The SLM strategy has benefited students in several ways:

- They have gained confidence.
- They are interested in educational activities, which has improved attendance and quality of education in the school.
- Improved the understanding of the subject.
- Improved retention rates due more practice.

Through the SLM strategy children learn on their own. Thus, this measure has also compensated for the shortage of teachers.

Enrichment of school environment

In order to provide better learning environment, classroom walls are decorated with educational charts, maps and pictures; school premises are made attractive, clean and beautiful, with the help of community. For example, in Desgaon cluster of Kelawan block (Nashik), the cluster head developed "greenhouses", which are sheds made with tree trunks and dry leaves, where children sit in summer and carry out their self learning work. Additionally, an environmental laboratory has been set up with the help of parents at Sinnar block in Nashik, where students collect materials like leaves, seeds, plants, clay, rock, and historical material.

Monitoring

A cohort study was conducted in 11 blocks of Asha project for cohort of students who were enrolled in class I in 1996. The study covered all schools with class I and offered instructions up to class IV or V by 1999-2000/ 2000-01. Independent analysis was held for four years of primary cycle and five years of primary cycle. It covered 1,589 schools and 37,001 students in Thane, and 1,243 schools and 30,232 students in Nashik. While the data analysis of the study is being conducted, however, preliminary findings indicate that in the tribal block completion rates are low and retention rates are relatively high particularly in case of girls students. Another study using 1998 as the base year has been also initiated. It is similar to the cohort study and aims to cover the complete project period. Similar study will also be undertaken in all other Janshala states.

Health and hygiene programmes

To achieve the goal of universal primary education, the Aamchi Shala programme has integrated health programmes to improve the health status of children in school. Initiatives in this regard include, regular health check-ups, education about personal hygiene and cleanliness. These programmes are monitored by PTAs. A workshop was organised by UNICEF's School Hygiene Education Programme at the Zilla Parishad school in Vikramgad from 10-15 April, 2000. One of the highlights was inculcating good habits of health and hygiene in children at a young age, creating awareness of cleanliness of environment among citizens, and informing about household remedies for common ailments[1]. The children also participated in the Pulse Polio drive. These health programmes have also improved the rate of attendance.

Child-centred and Gender-sensitive methods of teaching

As part of the community mobilisation, the mother-teacher associations (MTAs) were formed in two phases by 2000-01. The orientation of cluster coordinators for formation of MTAs and their working was completed in Thane and Nashik in July-September 2001. Two meetings were organised every month by headmasters of the schools, where members discussed problems of irregular attendance among girls with the parents, with special attention to ensure girls' education. A *Bal anand melava* (children's fair) and *balak-palak-shikshak* (a children-parent-teacher) get together in 31 schools in centres of Jawhar taluka, which was attended by 15,500 children, parents and teacher each, and 700 office bearers. *Mahila Melas (*women get togethers) are held every year at various places in the districts to focus attention on the importance of girls' education[2]. The programme aims to make children enjoy themselves; generate awareness through educational and cultural programmes; felicitate deserving students; develop hidden talents of children and parents and create positive attitude towards manual labour. In 2002, the Bal Anand Melava based on Bal Bhavan Training Programme organised with the help of Meljol, an NGO in the district of Thane taught children different activities like spray painting, printing, drawing and craft. About 1,000 children and 300 teacher-parents and villagers participated in this meet.

The gender sensitive approach includes measures like appointing girls and boys as monitors in class, seating boys and girls, and providing toilets in schools that are in densely populated villages, discussions on age of marriage for boys and girls, reducing or sharing of household responsibilities between the male and the female children in the households and treating girls and boys equally.

---

[1] The UNICEF's School Hygiene Education Programme at the Zilla Parishad school in Vikramgad also inculcated healthy habits such as washing hands before and after eating food and even after going to the toilet, cutting nails, brushing teeth and having a bath regularly.

[2] In December 2000, Bal anand melava (children's fair) and balak-palak-shikshak melava (children-parents-teacher get together) were held in 31 centre schools of Jawhar taluka, Thane district. About 15,500 children, 15000 parents and 15000 teachers participated in the meet.

Improving access and reaching difficult groups

The programme provided access to education by means of Vastishalas and Mahatma Phule Education Guarantee Scheme (MPEGS) centres. Remote habitations that are not served by any other government schools were provided with Vastishalas and MPEGS centres were established for working children.

Despite continuous development and expansion of formal education, children in the age group of 6-14 years belonging to the tribal community tend to be deprived of elementary education. In Nashik district, especially in tribal blocks, efforts to provide elementary education to such children through alternative schools (AS) and non-formal education (NFE) centres since 2000 were made. While local youths who have completed class XII and D. Ed were selected as volunteer teachers for Vastishalas, those who have completed class X or XII were selected as MPEGS instructors.

Impact

A team comprising representatives from the government of India and the UN jointly reviewed the Aamchi Shala programme, in 2001 and 2002. The points highlighted are as follows:

- During their visit to some of the Aamchi Shalas it was observed that all the children (from class I to class IV) with whom the mission interacted, could read and write. This is one of the major achievements of the programme by standards of most government schools in India.
- Relevant attempts were being made to collect data and to use this data in micro-planning exercises, although this aspect needed to be strengthened.
- There were no enrolment problems in schools even in tribal areas.
- Involvement of the community in schools had increased considerably since the implementation of the programme. Participation of women had also increased. The VECs were found to be active participants in the affairs of the Aamchi Shalas.
- It was observed that specific attempts were made to improve retention of adolescent girls in schools. It was felt that such an attempt would also require appointment of women teachers since girls need role models to stay on in schools.

The team also provided some recommendation based on their findings, which are follows:

- Schools would require certain additional facilities like libraries and few inexpensive scientific instruments like magnets, magnifying glasses, prisms etc.
- The teacher training components of the programme would have to be strengthened. Although the teachers could cope with classes I and II there was a need for additional training was required for classes III and IV.
- A synergy was required between different programmes of development intervention like health, tribal welfare, education etc., a need also expressed by officials in the field.

Summary

Aamchi Shala was initiated in 1998 as a measure to universalise primary education in areas not covered by the District Primary Education Programme. It is a holistic education programme to empower communities in an effort to bring them closer to schools, and make the formal school system more responsive to their needs and aspirations. The programme is not merely for students but for the community as whole. The programme was initiated in Nashik and Thane districts of the state. The criteria for selection of blocks were low female literacy, large tribal population, high drop-out rate, large-scale child labour and migration. One of the main features of the programme has been decentralisation and strengthening of blocks as a unit of planning and decision making in primary education. Community mobilisation and micro planning has enabled villages develop physical infrastructure as well as provide support to the Zilla Parishad in evolving strategies to improve enrolment, attendance and reduce absenteeism and drop-out rate. Specific community level initiatives have been designed to attract girls students and children belonging to socially disadvantaged section of the population.

Replicability

The Aamchi Shala programme is a pioneering attempt at achieving the objective of 'Education for All', to which the global community had committed itself at the Jomtien World Conference. The BRCs structure, the SLM and the mulitgrade system have been incorporated into Sarva Shiksha Abhiyan which is a national level education programme.

The programme introduced several strategies to ensure community involvement and provide quality education. Activities like training of teachers and regular consultation with the parents assured that the needs and priorities of the beneficiaries were considered. Special focus towards education of girls and tribals, cordial relations developed between teachers and the community helped in improving retention rates and reducing drop-out rates. Such strategies also helped in motivating children to enrol in schools and also to continue with the learning process. Several relevant cues could be drawn from the success of community based education programme in Maharashtra by other states.

Contact

State Programme Coordinator
Janshala Programme
Maharashtra Prathmik Shikshan Parishad
Jawahar Lal Bhawan
Netaji Subhash Chandra Marg
Charni Road
Mumbai – 400 004
Tel.: +91-22-363 6314, 367 9267
Fax: +91-22-363 7315
Email: mpspmah@bom5.nic.in

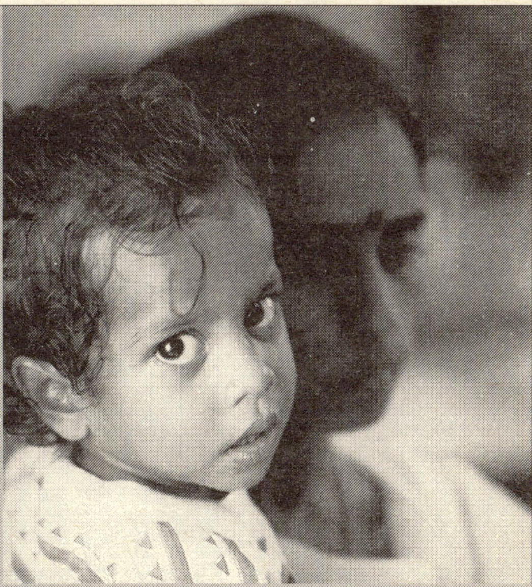

CHAPTER 13

Primary Education for All Village Children

Shishu Shiksha Karmasuchi, West Bengal

Background

In 1997, the Government of West Bengal formulated an alternate primary education system that was innovative in its populist appeal, as well as in its financial plan. Shishu Shiksha Karmasuchi (SSK) was initiated to meet the need for universal access to primary education within a time-frame. It solicited community action and initiative to run the schools. SSK was formalised and operated by the Panchayati Raj system, which represents liberalisation and decentralisation at its constitutional best. SSK is a low-cost, non-formal education system that aims to ensure quality education at the primary school level.

The Shishu Shiksha Kendra is a novel effort towards a community-centred approach to education that is both rights-based, as well as demand-driven. It operates through effective partnerships between organs of local self-government and the community, and has served to redress problems arising out of lopsided planning in education across West Bengal.

Objectives

SSK represents a partnership, based on the principles of decentralised management, between the government and the community. The system is designed to reach out to hitherto unserved and underserved areas. The SSK programme aims to universalise access of primary education and ensure quality education.

Salient features

Project set-up

A Shishu Shiksha Kendra can be opened in any village if:

- No primary school exists within a distance of one kilometre.
- Twenty or more children in the age-group five to nine years remain unenrolled or have dropped out from a formal primary school.
- The existing primary school suffers from infrastructural constraints (non-availability of rooms/ teachers) and is, therefore, unable to take the additional burden of unenrolled children and dropouts.

The SSK can be located in tribal/backward and remote areas.

Community initiative

Each SSK is started as a result of a community decision. The guardians/parents/villagers who are convinced of the need, suitability, and efficacy of SSK in their village and are willing to manage it locally, are required to pass a resolution towards this end. Subsequently, they are required to apply to the gram panchayat for approval. The gram panchayat scrutinises the eligibility of the application based on the above criteria and within four weeks, is required to either reject it or recommend it to the panchayat samiti. If there is no decision within five weeks, the villagers can re-route their application for an SSK to the panchayat samiti. If the panchayat samiti agrees, it recommends it for approval to the district panchayat. If the decision-making takes more than four weeks at any level, their clearance is automatically presumed and approval follows. Hence, throughout the process, a popular decision cannot be stymied by organisational/bureaucratic lethargy.

Implementation

A Shishu Shiksha Kendra depends on community decision and direct participation by the stakeholders in its management to ensure smooth functioning. Each SSK is managed by a nine-member management committee, out of which seven have to be guardians, elected from amongst the community. The local member of the gram panchayat is an *ex officio* member but, to safeguard the continuance of self-management, cannot be appointed as President or Secretary. The system is also gender-sensitive and stipulates that three members of the management committee have to be women.

Financing

The financial basis of an SSK is a mix of existing infrastructure, community efforts, and government aid. To secure financial assistance from the government, SSK's Managing Committee is required to:

- Arrange for building/rooms for setting up the SSK.
- Conduct a house-to-house survey and prepare a list of students who will attend the SSK.
- Engage one or more Shiksha Sahayikas (lady teachers) on a contract basis.
- Decide the timings and days when an SSK would remain open.
- Ensure attendance of the Shiksha Sahayika and supervise the quality of education.
- Arrange to mobilise community funding for running the SSK.
- Utilise, after obtaining permission, the existing secondary schools, public libraries, primary schools or any other public building for opening an SSK. If any private building is to be hired, the fund for this purpose is raised from the community.

If no public/community building is available, the gram panchayat/panchayat samiti may be requested to construct an SSK out of funds available under Jawahar Rozgar Yojana (JRY) and Employment Assurance Scheme (EAS). Each such structure has two classrooms and provision for a toilet and drinking water. Education infrastructure like furniture is supplied by the SSK Managing Committee, while the state government arranges to supply two blackboards, two hundred chalks and four dusters, as well as other teaching- learning materials at the time of opening of the centres. Textbooks are supplied by the state government as far as practicable. In case of a shortfall, funds are to be raised through community initiative. The requirement for such material is listed by the Managing Committee and forwarded to the district panchayat through the panchayat samiti. In addition, the government provides Rs. 500 each year to the Managing Committee for small-time expenditure and contingency needs.

Flow of funds

The flow of government funding is linked to community efforts, as well as to a steady growth of the SSK. Each school opens with the first grade only. On successful performance, the next grade is added each year, with not more than 40 pupils in each grade, to avoid overcrowding. In the first two years, up to two Shiksha Sahayikas can be appointed with government funding, and a third and fourth may be added on successful running of the school. Other teachers who may be appointed have to be paid out of community funding.

As a measure of administrative devolution and democratic decentralisation, the flow of government funds is routed through the panchayat system. The government places the funds with the district panchayat, which sub-allots them to each panchayat samiti, whose responsibility it is to supervise the maintenance of records and audit of expenditure incurred by the SSK. An internal audit takes place every quarter and an annual audit is organised at the end of each year.

Flexible enrolment

The functioning of classes in each SSK is a harmonious blend of the formal system and local needs. For example, though the clientele is primarily in the 5-9 years age group, dropout/unenrolled children in the 9-14 years age group are also admitted. An SSK has to run classes for at least 200 days in the year for three hours each day. The exact timings (as also selection of holidays) are decided by the Managing Committee in consultation with the community.

Accountability

The Shiksha Sahayika is fully accountable to the community. To obtain her remuneration, she has to achieve 90 per cent attendance each month. If the Managing Committee wants to pay her more than the government-approved amount (Rs. 1,000 per month), the additional amount has to be met from community funds. The Shiksha Sahayika has to be a resident of the village where the SSK is located. This ensures her regular attendance.

If suitable women teachers are not available, physically handicapped males may be appointed. Women or disabled males who have shown enthusiastic participation in the adult literacy campaign are given preference. These conditions, in addition to the mandatory women's representation in the Managing Committee, go a long way in ensuring equal opportunities for marginalised groups.

Training inputs

Training inputs are provided for the Shiksha Sahayikas. Having only secondary-level qualifications, they are understandably untrained in teaching methodology. District-level academic supervisors run 5-day capsules with government funding, for the benefit of the Shiksha Sahayikas.

The academic supervisor is invariably a retired school sub-inspector or an instructor of the Primary Teachers' Training Institute or headmaster of a primary school, and is engaged for SSKs on annual contract. She/he has to visit each SSK at least once in two months for inspection and technical supervision, and his/her tour expenditure is borne by the District Panchayat out of a special government fund.

Impact

All senior district officials from the District Collectorate have to monitor the progress of SSKs. The number of SSKs, as well as of enrolled students, has increased remarkably within a short span of time. Statistics of Murshidabad alone show more than 225 per cent increase in one year. Similar success has been reported all over the state (Table 13.1). The number of Shiksha Sahayikas increased from 484 to 1,572. However, the enrolment rate in the SSK was relatively lower at about 200 per cent. The teacher-pupil ratio has been relatively lower in the SSK at about 21 students per teacher.

Table 13.1 **Results of training provided to SSKs**

Year	SSKs	Shiksha Sahayikas	Students	Trained Supervisors
1999-2000	242	484	10200	8
2000-2001	786	1572	31431	34

Source: Department of Education, Government of West Bengal

Replicability

The success of the programme has been due to a large number of co-operant factors:

- SSK is a system of alternative education, which tackles the several ills of the conventional formal primary educational system, while addressing local needs.
- By acknowledging the importance of community involvement, initiative and management, SSK transforms guardians from passive observers to active doers. Accountability of teachers is guaranteed by a system of contractual appointment.
- By ensuring community participation, the programme elicits public support and taps the physical and financial resources of the community.
- It ensures the equitable participation of marginalised groups by carving out an organisational role for women and disabled men, as teachers.
- Finally, the SSK system is being implemented by the panchayats and Rural Development Department and not by the Primary Education Department. Its success is due to its non-formal and community-driven nature, a spin-off from the devolution of funds, functions and functionaries of the Panchayati Raj system.

The SSK approach has facilitated the progress towards universal access to primary schooling in West Bengal in a cost-effective and time-bound manner without compromising on the quality of delivery. From a legal perspective, being part of the Panchayati Raj set-up, the SSK can be replicated across the country whenever the 73rd Constitutional Amendment becomes an administrative and financial reality.

Contact

Rajiv Sinha
State Project Director
West Bengal Primary Education Programme
Bikash Bhavan, Salt Lake
Kolkata – 7700 091
Tel.: +91-33-334 3102
Fax: +91-33-358 5297
E-mail: wbdpep@cal3.vsnl.net.in
Website: www.wbdpep.org

CHAPTER 14

Management of Public Hospitals through Community Participation

Rogi Kalyan Samiti, Madhya Pradesh

Introduction

Health is a critical indicator of the quality of life of the population, and significantly contributes towards national development. Unfortunately, the provision of basic health care services to the population has remained an elusive objective, both at the empirical and the theoretical level. Although governments in developing nations have made concerted efforts towards improving health services, their policies, being devoid of a micro-perspective, have not created a sustained impact. Issues pertaining to health care in India are typically characterised by incomplete epidemiological transition, where diseases of poverty prevail, along with those due to affluent lifestyles. This has created a peculiar situation, wherein the rich depend on the private sector even as the poor, who are largely dependent on the public sector, are deprived of services of reasonable quality. The fiscal constraints faced by the central and state governments have added to the strain on the already low public expenditure on health care. Public hospitals suffer from poor facilities, which hampers the productivity of doctors. Ironically, these derelict public hospitals are still the only hope for a large majority of the populace in tribal and rural parts of the country.

Against this background, the Rogi Kalyan Samiti (RKS) initiative is a fine example of effective delivery of social services through decentralisation and community participation. The RKS's coordinated operations pertaining to plague eradication yielded management lessons, culminating in the user community managing hospitals. The project won the first annual Global Development Network (GDN) Award in the year 2000 in Tokyo, Japan.

The initial objective of the RKS project was to ensure the sanitation and remodelling of the Maharaja Yashwantrao Hospital, in order to check the spread of plague in Indore district of Madhya Pradesh. While this was achieved through concerted community action, there was also a need to revamp the public health care system. The RKS model institutionalised the levy of nominal user charges to create a stronger resource base. The nominal charges were accepted without any resentment by the people, and enabled each patient to exercise his/her right to demand and receive better medical attention. A management structure evolved and was operationalised to fulfil the objective of efficient and transparent administration through community participation.

Background

As panic of an impending plague epidemic spread across most of north India in 1994, the District Collector of Indore, along with the people of the district, decided to take effective steps to prevent an outbreak of the disease in the district[1]. One of the first places where attention was focused was the Maharaja Yashwantrao Hospital, a public hospital located in the town of Indore. An innovative plan was devised to overhaul the ailing health care system through an experiment that used no government funds and cost a little over Rs. 45 lakh.

Through a carefully calculated process of admissions and discharge, the 750-bed hospital, along with five other hospitals in the same campus, was evacuated of patients, who were shifted to 12 other hospitals, situated all over the town. A massive clean-up operation was undertaken in the hospital complex that involved clearing tonnes of rubbish and junk furniture. Rodents, pests and insects were eliminated through de-weeding, external and internal baiting, and finally disposed using an electric crematorium. After the clean-up, all physical facilities were restored and the hospital was renovated. Throughout the process, the involvement of the people of the town was sought in drawing up the policy framework for the operation.

Objectives

A process of participatory management was evolved, in which all hospital staff felt responsible for the improvement of health services through a process of mutual understanding, discussion, and problem-sharing. The objective was to ensure a degree of permanency and to prevent a relapse to its old state of decadence. This unique structure of hospital management came to be known as the RKS or Patient Welfare Committee.

The aim of the project was to create a model of the management of public service delivery based on public participation, with minimal recourse to the State exchequer. More specifically, the RKS undertook to achieve the following broad objectives:

- Improve the hospital, upgrade the equipment and modernise health services.
- Ensure discipline in the institution and mandate regular supervision of staff.
- Establish affiliations with private institutions to upgrade services.
- Undertake construction and expansion of the hospital building.
- Ensure optimal use of hospital land as per government guidelines.
- Improve participation of the committee in the running of the hospital.
- Ensure scientific disposal of hospital waste.
- Ensure proper training of doctors and staff.
- Ensure subsidised food, medicines and drinking water to patients and their attendants.

[1] The programme was initiated in the unified state of Madhya Pradesh in 1994. Despite the bifurcation of the state into Madhya Pradesh and Chhattisgarh in 1999, the programme continues in several regions of the newly formed state as well.

- Ensure proper implementation of national health programmes.
- Ensure proper use, timely maintenance and repair of hospital equipment and machinery.
- Ensure scientific reallocation of available space to improve efficiency.

It was decided to implement the following measures:

- Carry out a scientific reallocation of space to improve efficiency.
- Initiate redefinition of administrative responsibility.
- Introduce user charges in the hospital to strengthen the resource base.
- Establish a management structure that ensured permanency to the necessitated changes.

Salient features

Madhya Pradesh was the first state to devolve and decentralise responsibility in the health sector. The local administration of Indore spearheaded the formulation of this concept and its full-scale implementation. The active participation of hospital staff, along with representatives of the local population, was solicited. After elaborate discussions with eminent persons from the community, the hospital staff, elected representatives, environmental scientists, and the district administration evolved an operational policy for implementation.

The state government was approached for support to promulgate the concept by devolving rights and responsibilities pertaining to delivery of health systems to the local populace and to enable a framework for moving towards a performance-oriented regime. The implementation across the state involved a two-stage process. The state-level process included measures related to policy and framework of implementation, while at the district level, it pertained to formation of the Rogi Kalyan Samitis and other committees.

The experiment with the Maharaja Yashwantrao Hospital has since been replicated in over 450 government-owned hospitals in all the 61 districts of Madhya Pradesh and Chhattisgarh. The simplicity of concept, in addition to its core component of community participation, made for effective replicability. The results of this innovative project have been outstanding. In many hospitals in the backward districts and outlying rural areas, where often, basic amenities were not available, the Patient Welfare Committees have carried out physical improvements and provided equipment, as well as upgradation in services, which have been unprecedented in their scope and reach.

Project set-up

The RKS is a registered society that works like an NGO and has the mandate to take all functional decisions for the hospital. It has been set up in medical colleges, district hospitals, and community health centres throughout Madhya Pradesh and Chhattisgarh. The RKS comprises people's representatives, health officials, district officials, prominent citizens, representatives of the Indian Medical Association (IMA), members of urban local bodies and members of the Panchayat, as well as leading donors.

The RKS acts as an independent group of trustees for the hospital, while an Executive Committee, constituted for facilitating efficient administration, is expected to manage the affairs of the hospital.

Implementation mechanism

Implementation of the RKS concept began with the initial pilot experiment at Indore. Subsequently, replication across the state was effected in the following manner:

- Delineation of target areas and formulation of an RKS in each target area.
- Simultaneous devolution of rights and responsibilities to each RKS.
- Provision of infrastructure and commencement of operations and maintenance (O&M) management activities.
- Defining a support framework, policies and directives, and ensuring periodic review and revision of operations.

Fig. 14.1 RKS control chart

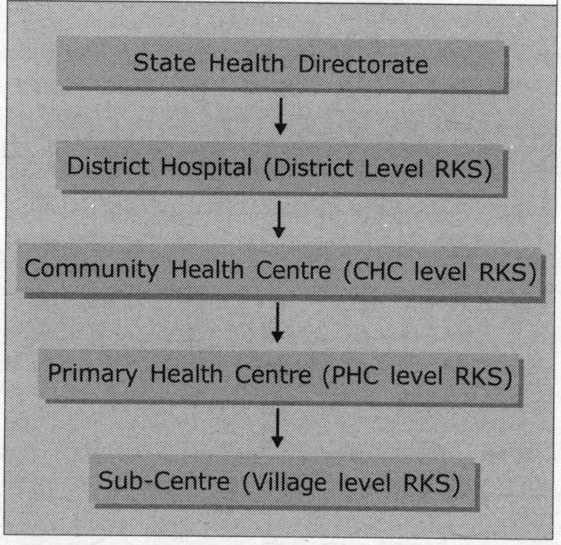

Source: *www.rogikalyansamiti.com*

Activities of RKS

RKS is free to use the funds at its disposal to its best judgement. RKS bodies have used the funds for a diverse set of purposes such as:

- Maintenance, repairs and necessary construction/expansion of the physical facilities in the hospitals.
- Sanitation, security, hospital waste management, medical information systems and other services in the hospital through private agencies.
- Upgradation of facilities such as operation theatre complexes, sonography units, burn units, paediatric wards, CT scan units, centralised pathological set-ups, etc.
- Purchase of equipment, chemicals, furniture and other necessities.
- Purchase of modern equipment through donations received and, if required, through loans from financial institutions.
- Improvement of hospital environment and facilities for attendants and patients.
- Free or subsidised medical care to the poor and needy.

Sources of funding

User charges

RKS is a service-oriented facility, which was permitted certain specific rights to allow freedom for operations and management. It was granted decision-making rights to invest in order to meet service requirements and the right to mobilise resources through the levy of user charges.

The rationale to introduce user charges was grounded on the belief that good health care on a continuous basis cannot be ensured without adequate financial provisions. However, broad guidelines were drawn up for the system to levy user charges:

- Charges must be levied for all facilities provided in the hospital, including outpatient facilities, pathological tests, beds, specialised treatment, operations, etc.
- The poorer sections of society and other groups as determined by the government would be exempted from the levy. Identification of such population would be based on self-certification. This would include persons below the poverty line, freedom fighters, etc.

- The charges for the general wards would be nominal, while higher charges would be fixed for private wards.
- Funds received from user charges would be deposited with the RKS and not in the government exchequer.

On the basis of the guidelines, RKS maintained the quantum of levy at a bare minimum. Initially, it was two rupees for the outpatient department ticket, which was later revised to Rs. 5. The user charges for specialised services like the intensive cardiac care unit (ICCU) are as low as Rs.150 per bed. Private organisations offering high-tech services like pathology, MRI, CT scan, sonography etc., have been permitted to set up their units within the hospital premises in return for providing their services at a rate fixed by RKS.

Other sources of revenue

Specific sources of funds for the RKS include:

- Fund raising through donations, loans from financial institutions, grants from the government, as well as other donor agencies.
- Utilisation of surplus land available in the hospital for commercial purposes or construction of shops and leasing them out (subject to broad guidelines issued by the government).
- Taking over and managing canteens, rest houses, bus stands, ambulance services, and other facilities within the hospital complex owned or managed by the government.

Note that RKS system will not affect the government's normal budgetary allocation for the hospital.

Impact

RKSs have been established in 604 hospitals across Madhya Pradesh, with 65-70 million beneficiaries and over 6000 people involved in its management. While most of the initial work was done at the district hospital level, there are several instances of local officials trying to bring around smaller hospitals across the state. After a review of the system in 1999, the government issued instructions that conferred greater powers to the RKS. The impact of the RKS can be analysed from both macro and micro levels.

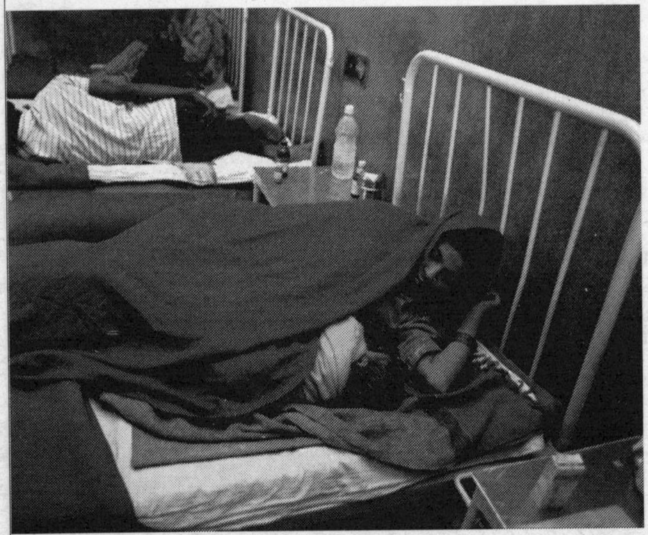

Macro-level impact

- Increased staff efficiency in government-owned health institutions.
- Empowerment of the community to contribute towards strengthening of public institutions.
- Inculcation of a sense of moral responsibility among the medical staff and a feeling of ownership in the minds of the patients through the system of user charges.
- Additional budgetary support for improvement of the health system.
- Manifold social benefits due to the restoration of safe and healthy surroundings in government hospitals.

- Upgradation and expansion of health care centres in rural and semi-rural areas from the internal resources generated by the RKS across the state.
- Improved working conditions for doctors and staff.
- Increased efficiency due to privatisation of medical services.
- Allocation of funds for improvement of health institutions from discretionary local area development funds by Members of Parliament and Members of Legislative Assemblies.

Micro-level impact

- Funds amounting to Rs. 35-40 crore have been collected by the districts through donations and user charges.
- District Red Cross Societies have been functioning in tandem with the RKS. During 1990-94, the Red Cross Societies spent around Rs. 40 lakh on hospital improvement, which increased to Rs. 7-8 crore during 1995-2000.
- A sum of Rs. 38 crore was raised by citizens through the RKS, during 1995-1999.
- RKS is expected to collect Rs. 75-80 crore over the period 2000-2002.
- Most hospitals are introducing the privatisation of ancillary services such as pathology, hospital sanitation, security and canteen services in a phased manner.
- The average daily collections of RKS range from Rs. 500 to Rs. 25,000 in each hospital, depending on its location. A conservative estimate would put the monthly collection at around Rs. 2.5 to 3 crore in all hospitals across the state.
- A fallout of the RKS experience is that medical colleges have been made into autonomous bodies, and their management handed over to RKS. Medical college fees have also been channelled into the RKS to improve the conditions of the previously decrepit medical college hospitals.

Future plans

The RKS experience has provided valuable insights into the process of governance and management of public institutions through participation of the community. The road ahead for the RKS is envisaged as follows:

- Programme formulation.
- Networking of the care centres, area/district centres.
- Upgradation and modernisation of facilities and hospitals.
- Capability building and training of staff.
- Regulation of RKS by an independent body.
- Benchmarking costs and benefits.
- Planning for resource mobilisation.

Summary

The RKS initiative was designed to combat the plague epidemic in 1994 in Madhya Pradesh. It aimed to improve the effectiveness of health services through decentralisation and community participation. It is a successful case study illustrating the manner in which a highly coordinated implementation could strengthen the delivery of services through efficient management and effective community participation.

The participatory management approach of the RKS through the introduction of user fees inculcated a sense of responsibility in the minds of the health care personnel, as well as a sense of ownership in the minds of the patients. Introduction of user charges has helped to raise substantial resources to improve the quality of services rendered in the RKS and improve the overall coverage of the services.

Replicability

The experience of Indore and subsequent experiences of other districts of Madhya Pradesh and Chhattisgarh where RKS has been replicated have served to teach many valuable lessons. It represents an effort to create a system that is self-sustaining and where active participation of hospital administration, motivation of staff and constant monitoring by the public can be ensured to guarantee better all-round performance of hospitals. To take the RKS concept across sections of the community, local representatives and the political regime, the concept had to be appealing and easy to replicate. The case for the replicability of RKS centres around two main features: (a) simplicity of concept; and (b) transition and adaptation with local support and political influence.

For replication across the state, implementation was effected through:

- Defining target areas and formulation of an RKS in each target area.
- Simultaneous devolution of rights and responsibilities to each RKS.
- Provision of facilities and introduction of O&M management.
- Defining a support framework – policy and directives, review and revision of policy, and framework for operations, from time to time as an ongoing process.

The RKS initiative signifies a paradigm shift from the 'top-down' approach to health delivery systems in the country. It has been successful in bringing together hospital staff and user communities through a process of mutual understanding and problem-sharing, for the common goal of improving local health service systems. Rather than assuming a zero sum relationship between government involvement and private cooperative efforts, the Rogi Kalyan Samiti has effectively drawn on the potential of micro-level social capital to construct a sustainable 'state-society' synergy.

Contact

Mr. S.R. Mohanty
Rogi Kalyan Samiti
D 2 / 11, Char Imli
Bhopal, India
Tel.: +91-755-552 409
E-mail: info@rogikalyansamiti.com
Website: www.rogikalyansamiti.com

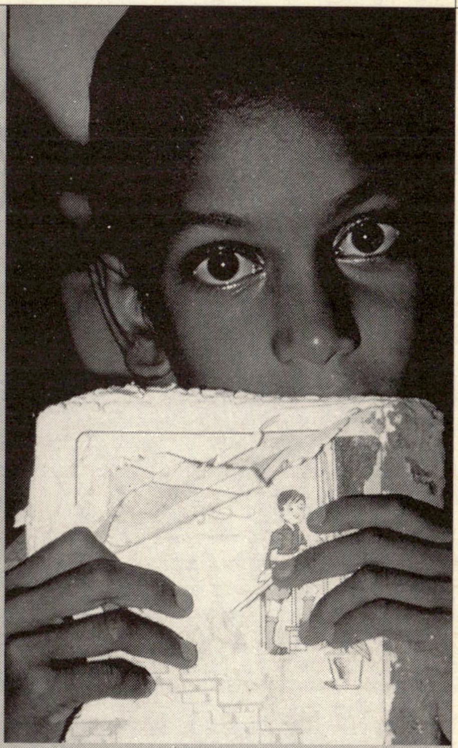

CHAPTER 15

Identification of Destitute Women and Children

A Case Study from Tamil Nadu

Introduction

In India, the only comprehensive survey is the decadal population census, which captures the demographic composition of the population. However, it fails to provide disaggregated information about the status of destitute women and children in the population. This issue assumes greater importance in the present context, where estimates indicate that there are about 100 million "missing women"[1] around the world, of which 50 million are in India alone. These would have been alive but for infanticide, neglect or sex-selective abortions (UNDP, 2002). Further, it is difficult to estimate precisely the size of the population of widows, deserted women, unmarried old women, handicapped women and orphan children in the total population, which also proves to be a constraint in providing assistance to such groups. Thus, the precondition to evolving a strategy of social protection for such groups would be to *identify the size* of the targeted group. In 2000, an initiative was undertaken by the district administration in the Nilgiri district of Tamil Nadu, to identify the number of destitute women and children through a survey. This survey also generated awareness about the existing government schemes for the destitute and helped in formulating steps to extend and modify provisioning to the identified destitute population.

Background

Women account for 50 per cent of the 11 lakh population in Nilgiri district. Official estimates indicate that about 5,660 persons, including 4,545 women, have availed of benefits from prevailing government schemes (Table 15.1). Under the National Social Assistance Programme, these persons have been receiving a monthly pension of Rs. 200 as old age pension, physically handicapped

---

[1] The term "missing women" is an alternate way of explaining the presence of gender gaps in the demographic composition of the population, often known as female-male ratio (FMR). The FMR in India is 930 per thousand males. Dreze and Sen (2002, p. 230) explain the process of missing women in India and in many other countries as being due to the relative neglect of health and well-being of women (particularly young girls, including female infants) resulting in survival disadvantage of females vis-à-vis males over long periods.

Table 15.1 Number of persons receiving pension in the Nilgiris district

Sl. No.	Taluka	Men	Women	Total
1.	Udhagai	262	1336	1598
2.	Coonoor	245	1220	1465
3.	Kotagiri	157	753	910
4.	Gudalur	158	545	703
5.	Kundah	79	408	487
6.	Pandalur	214	283	497
	Total	1115	4545	5660

Source: Collector, Nilgiris district

pension, destitute agricultural labourers' pension and deserted destitute wives' pension. This number is not indicative of people who deserve the pension; it only covers the number of people who are being assisted at present. The district administration has assisted those destitute women who presented petitions on "grievances days".

Several villages in the district had a number of destitute women, widows, and orphans, who were not receiving any form of social assistance. Further, women not covered under the schemes were unaware about them. The administration on the other hand did not have any planned effort to identify and rehabilitate all the destitute women. In order to extend the coverage of existing schemes there was an urgent need to design a comprehensive welfare plan for the district. Hence, the District Collector initiated a project titled *Neelamalai Mahalir Nala Thittam* (Nilgiri Women's Welfare Scheme). This involved a survey, which generated a comprehensive list of the destitute population in the area, and facilitated a paradigm shift from an ad hoc arbitrary approach to a more systematic and defined methodology.

Objectives

The specific objectives of the scheme were to:

- Draw a comprehensive action plan to uplift destitute women in the district.
- Ensure that every destitute woman child is provided assistance under government schemes.
- Bring a qualitative improvement in the lives of the destitute.

Salient features

Several steps were undertaken to identify the targeted population, including awareness generation about the survey and programmes for destitute women, census survey in all the villages of the district, and constitution of a team for primary data collection. The distinguishing feature of the initiative was its cost-effective implementation.

Awareness generation

There was a need to inform households about the objectives of the programme and motivate them to provide accurate information to the research investigators. The district administration publicised the survey and programme for destitute women through a massive awareness drive in the form of press releases and visual media in English and the regional dialect, wall posters, handbills, and slides in cinema halls. Handbills and posters carried catchy slogans to create awareness in the tribal and remote areas.

Local bodies and NGOs extended enormous support to the programme. The NGOs ensured that the survey teams did not miss enumeration of households even in remote areas, including tribal hamlets. Local leaders were also instrumental in generating awareness about the survey at the household level. As a result of such sensitisation, a number of women came forward to the Collector's office, seeking assistance under the pension scheme.

Survey

To identify the number of destitute women and prepare an exhaustive database, a survey was initiated for two days on 16-17 December 2000 in all the villages of Nilgiri district. Even though survey teams visited all households in the district, the exercise was confined only to the enumeration of women and children in the households.

Questionnaire

The survey was conducted using a pre-formatted questionnaire that captured essential information such as name, age group, health status, financial capability and needs of the target population. This format was designed in consultation with a select group of government officials, local body leaders and NGOs. The questionnaire was finalised based on two pilot surveys and field experience. The District Collector took special care to simplify the data format in such a way that the enumerators only had to tick the columns. This facilitated the completion of the survey in two days.

Implementation

The District Collector, in consultation with revenue officers, development officials, elected local body leaders, and NGO representatives, decided that the survey would be undertaken by government officials on a voluntary basis. Government employees from the Departments of Revenue, Education, Health, Development and Social Welfare were requested to contribute two days of their time. The dates also happened to be official holidays, thus ensuring wholehearted cooperation from the staff (Box 15.1). The survey generated an overwhelming response and the government officials

Box 15.1 **A remarkable team effort: survey in Nilgiri district**

The district administration realised that to capitalise on the enthusiasm of the research team and retain the interest of the households, the survey had to be completed within a span of two days. The villages were spread across six talukas, viz., Udhagamandalam, Kundah, Coonoor, Kotagiri, Gudalur and Pandalur. Each taluka had 4-15 villages, accounting for a total of 56 revenue villages and 459 hamlets (Table 15.2). Pandalur and Gudalur, under the Gudalur revenue division, had 12 revenue villages, while the remaining 44 revenue villages were under the Coonoor division. The revenue divisional officers in both the regions organised the survey on 16-17 December 2000.

The survey team comprised 2-3 government officials from five departments—village administrative officer, *Makkal Nala Paniyalargal*, anganwadi workers, noon-meal centre workers and a village health nurse. There were representative from other departments like *Arivoli Iyyakkam* volunteers, school teachers and bill collectors from municipalities and town panchayats.

The two-day survey, or census, was completed with the help of a large team of 3,464 government staff under the supervision of the Collector in the entire district. Each team of two enumerators had to cover 50-60 houses per day.

Source: Nilgiri Women and Children in Distress Survey and Rehabilitation Plan

Table 15.2 Villages covered by the survey

Taluka	No. of revenue villages	No. of hamlets
Udhagamandalam	13	107
Kundah	7	87
Coonoor	9	66
Kotagiri	15	119
Gudalur	8	48
Pandalur	4	32
Total	56	459

Source: Collector Nilgiris district

Table 15.3 Details of training classes conducted between 14–15 December 2000

Taluka	No. of classes	No. of Master trainees
Coonoor	3	5
Kotagiri	3	5
Kundha	2	4
Udhagai	3	11
Gudalur	1	8
Pandalur	1	4

Source: Collector Nilgiri district

agreed to work on a non-remuneratory basis. (Details of enumerators engaged in the survey in the *six* talukas of Nilgiri district have been included in Annexure 15.1.)

Training

The data collecting team was imparted special training in filling up of the questionnaires by master trainers. Two-day training programmes were conducted in each taluka prior to the survey. During the training, the Collector and Additional Collectors not only clarified the doubts of the volunteers but also motivated them (Table 15.3).

Expenditure

Resources were needed to train the survey teams, generate awareness, print formats, and build the database with the help of suitable software support, data entry and processing. These costs were met from the administrative head of the NSAP. The total exercise of enumerating over 2.10 lakh households was as low as Rs. 3 lakh, viz., a per household expenditure of less than a rupee (Table 15.4). The administrative cost of the teams was restricted to lunch for training and survey teams and provision of kits for survey, which accounted for 45 per cent of the total expenditure (Annexure 15.2). Over one-fourth of the total expenditure was towards the awareness programme.

Table 15.4 Absolute budget expenditures on the survey

Items	Amount in Rs.	% share
Total expenditure	300,000	-
Lunch for training and survey teams	60,000	20.00
Awareness generation	78,000	26.00
Kit materials for the survey team	75,000	25.00
Other contingencies	45,000	15.00
Stationery	20,000	6.67
Data entry in computer	12,000	4.00

Source: Nilgiri Report

Findings of the survey

The survey succeeded in generating awareness about the existing schemes for destitute women. The number of women visiting the Collector's office increased manifold and many deserving women were assisted by the pension scheme. Official estimates of the total destitute women in Nilgiri district indicate that out of the 3.15 lakh women in the district, nearly 74,117 are destitute, viz., about 23.48 per cent of the population.

The absolute values of each category of destitution indicates that the proportionate share of destitute women and children in the total population of the district is about 21.82 per cent and 1.79 per cent, respectively (Table 15.5). In the total women's population, the percentage share of widows was highest at 11.25 per cent. A mere 0.30 per cent women were protected by pensions. Destitute children were mainly the physically disadvantaged and mentally challenged children. There were about 356 orphan children in the region.

Table 15.5 **Information on destitute women and children generated by the survey**

Sl. No.	Category	Number	Percentage
1.	Blind children	198	0.11
2.	Blind women	3005	0.95
3.	Deaf children	406	0.23
4.	Deaf women	1991	0.63
5.	Deserted women	6207	1.97
6.	Dumb children	413	0.24
7.	Mute women	617	0.20
8.	Mentally retarded children	691	0.40
9.	Mentally retarded women	1586	0.50
10.	Obtaining Pension	952	0.30
11.	Orphan children	356	0.21
12.	Physically handicapped children	1019	0.59
13.	Physically handicapped women	3314	1.05
14.	Unmarried women	15338	4.86
15.	Widows	35514	11.25

Total women surveyed: 3,15,631
Total children surveyed: 1,73,270
Women and children in distress: 74,117 (23.48%)

Source: Collector Nilgiris district

Follow-up plan for rehabilitation

The data generated from the survey was disseminated through presentations to officials and local body leaders. Several NGOs, private individuals, charitable institutions, and other institutions participated in the presentations, followed by sessions to plan for the rehabilitation of the destitute population. The rehabilitation plans have been prepared in terms of identification of the cause of deprivation, improving the provisioning of existing facilities and starting new facilities under the following heads:

- Blind children and women: The number of blind women and children was as high as 3,005 and 198, respectively. To provide any treatment to them, it was felt necessary to identify the reasons for blindness and classify them according to the cause. Suggestions included distribution of excess supply of medicines for night blindness from government hospitals to night blindness camps; issuing of bus passes and conducting awareness campaigns for eye donations.
- Deaf-mute children and women and physically handicapped children and women: Options such as enrolling such children in regular schools and provision of physical aids were suggested.
- Mentally retarded children and women: It was felt that measures to extend government schemes for such groups would have to integrate provision of better medical facilities like provision of equipment for physiotherapy, along with existing basic needs such as food, clothing and shelter and improve utilisation of existing facilities. It was felt that there was need to transfer the facilities to primary health care centres to improve accessibility of services, and provide monthly monetary support in the form of grants to these children.
- Widows: It was felt that instead of a monthly pension scheme, it would be more meaningful to provide welfare measures such as permanent job opportunities or self-employment opportunities. Suggestion for widow remarriages was given as well.
- Orphan children: It was felt that there was an urgent to need to explain procedures of adoption to childless parents and provide a family environment to such children.

Summary

In 2000, the district administration of Nilgiri formulated the *Neelamalai Mahalir Nala Thittam* (Nilgiri Women's Welfare Scheme) to identify the number of destitute children and women in the district. The underlying rationale of the scheme was to extend the coverage of existing government schemes, which were otherwise reaching out only to a minuscule proportion of the needy population. The identification process was conducted in a sequential manner, which involved generating awareness of government schemes for destitute women and children, and enumeration of destitute women and children through a survey of households. The survey was carried out within a span of two days with the help of a team consisting of government employees from various departments on a non-remuneratory basis. This strategy made the survey an extremely cost-effective exercise, keeping the expenditure to three lakh rupees, that is, less than a rupee per household enumerated.

The survey was followed by rehabilitation meetings, where strategies were chalked out to ensure wider coverage and improve the quality of life of the vast destitute population identified through the survey. The impact of the awareness programme was also found at the household level (Box. 15.2)

Box 15.2 **Impact of awareness programme**

On 16 December 2000, a middle-aged official with a pad and set of papers reached a household to conduct the survey. The official, who worked at the Agricultural Engineering Office in Coonoor, briefed the household members about the purpose of the survey. The official stated that 'among all the social activities I have done so far, this survey work is the most satisfying to my mind. I am glad to be part of a scheme that aims to rehabilitate women and children.' Such sincerity was seen among all government officials, thus, making the data generated extremely reliable.

The awareness programme also generated social awareness about caring for the physically disabled, mentally challenged, widows and orphans. It also raised relevant issues of special attention to destitute women and children. It was felt that support to the destitute need not be linked to the economic status of the household but should be provided by the government by issuing relevant certificates to the 'physically and mentally challenged'.

Source: Indian Express, Coimbatore edition, 20-12-2000, p. 4

Replicability

The Nilgiri experiment, by enumerating the women-related profile of the district, has broken new ground in redressing the inequities in gender development. The survey undertaken by government officials generated valuable primary data. This has built a strong foundation on which the district administration can build its plans for providing government assistance to destitute women and children. Such initiatives have often been suspended on the pretext of entailing high costs. The Nilgiri experience has demonstrated a cost-effective means of identifying target groups, and utilising resources allocated to government schemes. Based on the data, a rehabilitation plan has been drawn up for the district. The programme of rehabilitation is now underway in each village. This scheme has highlighted the importance of government's role in providing assistance to the targeted population.

The rehabilitation of destitute women and children is accorded very low priority in most plans at the state level. As a result of this, the benefits to such sections of the population under various government schemes are left largely underutilised. The success of the Nilgiri model in bringing the destitute population under the welfare net is well worth replicating in districts across the country.

Contact

Supriya Sahu, IAS
District Collector
Nilgiri district,
Udhagamandalam – 643001, India
Tel.: +91-423-442 233, 442 344
Fax: +91-423-442 344
Email: collrnlg@tn.nic.in

Annexure 15.1 **Details of enumerators engaged in the survey**

1. Coonoor
   a. Teams 1355
   Enumerators 2710
   Reserve 167
   2877
   b. Details taluka-wise

Taluka	Team	Persons
Coonoor	412	824
Kotagiri	267	534
Udhagai	511	1022
Kundah	165	330

2. Gudalur
   a. Teams 377
   Enumerators 754
   b. Details taluka-wise

Taluka	Team	Persons
Gudalur	207	414
Pandalur	170	340

c. Details of the enumerators (department-wise) deputed for survey
   1. Makkalnala Paniyalargal
   2. Volunteers of Arivoli Iyakkam
   3. Anganwadi workers
   4. Village administrative officers
   5. Village health assistants
   6. Revenue inspectors and village assistants
   7. Bill collectors in village panchayats and town panchayats
   8. Teachers
   9. Noon-meal organisers

d. Supervising officers for entire survey
   1. District Collector
   2. Additional Collector (Development)
   3. District Revenue Officer

e. Details of census formats, wall posters, appointment orders for enumerators, etc., that were printed

1.	Census formats	3,00,000
2.	Notice	7,000
3.	Wall Posters	5,000
4.	Appointment Orders for Enumerators	17,000
5.	Question and Answer sheets to formats	6,000
6.	Appreciation Letters to Enumerators	5,500

Source: Collector, Nilgiri district

Annexure 15.2 **Budget for conducting the survey (Rs.)**

1.	**Total number of households in the district** (as per 1991 census) with added four per cent increase, i.e. 2.10,000 formats	**1,95,845.00**
	Cost of the survey formats	10,000.00
2.	**Lunch for Training and Survey Teams**	
	i) Gudalur teams: 150 x 2 people	300.00
	ii) Coonoor teams: 600 x 3 people	1,200.00
	Total no. of people to be involved in survey	**1,500.00**
	a) Training lunch: 1500 x Rs. 20	30,000.00
	b) Survey lunch: 1500 x Rs. 20	30,000.00
	Total	60,000.00
3.	**Awareness generation**	
	Printing of posters:	
	Village Panchayat hamlets : 600 hamlets x 10 posters	600.00
	Ooty Municipality: 36 wards x 10 posters	360.00
	Coonoor Municipalities: 32 wards x 10 posters	320.00
	Town Panchayats:13 x 200 posters	2,600.00
		9,280.00
	or approx.	10,000.00
	Cost of the posters	10,000.00
4.	Cost of the posters: 6000 x Rs. 3	18,000.00
5.	Paper advertisement	50,000.00
6.	Kit materials: 1500 x Rs. 50 for survey team	75,000.00
7.	Other contingencies	45,000.00
8.	Stationery	20,000.00
9.	Feeding of data entries in the computer	12,000.00
	Total	**3,00,000.00**

Source: Collector, Nilgiri district

48
49
50
51

Section III

Public Interface with the Government

Introduction

Since the beginning of planned development in India, both central and state governments have implemented several development programmes. With liberalisation, there is an ongoing paradigm shift at the state level, with the government increasingly playing the role of a facilitator. At the same time, there remain large areas of direct public interface with the government, and small improvements in the functioning of these areas can contribute significantly to public well-being. Better governance and implementation of programmes within a pro-poor framework are needed for effective results on the ground that visibly benefit the people. The case studies included in this section include such efforts drawn from areas where there is a high degree of interface with the government, ranging from improvements in municipal governance to agricultural markets to rural credit to innovative application of information technology for rural development.

The first initiative relates to the Municipal Corporation of Ludhiana, which in an attempt to evolve into a more efficient organisation, initiated several reforms relating to managerial capacity building and increased community participation. In doing so, the corporation aspired to improve the quality of life for the citizens of Ludhiana, by promoting a strong, effective and accountable municipal government.

The domination of middlemen in agricultural markets in India has reduced the producer-consumer relationship to the weakest link in the marketing chain. Lack of market intelligence, credit facilities and ad hoc marketing techniques have reduced the benefits of marketing of agricultural produce for the farmers. The consumers, on their part, are often dissatisfied with inferior quality, spiralling prices and malpractices. To combat these problems, the Government of Andhra Pradesh evolved an alternative marketing strategy where both the farmers as well as the consumers are beneficiaries. These Rythu Bazars or farmers' markets were conceived of as price stabilisation centres, in order to promote direct interaction between consumers and growers and eliminate interference from middlemen. Following the success of these regulated markets in Andhra Pradesh, neighbouring states have also attempted to replicate the concept.

The empowerment of women as agents of socio-economic change and development has been a focus of successive Five-Year Plans. The Tamil Nadu Women's Development Project is a unique partnership between the government, non-governmental organisations, and commercial banks to implement a massive development programme for women based on the formation of a network of self-help groups (SHGs) across the state. The project illustrates that empowerment of women based on the SHG model can have far-reaching results and that the institutionalisation of SHGs as agents of rural development enhances women's bargaining power and decision-making responsibilities towards the overall development of communities.

The use of information technology (IT) for development, first envisaged in the computer policy in 1985, has seen several successes in India. However there has been some scepticism about the use of IT in an agrarian context in view of the terrain, absence of adequate infrastructure and the alleged lack of awareness among the rural population.

Against this background, the Gyandoot project is an example of a low-cost, self-sustainable and community-owned rural Intranet project that has catalysed a social revolution in the Dhar district of Madhya Pradesh. Through its innovative government-to-citizen (G2C) model, it aspires to cater to the developmental needs of the resource poor and bridge the urban/rural digital divide. It is encouraging to note that this initiative has helped dispel some of the scepticism about the use of computers and the Internet in rural settings, and demonstrated the relevance of a demand-driven approach, which also incorporates a revenue stream for the information provider/kiosk operator.

The Bhoomi project, aimed at computerisation of land records by the Government of Karnataka, has been a successful attempt at introducing an efficient system of land record maintenance as opposed to the traditional manual system of management of land deeds, with all its attendant weaknesses. The Karnataka experience has proved the potential of IT as a tool of transparent governance in the all-important area of land record management.

CHAPTER 16

Municipal Management and Capacity Building
A Case Study from Punjab

Introduction

Within a span of about 50 years, Ludhiana has grown into the largest city in Punjab with a population of 14 lakhs spread over an area of 169 sq.km. Also known as the 'Manchester of India', Ludhiana is the industrial hub of the state and amongst the fastest growing cities of the country. This growth has been accompanied by a corresponding demand for infrastructure resulting in a serious shortfall in essential municipal services. In a scenario of increasing demands and shrinking government grants, the Municipal Corporation of Ludhiana (MCL) had to face the challenges of rapid urbanisation, haphazard development, political interference, poor work culture, eroding accountability and a declining public image due to the increasing gap between service delivery and public expectations. The MCL is dedicated to improving the quality of life of the community by promoting strong, effective and accountable municipal governance.

To revamp the derelict system, MCL initiated various reforms related to managerial capacity building and community participation. The reform measures include privatisation, asset management, monthly appraisals, organisational restructuring, human resource development, management information systems and financial overhauling. The reforms focused on increasing work accountability and transparency, using innovative e-governance techniques, implementing zero-based budgeting, promoting confidence building with stakeholders and cutting down establishment expenditure. As a result, MCL has become a more efficient, clarified organisation. By pruning administrative expenditure and using innovative methods to generate additional financial resources, MCL's income has increased by 221 per cent and expenditure on infrastructure development works increased by 644 per cent.

Background

The MCL, by virtue of being the first point of contact of the general populace with the public sector, is the first order of government for the people. Like many other local bodies, it was functioning within an 'equilibrium trap' (Fig. 16.1) where poor service delivery resulted in poor willingness-to-pay by the citizenry and consequently, poor recoveries by the corporation. The management techniques of MCL were outdated, inefficient, non-transparent and frequently plagued by allegations of corruption. Financial resources were meagre, thereby limiting the extent of duties that could be undertaken by the corporation. Furthermore, disgruntled by the work ethic of MCL, the urban population grew increasingly cynical of the nature and scope of the corporation as the true voice and advocate of the city's requirements.

Fig. 16.1 Equilibrium trap due to poor capacity-building

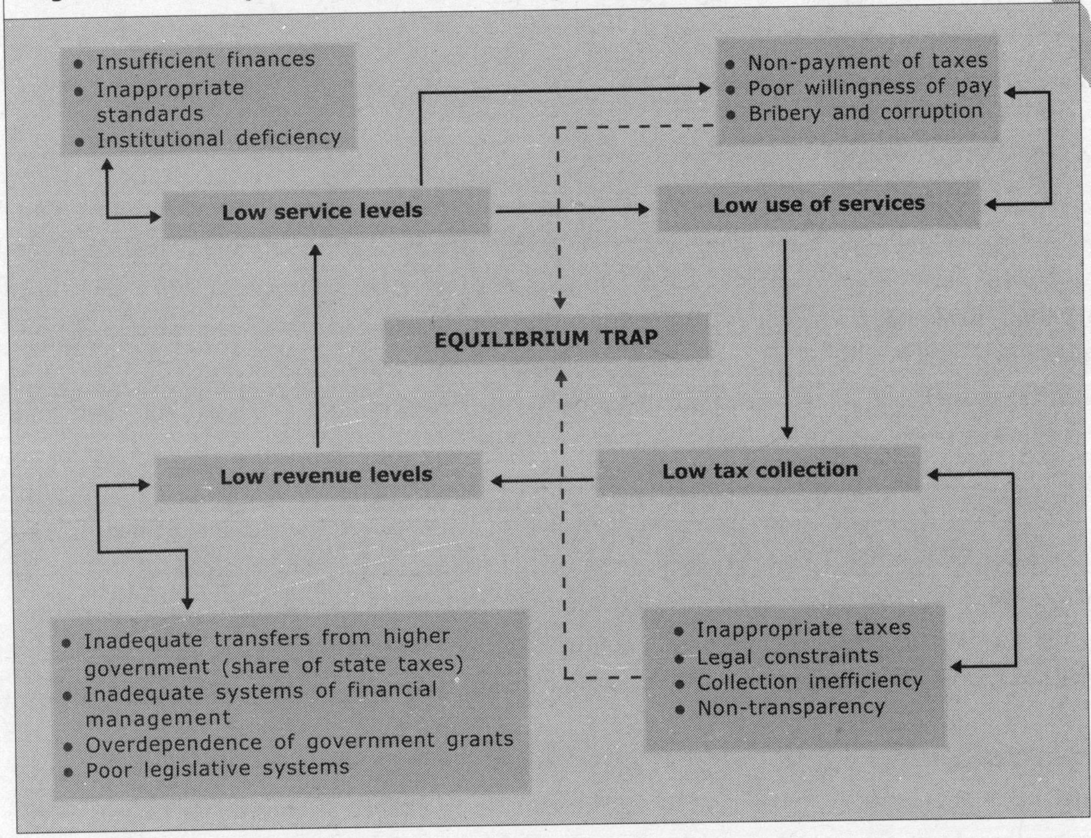

In the past, MCL had been plagued by several administrative and management issues. Primary among them were:

- Rapid urbanisation resulting in mushrooming unauthorised colonies.
- Outdated manual record-keeping systems that collapsed under pressure from increasing documentation, leading to litigation and heavy losses to MCL.
- Political interference and official connivance leading to apathy, demotivation, unionism and corruption amongst employees.
- Ineffective performance appraisal systems and poor accountability in work transactions.
- Limited in-house skill upgradation.
- Weak accounting, planning and budgetary methods with no lucid criteria for appraisal and prioritisation of investment projects.
- Lack of citizenry involvement.

To meet this challenge, it became imperative to introduce capacity building reforms towards the improved management and self-sufficiency of the corporation.

Objectives

The reforms initiated by MCL had the following objectives:

- To provide efficient and quality services at minimum cost.
- Institutional strengthening and human resource development.
- Inculcate a sense of accountability amongst all employees.
- To ensure better management of the city through community participation and privatisation.
- Improved municipal planning and asset management.
- Better financial management.

Salient features

Community participation

MCL did not have a sufficient number of effective supervisors and managers and hiring more supervisors meant a significant increase in their overhead cost. Moreover, municipal employees were desensitised towards the needs of the community being accountable only to their immediate supervisors. Realising the potential of the community to contribute to the improvement of their neighbourhood and work as 'managers without salary' MCL promoted the concept of 'Manage your Neighbourhood'. The management of parks was handed over to Neighbourhood Park Management Committees, whose tasks included the hiring of gardeners, supervision of gardening activities and the overall upkeep of gardens. MCL reimbursed the expenses of the management committee @ Re. 1 per sq. metre per month. Of its total 830 parks, 427 are maintained by Park Management Committees. Through its novel scheme, 'Manage your Neighbourhood', MCL not only overcame the problem of staff shortage but also ensured 80 per cent savings. It also eliminated the problems of absenteeism, unionism and continuous supervision. For instance, under the round-the-clock supervision by stakeholders, the condition of parks has improved significantly.

Privatisation

To avoid the problem of monopoly and to provide efficient and cheap services to the citizens, MCL privatised the various activities (Box 16.1). MCL is the first corporation in India to get locally fabricated big vacuum cleaners for sweeping main roads. The output of each cleaner is equal to that of 20 sweepers. The Corporation thus saves 50 per cent of its costs apart from having much cleaner roads.

Box 16.1 **From eyesores to eye-catchers**

Overflowing garbage containers are a common eyesore in big cities. To tackle this problem MCL launched an innovative scheme whereby advertisement agencies undertake to maintain garbage containers by covering them with advertisements/ hoardings on a 'Build-Operate-Own' (BOO) basis. In the bargain, MCL does not spend money on the maintenance of the garbage dumps and advertisement agencies, in lieu of advertising rights, aesthetically maintain these container sites and prevent spilling of garbage by posting container attendants.

Street-light maintenance

MCL is the first urban local body in Punjab to completely privatise street-light maintenance, on independent as well as composite lines. This has helped reduce cost by nearly 50 per cent as compared to maintenance costs incurred by the Punjab State Electricity Board (PSEB). Additionally, by making the contractor pay a penalty of Rs. 50 per day per point for every non-functioning street-light, the process of privatisation has led to increased efficiency of street-light maintenance.

Tubewells

Water supply too has been handed over to a private contractor. Hundred and ten new tubewells with the latest technologies such as time switches have been installed which do not require any manpower to run them (Box. 16.2).

Box 16.2 The Neighbourhood Tubewell Operator Scheme

MCL launched the Neighbourhood Tubewell Operator (NTO) Scheme wherein a competent person (may be a shopkeeper or a housewife) from the neighbourhood where the tubewell is located is selected and given a brief training about its operation. In lieu of services, they are compensated by MCL at Rs.1,500 per month, which becomes an additional income for them. About 5-10 tubewells are under the supervision of a technically qualified municipal supervisor to ensure their smooth running. Thus MCL saves about 85 per cent of expenditure on salaries through community involvement.

Additionally, the chlorination of water, desiltation of sewers, night sweeping in congested areas, and maintenance of roads are undertaken by private contractors. Competition among private contractors to obtain assignments from MCL, has benefited the Corporation by way of efficient services and increased savings which range from 50-85 per cent.

Asset management

The Estate Department of the MCL had been a liability rather than an asset to the Corporation. It did not have a complete inventory of its lands, many of its properties were not mutated in revenue records, encroachments were a frequent phenomenon and most of its valuable properties were under litigation. To tackle these problems, the following reforms were carried out:

Land inventory, database development and analysis

MCL, with technical support from their consultants, unearthed hidden properties belonging to MCL through reconciliation with very old land/revenue records of the Revenue Department. As a result, MCL was able to add more than 800 additional properties to its land inventory, valued at about Rs. 190 crore. Part of this property is vacant and part of it is encroached/occupied land. The MCL is now in a position to develop/dispose off the vacant properties and announce an amnesty scheme to regularise the occupied properties. This will enable MCL to raise around Rs. 117 crore.

A comprehensive software for database management of lands has been developed which enables MCL to keep a record of the status of all its properties and prevent any tampering of land records.

Geographical information system (GIS)

MCL has developed a GIS for the city with the help of which data pertaining to different locations (including its own properties) can be ascertained instantly.

Financial management

Financial reporting by means of single-entry cash-based accounting against the budgetary outlay system fails to give a holistic financial picture, questioning the authenticity of the data on record. Realising this, MCL switched over to the double-entry accrual-based accounting system.

MCL is also the first corporation in the state to raise Rs. 17 crore from the capital market through municipal bonds on the basis of a credit rating of AA-(SO), without any government guarantee. Further, the method of Zero-Base Budgeting introduced in MCL has saved substantial resources.

Organisational management

Monthly performance appraisal for employees

Earlier, MCL had the Annual Confidential Roll (ACR) system for judging the performance of employees. The criteria for appraisal of the employees were generic and based on individual assessments. Further, the appraisal being annual, took note of employee performance only at the time of promotion. This affected accountability and transparency in the system.

A monthly performance appraisal system has been introduced where all employees are given job charts according to their placement in the hierarchy. Each job carries certain weighted marks and the employee's performance is judged at the end of every month. Based on cumulative monthly scores, final marks are awarded. The employees are now more accountable, competitive and conscious of their performance. To score the desired marks they are constantly under pressure to perform their duties and realise targets.

Management information system (MIS)

Previously, MCL had an information system, which was unstructured and prepared on the basis of immediate requirements. The reports were unformatted with no scope for cross-checking and verification. None of the departments had any synchronised and comprehensive databases for the expeditious delivery of information, resulting in delays.

An MIS was devised with the help of consultants, where the critical levels of decision-making, planning and information needs were identified. A system of management audit with reference to a set of key indicators for policy-making, administration planning, responsibility/accountability and community development has been set in motion. The new MIS now presents results in the form of specific information, comparable parameters and departmental as well as individual performances that leads to quick decision-making. As a result of improved information channels, several bottlenecks in departments have been identified and removed, resulting in greater efficiency in management.

Computerisation

The manual systems by virtue of being non-tamper proof, resulted in lost records and frequent public complaints about faulty postings and inflated bills. To redress the problems associated with incorrect billing, payments and receipts with respect to water/ sewerage and house tax were computerised. As a result, arrears worth Rs. 40 crore were brought to light. Additionally, details of employee provident funds, gratuities, along with salary details and increments, have been computerised. As a result there is proper record management, no scope for indiscretion and connivance, quick delivery and increased efficiency.

MCL was the first local body in Punjab to launch its website (www.ludhianacorp.com). This website provides MCL-related information and has opened up new vistas for dialogue between the elected municipal officials and the residents of Ludhiana. The dissemination of information regarding the working of the municipality provides a forum for communication and strengthens public participation. Providing web-enabled services is the next step in this exercise.

Organisational restructuring and staff rationalisation

- Zonal system: Ludhiana, being a large city, was difficult to manage from a single head office. To remedy this, the entire municipal area has now been divided into four zones and the organisational structure has been revamped. Redressal of complaints, tax collections and most other functions have been decentralised to the zonal level.
- Staff optimisation: The organisational structure of MCL was obsolete and redeployment of staff at appropriate places had become a necessity. Consequently, after privatisation of the bill distribution operation, employees performing this function were redeployed as tax collectors, thus improving tax collection without adding to the salary bill.
- Single window inspectorate: Previously, the taxation department comprised seven inspectors handling seven different portfolios—house tax, water and sewerage, license, tehbazri, advertisement, building and sanitation within the same area. The system was inconvenient as the public had to deal with seven different inspectors and the inspectors had huge territorial jurisdictions. To improve the efficiency in the functioning of the taxation department, a single window system was introduced, where only one inspector has been made responsible for all the seven activities in a particular area.

Impact

- The municipal reforms introduced in Ludhiana succeeded in achieving the broad objectives of better municipal management and capacity building.
- By encouraging community participation in schemes like Park Management Committees, Neighbourhood Sanitation Committees, Neighbourhood Tubewell Operator Schemes, etc., the delivery of services improved by a great extent. By involving the community, particularly senior and retired citizens who were

willing to contribute their services for the betterment of their localities, MCL launched a cadre of 'managers without salary'. This concept has been very successful and has led to increased administrative efficiency.

- By opening several of its functions to private operators MCL introduced competition among private partners, which has led to more efficient and quality services at cheaper costs.
- Institutional strengthening was achieved through the introduction of the zonal system, where 90 per cent of the workload was tackled at the zonal level and only policy matters were taken up to the head office. The single window system has reduced the territorial jurisdiction of the inspectors by placing one inspector in charge of jobs that were being carried out by seven different inspectors. Computerisation has streamlined most of the functions of MCL enabling it to work more efficiently and needing very few employees as compared to manual systems.
- The introduction of the score-based monthly appraisal system enhanced performance levels of employees making them accountable to the Council every month rather than only at the time of the yearly appraisal.
- The introduction of MIS and computerisation helped senior management to take quick and well-informed decisions as the flow of information at different levels became easier and more reliable.
- The double-entry accrual-based accounting System helped in better decision-making due to the management and monitoring of the financial situation on a day-to-day basis.

Summary

The MCL initiated various reforms related to managerial capacity building and community participation. Privatisation has been the key to reforms agenda in the programme. Several organisational restructuring measures were incorporated. The reforms focused on cutting down establishment expenditure, increasing work accountability and transparency, using innovative e-governance techniques, implementing zero-based budgeting and promoting confidence building with stakeholders. As a result of the implementation of these reforms, MCL has become a more efficient organisation.

For the first time, MCL has completely privatised street-light maintenance, on independent as well as composite lines. This has helped reduce cost by nearly 50 per cent as compared to maintenance costs incurred by the Punjab State Electricity Board (PSEB). To strengthen asset management measures such as land inventory, database development and analysis, the creation of a geographical information system has been critical.

These measures have not only encouraged community participation but have also improved the quality of services. Institutional strengthening was achieved through the introduction of the zonal system where 90 per cent of the workload was tackled at the zonal level and only policy matters were taken up to the head office. The single window system has reduced the territorial jurisdiction of the inspectors by placing one inspector in charge of jobs that were previously carried out by seven different inspectors. Computerisation has streamlined most of the functions of MCL enabling it to work more efficiently with very few employees as compared to manual systems. The introduction of MIS and computerisation has helped the senior management to take quick and well-informed decisions as the flow of information at different levels has become easier and more reliable.

Replicability

There has been a metamorphic change in the Municipal Corporation of Ludhiana to an efficient and responsible intermediary between the citizens and the elected local government. MCL is dedicated to improving the quality of life of the people by promoting a strong, effective and accountable municipal government.

Some key aspects are responsible for the successful implementation of municipal reforms by MCL:

- Such reforms must be part of the agenda of the top leadership of an organisation. The credibility of the MCL leadership played an important role in acceptability of reforms.
- Community involvement is essential for implementing reforms. Mechanisms to ensure the participation of all sections of society in public life have been developed by the MCL.
- To carry out reforms in a time-bound manner, it is important that the progress of reforms is monitored at appropriate levels on a day-to-day basis and sorted out immediately. MCL introduced reforms in a phased manner involving all the stakeholders.
- Technical training of staff while introducing new systems like computerisation of various functions, implementation of MIS and GIS and switching over to double-entry accrual-based accounting system, is crucial. Many employees, unhappy with a shift in the traditional mode of service delivery, resisted these training exercises. MCL resolved this issue by offering incentives to employees to undergo training and thus averted attempts to sabotage the reform process by employee inertia.
- In addition to employee disapproval, resistance was also experienced at the political level as the new system ruled out scope for granting favours by politicians. Political resistance was minimised by informing the public (voters) of the benefits, which would accrue to them after reforms. This awareness campaign made it difficult for the politicians to go against public opinion and oppose the reforms. The press and other media played an important role in the implementation of reforms. To generate strong public opinion in favour of the reforms, MCL held regular media briefings. This helped in allaying fears and overcoming resistance to change by politicians and the public.
- Major resistance also came from employees' unions, who opposed the privatisation initiative as well as the introduction of score-based monthly appraisal system. The employees were resistive of such processes, as they were not used to such a high level of accountability. However, MCL enforced the system by ensuring that the appraisal system applied to all levels of the organisational hierarchy. Moreover, the offer of incentives for better performance also brought acceptance by employees.
- Municipal bodies are different from government departments in two respects. First, they have a large number of elected councillors, many of them full-time politicians who interact with the officials in almost every transaction. Second, there is a large number of Class IV employees (sweepers, sewermen and gardeners, etc.) who are members of unions. These two factors—aggressive unionism and frequent political interference—make the task of carrying out reforms much more difficult as compared to any other government department. Both factors needed to be considered when introducing reforms in Ludhiana. For example, if the community representatives who are given the responsibility to implement schemes have a different political affiliation from the elected councillors from that area, the councillor may try to resist such schemes. Intervention from the highest echelons

of the political system, including the Chief Minister and the Chief Secretary, was necessary to implement many of the reform schemes in the MCL.

- Community participation in managing the neighbourhood is the best way to deliver municipal services. On the one hand, there is always a shortage of committed and effective supervisors in municipalities, and on the other, there are always citizens, particularly senior and retired members of the community, who are more than willing to contribute their might for the betterment of their neighbourhood. Bridging this gap proved to be an effective strategy in the management and delivery of municipal services in Ludhiana.

By striving to undertake continuous policy and operations reform, the MCL has emerged as an organisation that aspires for better, cheaper and more efficient systems to deliver services and to bridge the gap between prevailing delivery systems and citizens' expectations. Thus, there is a transparency of public purpose and no room for partisan politics and corrupt practices. This successful restructuring of the Municipal Corporation of Ludhiana merits replication in municipal organisations across the country.

Contact

Municipal Commissioner
Ludhiana Municipal Corporation, Corporation House
Opp. Guru Nanak Stadium, Civil Lines
Ludhiana – 141 001
Tel.: +91-161-441 333/34
Fax: +91-161-421 629
Email: mcldh@satyam.net.in
Website: www.ludhianacorp.com

CHAPTER 17

Linking the Producer and the Consumer

Rythu Bazars, Andhra Pradesh

Introduction

Andhra Pradesh is the second largest producer of fruits, vegetables and flowers in the country. However, the marketing of the agricultural produce is constrained due to scanty availability of regulated market yards and presence of a large number of middlemen between the farmer and the ultimate consumer. Absence of infrastructure and improper management coupled with the lack of market intelligence and credit systems has rendered the marketing system unviable to the farmer. The estimated losses in the handling of vegetables in the traditional channel of marketing are about 30 to 35 per cent. A study conducted by the Food and Agriculture Organisation (FAO) has revealed that the farmer's share in the consumer rupee in India is about 64 per cent for rice and his share in the case of perishable produce like fruits and vegetables is much lower.

Small farmers have not been able to bargain effectively for a better price in the wholesale markets. Inefficiency in these markets has resulted in problems of multiple handling, loss in quality and an increased gap between producer and consumer prices. A large number of small retailers, each handling small quantities, create high overheads leading to high margins on produce. Furthermore, attempts by small retailers to market limited produce have increased overhead costs and have isolated them from benefiting from the economies of large-scale marketing.

Much to the dissatisfaction of both the producer and the consumer, the traditional marketing system has failed to be an equitable medium for commodity exchange. While farmers complain of non-remunerative pricing, high commission charges and lack of facilities, consumers are dissatisfied with inferior quality, spiralling prices and malpractice in weighment.

The provision of marketing facilities for agricultural commodities in urban areas has not kept pace with the rate of urbanisation. Very few wholesale markets cater to urban areas. Some farmers who reside in villages surrounding urban settlements regularly commute to urban centres to market their products, making their marketing technique ad hoc and unorganised. In 1999, the Government of Andhra Pradesh evolved an alternate marketing strategy called Rythu Bazars, to benefit both growers and consumers.

Background

Rythu Bazars were formulated by the Government of Andhra Pradesh in 1999 as a direct interface between the farmers and consumers, and to eliminate middlemen. They were instituted to act as price stabilisation centres. Rythu Bazars operate outside the purview of Agricultural Market Committees, and are managed by Estate Officers, under the control of Joint District Collectors. In 2001, there were 97 such bazars in Andhra Pradesh. Following the success of these regulated markets in Andhra Pradesh, the neighbouring states of Tamil Nadu and Orissa have begun replicating this concept.

Objectives

Rythu Bazars were initiated in 1999 with the following objectives:

- To ensure remunerative prices to the farmers and provide fresh vegetables to consumers at reasonable rates on a daily basis.
- To facilitate prompt realisation of sale proceeds to farmers without any deductions.
- To curb malpractices and provide vegetables with correct weighment to consumers.
- To provide a direct interface between farmers and consumers—eliminating intermediaries from the system.

Salient features

Project implementation

Rythu Bazars are located on government-owned lands that are identified by the District Collectors and a location that is convenient for both farmers and consumers is chosen. The criteria for the opening of a new Rythu Bazar are the availability of at least one acre of land in a strategic location, and the identification of 250 vegetable growing farmers, who are willing to participate in the Bazar. The establishment of marketing linkages between the buyer and the seller is critical to the successful functioning of a Rythu Bazar.

Infrastructure facilities are provided for all Rythu Bazars through funds from the Agricultural Market Committees. Temporary structures (such as vegetable containers and vending stalls) have been replaced by semi-permanent structures in Rythu Bazars to provide adequate protection against sun/rain to both producers and users alike.

Each Rythu Bazar ensures the provision of the following facilities:

- Adequate number of sheds for farmers to store and sell their produce.
- Adequate arrangements for supply of drinking water.
- Toilet facilities with proper sanitation.
- Proper arrangements for parking of vehicles.
- Arrangements for periodic removal of garbage and regular cleaning of the market.
- Facilities for storage of unsold produce including refrigeration facilities like the Zero Energy Cool chambers.
- Provision of tamper-proof weighing scales for all the farmers.

Identification of farmers

Farmers from a cluster of 10–15 predominantly vegetable-growing villages, who are willing to participate in the Bazar, are identified by the Horticulture Department. This enables the systematic provision of horticulture services, inputs and transportation arrangements to the farmers by the Horticulture Department.

Farmers are identified by a team consisting of a Market Research Officer, Horticulture Officer/ Consultant, Village Agricultural Officer. The team finalises the schedule of visits to the villages and publicises the same among the vegetable-growing farmers. As per the schedule, the team visits the villages and convenes a meeting of vegetable-growing farmers. At the meeting, the farmers are briefed about the advantages of the Rythu Bazar, namely, the benefits that will accrue to them through provision of horticultural services, seed supply at subsidised rates, transportation arrangements, pricing mechanism and elimination of middlemen, in order to motivate them to reap the benefits of cooperative marketing. After the meeting, the team visits the fields of willing farmers and issues temporary identity cards to them on the spot. These are subsequently replaced by laminated photo identity cards, within a week of their issue. Tenants are also eligible for identity cards on field verification. Farmers are divided into groups as per their choice and each group can send one or more members on rotation for sale of vegetables to the Rythu Bazar. The benefits given to self-help groups (SHG) by the government are also extended to these groups.

Price setting

The price difference between the wholesale market and the retail outlet in perishables is sometimes more than double. In most cases, the consumer is made to pay prices in the retail market that are much higher than what is considered fair. To combat this variation in price and to protect the interests of the consumer, a system of price fixation has been put in place in Rythu Bazars. The price fixation in Rythu Bazars is done through a committee of farmers and the Estate Officer. Every day's wholesale market and local retail market prices are collected and the prices fixed in the Rythu Bazar which are generally between the wholesale and retail rates. If the prices in the Rythu Bazar are higher than the local market rate there is no incentive to the consumer, and if the prices fixed are lower than the wholesale market rates, there is no incentive to the farmers. Keeping this in view, the prices are generally 25 per cent above the wholesale price and 25 per cent below retail prices.

Organisational set-up

Photo identity cards

The farmers participating in the Rythu Bazars are provided with photo identity cards. These cards help identify sellers in the market and prevent unauthorised personnel from misusing the facilities that are provided to the farmers registered at the Rythu Bazar, by unauthorised personnel. The photo cards contain details of the farmer, like name, postal address, extent of land under cultivation, details of vegetables cultivated, photograph of farmer/farmer with his family members, and photograph of the group members.

These photographs are attested by the Horticulture Consultant and laminated before they are given to farmers. A register containing the details of the identity cards issued is maintained by the Horticulture Consultant and Estate Officer. The identity cards are valid for six months from the date of issue. Renewal of the identity cards has to be completed at least 15 days before expiry. Only farmers/groups with valid photo identity cards are permitted to trade in Rythu Bazars. This verification system has eliminated the exploitation of the consumer/producer by middlemen and intermediaries. If any farmer comes to a Rythu Bazar without an identity card, he/she is directed to the Horticulture Consultant to obtain a card. Farmers are allowed to sell vegetables grown only by them.

Allotment of shops

The daily allotment of shops is on a 'first-come-first-served' basis and on rotation. No farmer is allowed to occupy the same shop continuously and neither are allowed to reserve the shop by keeping vegetables there at night.

Transport arrangements

Joint District Collectors ensure adequate transport arrangements for the farmers (to and from the Bazar) in consultation with the Andhra Pradesh State Road Transport Corporation after ascertaining the specific requirements from the Estate Officers and farmers. This is reviewed once in 15 days and changes are made whenever necessary.

Sanitation

Enormous effort is put into the maintenance of a sanitised atmosphere in the Bazar. Removal of garbage, cleaning the market place, maintenance of toilets is entrusted either to the local body, a private agency, or a SHG. This activity is financed from the income generated through auction of parking space, profits from the market canteen and lease of private nurseries.

Duties of estate officers

The Estate Officers who are appointed on a contract basis (of Rs. 4,000 a month) are responsible for:

- The upkeep and maintenance of Rythu Bazars.
- Daily allotment of space on first-come-first-serve basis.
- Providing weighing scales to farmers on a daily basis and collecting them in the evening.
- Formation of price fixation committees and the actual fixation of prices every morning.
- Ensuring that sales take place at the prices fixed.

The prices are displayed at prominent places in the Bazar so that customers are able to see the day's prices and the transactions are completely transparent.

The Estate Officers conduct a meeting with all farmers once a week to assess the functioning of the Bazar. The minutes of these weekly meetings, along with a proper recording of daily arrivals and sales, are sent to the Joint Collector and Director of Marketing in order to keep them fully updated about the activities in the market. It is also the primary duty of the Estate Officers to encourage sale of vegetables not grown locally, through SHG. They also coordinate with Horticulture Officers/Consultants for the timely distribution of seed material/inputs to promote horticulture production. Problems of transportation, interference from middlemen, additional infrastructural requirements and assorted concerns of the farmers are promptly brought to the notice of the Joint Collectors (Fig. 17.1).

Fig. 17.1 **Organisation of Rythu Bazar**

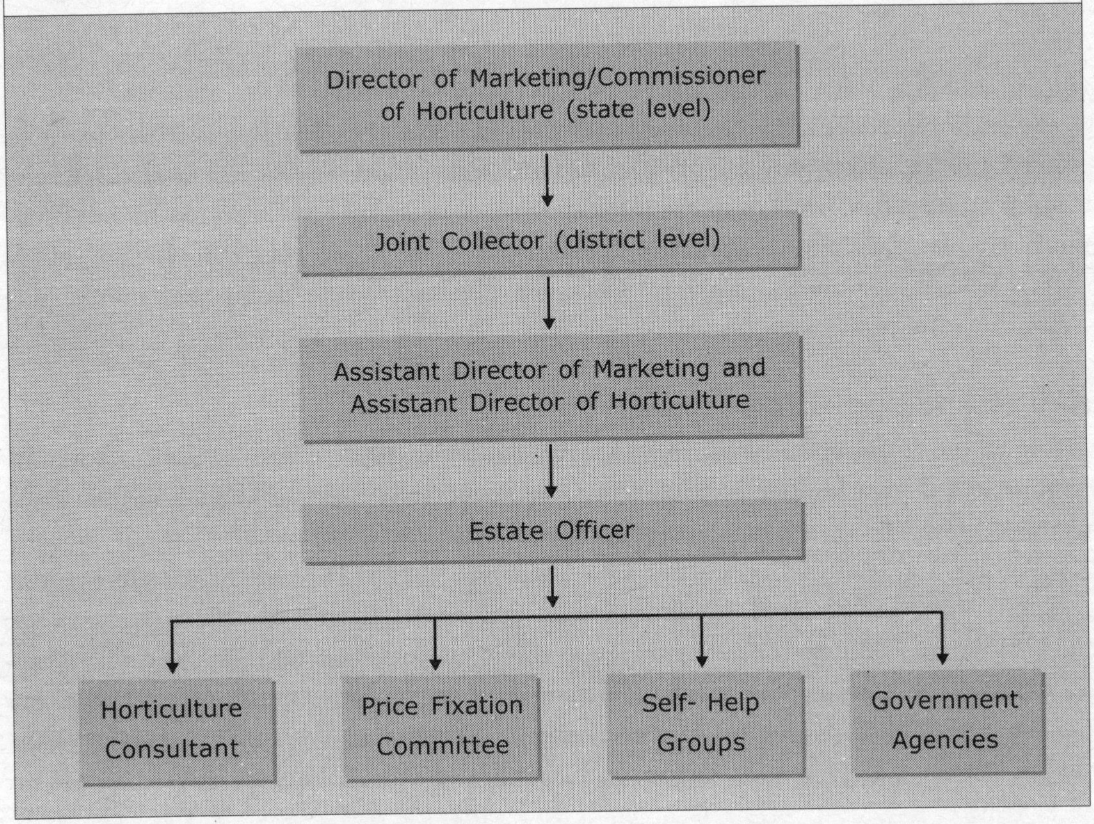

Role of horticulture consultants

Horticulture Consultants are appointed on a contract basis (Rs. 5,000 a month), the cost of which is met by the Horticulture Department. Their responsibilities include:

- Ensuring adequate participation of farmers which is essential for the successful functioning of Rythu Bazars.
- Identifying, motivating and ensuring regular attendance by vegetable growers in order that they reap the benefits that arise from cooperative marketing.
- Visiting Rythu Bazars regularly and assessing the daily requirement of vegetables, and on the basis of these requirements, preparing action plans for the production and regular supply of vegetables by identifying willing farmers.
- Visiting identified villages periodically and conducting pre-post-harvest consultations with the identified farmers.
- Ensuring timely supply of quality seeds at subsidised prices to the farmers.
- Providing expertise to farmers towards the production of off-season vegetables and organising training session for vegetable growers.
- Maintaining farmer-wise, village-wise, mandal-wise inventories for different vegetables (variety and quantity) produced and sold in Rythu Bazars.

Role of agriculture officers

The Agriculture Officers who are departmental officers, coordinate with Horticulture Consultants for the distribution of seeds to farmers. They are focal points for implementation of the horticulture production plan. They also assist the Horticulture Consultant in proper identification of villages/ farmers for Rythu Bazars.

Arrangements for sale

All varieties of vegetables are not grown in the area identified for each Rythu Bazar. To enable consumers to purchase all varieties of vegetables and fruits under one roof, it is envisaged that SHGs will procure these items from the wholesale market or tie up with importers for sale in the Rythu Bazars. Similarly, other essential commodities like oils, pulses, tamarind, etc., are sold by the SHGs who are identified by the Joint Collectors. Prices in Rythu Bazars must invariably be less than the prices in the retail market.

Funding and operation

The cost of the entire operation is met through funds provided by the Agricultural Market Committee and the Horticulture Development Department. Infrastructural facilities such as shops, drinking water, electricity, parking, storage for unsold produce, weighing scales, etc. are provided by the Agricultural Market Committees from their own funds. The cost of the Horticulture Consultant is met out of the Horticulture Department funds. Each Rythu Bazar employs one Estate Officer, one computer operator, five supervisors, one store assistant, one electrician-cum-office attendant, and five security guards. The number of employed personnel may vary from one Rythu Bazar to another depending on the volume of business. All the staff members of Rythu Bazars are hired on a contract basis and are paid consolidated salaries. They are not eligible for any other benefits.

Rythu Bazars generate sufficient income for their sustenance through auction of parking space, lease of private nurseries and profits from the market canteen. The Joint Collector is the competent authority to arrange and finalise the auction. The money realised through the auction is credited to the Rythu Bazar funds and can be used for provision of sanitation, drinking water facilities, purchase and repairs of weighing scales, and general maintenance of Rythu Bazars. Experience has proved that most Rythu Bazaars in cities function as self-sufficient financial entities.

Reporting and monitoring

The Estate Officers ensure proper maintenance of registers/records. They furnish daily reports of transactions in the Bazars, appended before 11 a.m. everyday. They also furnish weekly returns of transactions as per proforma every Friday. They also have to send a fortnightly report every month on the Rythu Bazar as per the prescribed proforma. The reporting system is thus quite comprehensive and enables the Joint District Collectors to closely monitor the functioning of the Rythu Bazars.

Communication facilities

Telephone, fax and computers are provided in all Rythu Bazars. Each Rythu Bazar has a computer operator-cum-assistant (on a consolidated salary of Rs. 2,500 per month) and all price data are completely computerised. The Estate Officers use the computer facilities for prompt submission of returns and the receipt of information contributing to the better management of the Bazar. Networking amongst Rythu Bazars enable Estate Officers to fix realistic prices and help the farmers and SHGs to take advantage of the prevailing prices in different markets.

Training

The Commissioner, Horticulture Department, and Director of Marketing organise training programmes at periodic intervals for Estate Officers and Horticulture Consultants.

Administrative arrangements

Joint District Collectors are responsible for the effective functioning of Rythu Bazars in the district. These collectors conduct periodic meetings with the Estate Officers, farmers and consumers to assess the needs and concerns of the producer/seller arrangements. They also hold weekly meetings with Estate Officers and inspect at least one Rythu Bazar each week and monitor its performance over time. This also helps them to ensure proper coordination between Departments of Agriculture, Horticulture, Revenue, Marketing and Transport for the smooth functioning of the Rythu Bazar.

Status of Rythu bazars

The status of Rythu Bazars in Andhra Pradesh is given in Tables 17.1 and 17.2.

Table 17.1 Profile of Rythu Bazars in Andhra Pradesh

Indicators	1999	2000	2001
No. of Rythu Bazars	92	97	97
Permanent Rythu Bazars	7	28	34
No. of Farmers	4500	4888	5871
Weekly arrivals (quintal)	51142	75389	101111
Value of weekly arrivals (in Rs.)	375	550	743
Computers	12	29	34
Fax machines	76	82	82

From tables 17.1 and 17.2, we can infer the following:

- About 97 Rythu Bazars are functioning in Andhra Pradesh where one lakh quintals of vegetables are sold per week.
- About 6,000 farmers are availing the benefiting from Rythu Bazars.
- Total turnover of vegetable and other essential commodities is about 7.5 crore per week.
- Rythu Bazars have facilitated direct marketing. This has cut short marketing channels by eliminating middlemen and brought producer/sellers in direct contact with the consumer.
- The producers of perishable goods around the cities and urban towns are able to get the benefit of direct selling to the consumers.

Table 17.2 Arrivals of vegetables in Rythu Bazars

Weekly Arrivals (quintal)	No. of Rythu Bazars
> 1000	20
500–1000	28
300–500	16
200–300	15
100–200	12
< 100	6
Total	**97**

- Rythu Bazars have, therefore, increased the returns to producers, while providing vegetables, fruits and essential commodities to the consumers at economical prices.
- Efforts are on to provide all Rythu Bazars with 'zero-energy storage units' of appropriate capacity to store unsold stock.
- Training-cum-appraisal programmes for Estate Officers, Horticulture Consultants and Assistant Directors of Marketing and Horticulture every quarter are also being initiated to help resolve operational bottlenecks and further improve the efficacy of Rythu Bazars.

Evaluation

Rythu Bazars have been an outstanding success in Andhra Pradesh and have brought immense benefits to the farmers participating in them. However, modifications in the present market framework are necessary to strengthen the existing Rythu Bazars and to ensure their sustainability. The Government of Andhra Pradesh is paying particular attention to the following aspects:

- It is recognised that location is very important for the successful functioning of Rythu Bazars. Experience suggests that the location of the Bazars should be away from the existing wholesale markets and in the neighbourhood of consumers. They should also be accessible by direct transport, for the benefit of farmers. Therefore, it is necessary to shift/close those Rythu Bazars that are located near wholesale markets.
- Consumers prefer markets where all varieties of vegetable and fruits are available. SHGs are being encouraged to play a useful role in promoting the sale of vegetables not cultivated in the district. Rice and other essential commodities are also being made available through government agencies, rice millers' association or through the wholesalers. Thus, efforts are being made to provide a holistic marketing environment for consumers.
- Transport facilities that are available in the early hours of the day are essential for farmers to come to the Rythu Bazars from their villages. The government, on its part, must make sure that these farmers are provided efficient and regular means of transport reaching the Bazars.
- Some Rythu Bazars have been able to generate adequate income through auction of parking spaces and canteen facilities for the maintenance of the Bazar. Since infrastructure facilities are provided free of cost by the Marketing Department, all Rythu Bazars are being encouraged to generate their own income towards recurring expenditure. In order to achieve this, all Rythu Bazars should eventually be converted into mutually aided cooperative societies so that their management can be handed over to farmers themselves.

Summary

Rythu Bazars were conceptualised to provide better marketing avenues for agricultural produce, as well as bridge the gap between the farmers and the consumers. Farmers from a cluster of 10–15 predominantly vegetable-growing villages, who are willing to participate in the Bazar, are identified by the Horticulture Department. Rythu Bazars help to reduce variations in prices and protect the interest of the consumer. A system of price fixation has been put in place in Rythu Bazars, which is done through a committee and the Estate Officer. The Estate Officer conducts meetings with all farmers once a week to assess the functioning of the Bazar.

However, there is a need to improve the accessibility of Rythu Bazar to larger sections of the population. It is recognised that location is very important for successful functioning of the Rythu Bazar. Experience suggests that the location of the Bazar should be away from the existing wholesale markets and in the neighbourhood of consumers. They should also be accessible by direct transport, for the benefit of the farmers. Therefore, it is necessary to shift/close those Rythu Bazars that are located near wholesale markets.

Replicability

Agencies like the Reserve Bank of India, the Research and Analysis Wing of the Civil Supplies Department as well as teams from neighbouring states have conducted studies on the functioning of Rythu Bazars. These studies have revealed that creating a direct interface between the farmers and the consumers accrue mutual benefits for both the groups involved, while eliminating exploitation from intermediaries. Tamil Nadu and Orissa have already replicated this novel example of regulating producer/consumer markets. At the national level, the Agriculture Division of the Planning Commission envisages promoting the concept of Rythu Bazars, evolved by the state of Andhra Pradesh, as an innovative example of creating a viable alternate market structure.

Contact

Director
Department of Marketing
BRKR Bhavan, 1st floor, 'C' Block
Tank Bund Road
Hyderabad – 500063, India
Tel.: +91-40-322 1307, 322 2161
Fax: +91-40-322 1084
Website: www.gist.ap.nic.in/cgi-bin/mkt/mktfrm.cgi

CHAPTER 18

Women's Empowerment through Self-Help Groups

TNWDP, Tamil Nadu

Introduction

The Tamil Nadu Women's Development Project (TNWDP) represents a unique partnership between the government, NGOs and commercial banks. Initiated in May 1989, the project envisaged the development of poor rural women with assistance from the International Fund for Agricultural Development (IFAD). It has evolved as an inspirational model for self-help programmes for women and is being implemented in other parts of the country as well.

Background

TNWDP is implemented through a network of women's self-help groups (SHGs) which have been established and nurtured with NGO support at the village level. The overall responsibility for coordination lies with the Tamil Nadu Corporation for Development of Women on behalf of the Government of Tamil Nadu. Initially, 75 pre-selected blocks from eight districts in Tamil Nadu were taken up for coverage in a phased manner. As on 31 December 1998, 5207 SHGs were formed, covering 1,20,960 women. Encouraged by the success of the scheme, the project has been extended to the remaining districts under state funding through a phased programme. By March 2000, about 26,220 SHGs had been formed with a membership of 4,81,733 women.

The project illustrates that empowerment based on the SHG model can have far-reaching results. Further, the institutionalisation of SHGs for development of village has been recognised in many districts. The Government of India, the Government of Tamil Nadu, the World Bank and others have imbued the core of various new programmes and activities aimed at women's development with the SHG model. SHGs provide an effective instrument through which women can build self-reliance, solidarity and confidence, as well as contribute to the overall development of their families and societies. They also enhance the women's bargaining power and consolidate their decision-making responsibilities, towards the overall development of the communities. Cohesion within a group provides women with a sense of identity, status and security, and also provides them access to credit and institutional support services, which otherwise might have been denied to them.

Objectives

The TNWDP was initiated with the objective of:

- Ensuring economic and social upliftment of women.
- Enhancing the welfare of their families and improving their status in the community.
- Generating income mainly through credit.
- Establishing and consolidating women's groups.
- Fostering beneficiary participation and group responsibility for development through credit.

Salient features

Eligibility

Under this project, women below the poverty line within 21–55 years of age are eligible for assistance. Preference is given to women-headed households, widows and destitutes. Independent NGOs are actively associated in the selection of project beneficiaries.

The selected women are organised into informal groups of about 20–25 members with the help of NGOs. They are encouraged to contribute regularly to a savings fund managed by the group. Once a reasonable amount is saved, the group is then encouraged to provide petty loans, which are often given for urgent, short-term needs like food, health, education and crop production and the group decides who should get the loans and rate of interest. The interest rates tend to be around 2–3 per cent per month, which translates to 24–36 per cent per annum. These rates are significantly lower than the rates charged by the local money lenders. The velocity of money is rapid and repayment by the borrowers are prompt as well resulting in disbursement of loans three to four times greater than the amount saved. A medium-size loan ranges from Rs.100–500.

A woman is eligible for loans and subsidies for economic activities only on completion of a minimum of three months as a member. During this period, she has to make regular contributions to the group's savings fund. The loans are arranged from the nationalised Indian Bank and subsidy is given as per the Integrated Rural Development Programme norms.

Economic activities

The TNWDP assistance is provided for land-based activities like agriculture, horticulture, sericulture and oilseed cultivation, to women who have sole or joint title to the land or to women who have taken land, on lease. For landless women, assistance is provided for taking up animal husbandry programmes or cottage and village industries.

The average loan assistance under the project has been gradually increasing due to rising costs and concerted efforts are being made on behalf of all project and bank staff to identify activities capable of increasing the women's income, in accordance with project objectives. Serious efforts are being made at all levels to identify non-traditional activities as well as combinations of activities which can provide the income required. Supplementary doses of assistance will also be provided for beneficiaries who obtained only a nominal loan in the first borrowing cycle.

Monitoring and coordination

One village-level worker (animator) is engaged per village to look after the various aspects of the group. This worker, a woman from the group, is paid an honorarium of Rs. 180 per month, from the project. There is a supervisor for every 17 animators. At the district-level, a Project Officer heads the project implementation unit (PIU). At the state level, there is a project management unit (PMU) headed by a Project Coordinator. All policy decisions are made by the Project Director, who is the Managing Director of the Corporation.

Since the programme involves several line departments of the government and NGOs, it is important to maintain close coordination at all tiers. At the district level, there is a district Project Coordinating Committee headed by the District Collector which meets every month to review the progress of the schemes. At the state level, there is a Central Project Coordinating Committee, that concerns itself with regular appraisals of the project, with the Chief Secretary to Government of Tamil Nadu as Chairman.

Group savings

This is an important aspect of the project and is an indicator of the performance of the group. The total savings amongst the various groups, at the end of the IFAD project period in 1998 stood at Rs. 13 crore. With the extension of the project to all 30 districts of the state under state funding, this had increased to Rs. 33.43 crore (by 31 March 2000).

Strategies

Since the time of its inception in 1989, the TNWDP has evolved over a 12-year period. Various strategies have been refined and a set of best practices arrived at in order to ensure quality and minimum standards in implementation and a high degree of responsiveness to local needs arising among poor communities. The project has transformed itself from a supply-driven approach to a demand-driven one.

Absence of target approach

The project was initiated as a pilot study in one district, on an experimental basis through external funding from the IFAD. It expanded in phases, following a 'process approach' without any statistical expenditure or physical target orientation. This was one of the key factors contributing to maintaining quality in implementation. After closure of IFAD funding, the project has expanded and consolidated under the state budget, on lessons learned. Over the 12 years, the project has expanded to cover all the 30 districts in Tamil Nadu.

Self-help

The earlier 'welfare' or provisioning approach of the government led to poor initiative on the part of the deprived. This approach worked against the sustainability of schemes. Realising this, TNWDP has consistently striven to achieve the 'equity' of the poor by empowering them through savings and self-help schemes.

Stakeholder analysis/participatory approach

The project is a unique partnership between (a) an independent government agency, the Tamil Nadu Corporation for Development of Women (DeW); (b) NGOs selected on the basis of pre-determined criteria; and (c) banks—commercial, cooperative and National Bank for Agricultural and Rural Development (NABARD). This partnership ensures that the strengths of each of the agencies are pooled for the benefit of women from poor households. The wide reach of the programme and fund access through development of women are combined with the financial knowledge and credit access of the banking system. Moreover, the existence of these three distinct categories of partners minimises the domination of any one, translating into benefits for the intended beneficiaries.

NGO selection

Recognising that NGOs come from heterogeneous backgrounds with varying strengths, skills and bonafides, a transparent two-stage selection process has been instituted:

Stage I: NGOs interested in participating in the project apply on a pre-designed form. A table check is made to shortlist eligible NGOs for a detailed verification.

Stage II: A three-person team is sent for inspection of the NGO, its records, premises and activities. The team consists of a government officer from a different district, representative from another NGO, and a local staff member. This process ensures that neither the inspecting team nor the NGO has any complaint about biased judgement, unauthorised payments for NGO approval/rejection or bureaucratic harassment.

Credit rating for SHGs

Credit is an incentive for performance. Credit rating guidelines have been evolved, approved by the state-level Banker's Committee after consultation with all member banks in order to separate credit-worthy SHGs from others (which may require still more time to become credit-worthy). A bank officer is involved in the process of assessing each SHG during the credit rating process. Only those groups that pass the credit rating exercise are eligible for bank credit.

Systematic training for capacity building

Training is divided into three broad-based categories, such as beneficiary training, training for project partners, and capacity-building for sustainability.

Beneficiary training

- SHG members' training comprises 10 modules—each module lasts one day and is spaced out over a period of 45 days.
- Animators' and representatives' training consists of 12 modules—each module lasts for two days. The training is spread out over a period of two years.
- Cluster level federation training comprises seven modules—each module lasts for two days.

Training for project partners

Training is also carried out for functionaries of different project partners to sensitise them on SHGs and to ensure that the entire team develops a common mindset. The following categories of training are in place:

- Bankers' training, including Primary Agricultural Cooperative Banks (PACBs).
- Project staff training.

- NGO staff training.
- Training for PRIs (Panchayat Raj Institutions) and ULBs (urban local bodies).
- Training for *anganwadi* (preschool) workers.

Capacity building for sustainability

To facilitate delivery of quality training inputs in consonance with the massive training needs, training of trainers (TOT) is also conducted. DeW has shifted its focus to capacity building at the community level by identifying capable women among SHGs and training them as trainers.

Working manual

In order to understand the vision and mission of the project, and also to imbibe the lessons learned during the implementation of the IFAD-assisted project, a comprehensive Working Manual was prepared in 1998 which explains basic concepts, approaches and strategies, while allowing for flexibility and innovation in implementation. The manual was revised in March 2000, incorporating topics such as (1) status of women and empowerment; (2) participatory monitoring & evaluation; (3) sustainability of schemes; (4) changing role of SHGs and NGOs; and (5) platform for action (PFA) based on the Beijing Declaration.

Handbook for SHG members

An easy-to-use handbook in the local language, Tamil, has been prepared and distributed among all the groups so that the operational process is well understood and known to every member of the group. A radio programme has also been launched to reach out to the illiterate SHG members.

Democratic empowerment

Democratic empowerment among the SHG members is a goal that guides not only internal working principles, but is visible from the large number of women participating in Gram Sabhas. Over 48 per cent of the existing 13,47,000 women SHG members participated in the last Gram Sabha. The democratic structure of the programme also encourages members to contest the local body elections.

Continuous learning from feedback

The project continuously endeavours to respond to issues and needs arising during implementation of schemes, as articulated by the beneficiaries, i.e., the women members. For example, when insurance was identified as a need, an insurance scheme for women was specifically introduced after a series of discussions with SHG representatives.

Lessons learnt

Financial operations

The project successfully introduced informal financial operations built on group-based lending and saving, and integrated rural women with formal credit channels. *Sangha* (group) loans were used to meet the emergency and consumption requirements of women, and replaced their dependency on moneylenders who charge exorbitant interest rates. The savings mobilised within groups are first deposited in a bank account in the name of the groups and then transformed into loans to members. Each member, on an average, has benefited from three to four such loans.

Recovery rates of such internal group loans are over 90 per cent. After an initial period of such credit operation, individual women were given access to credit from formal sources, depending on their track record. This led to a borrower outreach from 40,320 to 87,539 beneficiaries. Institutional credit has been useful in establishing small enterprises, and other related activities (Box 18.1).

Box 18.1 **Economic prosperity through SHGs**

Sarasu, from Kayathur village in South Arcot district, has had a long history of domestic and marital problems, ranging from extreme poverty with seven children to raise, and an uncertain income of Rs. 20 a day. She joined the SHG in her village in 1992, managing to make up the minimum savings required by the group, and three years later was able to take out a bank loan and purchase two dairy cows. The yield from the two cows averaged 15 litres per day, which she sold at Rs. 8 per litre. Thus, she could earn over Rs. 100 per day. In 1996, she took a loan from her group and started a small firewood business. Both loans have now been repaid and two of her children have graduated from the university. Sarasu considers the group and the Indian Bank as the central influence in her new life today.

Although the project has proved to be highly cost-effective, the lender transaction cost could be further reduced if the option of institutional lending to groups for on-lending to individuals, rather than directly to individuals within the groups, is considered. This is clearly an attractive option for the banks, but in such an eventuality care should be taken with regard to group dynamics, particularly with regard to loan distribution within groups to ensure that the poorer women are not marginalised.

Institutional arrangements

The key to the project's success has been the institutional arrangement and excellent cooperation among the principal project partners—the Government of Tamil Nadu, Tamil Nadu Corporation for Women's Development, the Indian Bank, and various NGOs. Although the agency responsible for implementing the project (the Tamil Nadu Corporation for Women's Development) is a government undertaking, it enjoys a semi-autonomous status in decision-making which has greatly facilitated implementation.

DeW brought legitimacy, resources and overall vision to the project; the Indian Bank brought in resources and helped institutionalise efficient systems; the NGOs brought in commitment and local knowledge in reaching rural women and mobilising them into groups; and the government played a facilitating role and provided overall moral support. The administrative positioning of the implementing agency was also a central factor, as the corporation was able to benefit from the support of government authorities and line departments while minimising delays and interference.

The Indian Bank's commitment to advancing the cause of rural women in Tamil Nadu prompted them to take the risk of providing physical collateral-free bank credit to the groups. In the follow-up phase of the project, various other financial institutions have come forward to participate in the project.

NGOs have played a central role in project activities. Although only one NGO was involved in the beginning, by the end of its implementation around 30 NGOs were cooperating actively with the project. NGOs helped to identify potential beneficiaries, involved them and trained them in a variety of areas according to the requirements and priorities of the target group, including social, technical and credit-related topics as well as in group management and operations. More than 150 NGOs are involved in the second phase of the project which is financed by the state government, covering all districts in Tamil Nadu.

Women's empowerment

The project demonstrates that women's empowerment through SHGs enables members to exercise control over their labour, mobility, interaction, resources, decision-making processes and identity (Box 18.2).

Box 18.2 **Women's' empowerment through SHGs**

Indrani became the animator of an SHG in Maruthagam village in 1994. She decided to contest the panchayat (grassroots-level committee) presidential elections in 1996 and won through the support of the local SHG member, who campaigned on her behalf. As panchayat president, she has been responsible for major development initiatives, including the asphalting of local roads, the construction of a wedding hall, the drilling of numerous water boreholes, the setting up of ration shops in villages where none previously existed, curbing the sale of alcohol, and various other measures that have improved the well-being of the rural women in Tamil Nadu.

Suguna of Kasimapatti village in Dharmapuri district joined an SHG in 1995 and took a course in photography the same year. She then obtained a bank loan of Rs. 10,500 for the purchase of a camera and set herself up as a photographer. Since then, she has become well known in her neighbourhood and also works in Hosur and Bangalore, covering private functions such as birthdays and marriages. She repaid her loan within two years, makes a significant contribution to the household income and enjoys the support of her husband.

The project has increased opportunities for disadvantaged women to come out of their homes and interact with institutions and people, including NGOs, loan officers, local authorities and others. Women travel independent of their spouses, unskilled women-wage labourers have become partly/fully self-employed, having assimilated new skills and strengthened existing ones. Men have observed tangible benefits of the involvement of their spouses in SHGs, and have started helping their wives in domestic tasks by fetching water, gathering fuel and taking care of children. The access to and control over resources by women has empowered them towards asserting their own rights. Although gender division in decision-making still persists in the project districts, there is an increase in the intra-household decision-making powers of women. This empowerment has percolated into decisions regarding credit activities, children's education, health care of family members and use of household assets.

Group formation and sustainability

Three groups were formed under the auspices of the local NGO in Metholodai village. These groups are stable and cohesive and are distinguished by the smart uniforms worn by the members. Women unable to join these groups (as they were already fully subscribed) formed two more groups on their own initiative. The animators of these new groups have learned the process of savings management and book-keeping from animators of the existing groups. The new groups meet twice a month and have already started credit operations, providing loans to individuals upto approximately Rs. 20,000. There are over 5,000 groups that were formed under the project that provide ample information on group formation and help identify factors that are critical for effective group operations and sustainability.

Primarily, a steady pace for group formation is an important factor for efficient functioning. The crucial factor for group cohesion is that before receiving institutional loans, there should be a 1–2 year period during which the groups systematically save money and rotate their funds in the form of petty loans for production, consumption and social purposes. This process creates solidarity and self-reliance and may also play an important role in sustainability of the group. Other dimensions for effective group operations include optimal group size, rotation of leadership responsibilities, economic homogeneity of group members, continuity of members in groups, and rules governing group operations. The project also illustrates that pro-poor, equitable and transparent savings, and lending practices contribute to efficient group functioning and in the collective engagement of the group in socially productive activities.

Sustainability of groups may be enhanced by the formation of cluster-level federations of groups. Such federations can eventually take over the motivating role played by NGOs and serve as an important aid to sustainability. In the project, more than half the groups have formed cluster-level federations, that are gradually dealing with some of the functions of NGOs. Cluster-level federations contribute to improving savings and loan recoveries, resolving conflicts and cases of financial mismanagement in groups, mobilising government programmes, and addressing the common social and economic needs of villages in the cluster. In some cases they could even act as financial intermediaries for mobilising capital from some groups and channelling it into others. Federation membership also gives groups a sense of belonging to a larger organisation. In short, federations contribute not only to the sustainability of groups, but also assist in reducing overall transaction costs.

Income generation

The project created a number of income-generating opportunities. The evaluation's analysis established that around 50 per cent of the households engaged in the project reported a significant improvement in their income. In contrast, only seven per cent of non-member households from the same village registered an improvement in their income.

Apart from animal husbandry, other income-generating activities included bee-keeping, cultivation of jasmine, mangoes, betel, grapes and coconut seedlings, rope making, fishnet production and repair, mat weaving, tailoring and pottery. Loans enabled women to manage their activities independently and to have greater control over their assets and income. The assumption that women would generally make wise choices because their expertise and knowledge of local market conditions was sound, combined with healthy repayment rates, are proof that their choices were generally realistic (Box 18.3).

Box 18.3 **Breaking gender barriers**

Narasamma, of Sivasakthi Magalir Manram, works as a mason in Naganoor, Dharmapuri—a special achievement for a woman in a profession that is usually dominated by men. She was given training for three months in masonry work and consequently started taking up small assignments like the construction of tanks and bathrooms. She slowly graduated to construction of small houses, granaries, community halls and village wells. As a mason, she is able to earn almost Rs.60 a day and has become an icon in her chosen field of work.

Contrary to expectations at appraisal, that most of the loans would be used for crop improvement purposes, more than half of the principal was utilised for livestock activities (purchase of dairy cows, goats and ewes) that provided the landless and small-holder women a daily income. It was also foreseen that income-generating activities promoted by the project would primarily be land-centric and that increased agricultural and horticultural productivity in project areas would be a primary aim. Integrated packages of soil and water conservation measures were also envisaged, although greater majority of income-generating activities have focused on animal husbandry and village industries.

Summary

The TNWDP was initiated in 1989 as an enterprising partnership between the government, NGOs and commercial banks. The project envisaged the development of poor rural women. TNWDP is implemented through a network of women's SHGs through the support provided by the NGO in the villages. Although, 75 pre-selected blocks from eight districts in Tamil Nadu were taken up for coverage in a phased manner the project now covers all the districts. In 2000, 26,220 SHGs had been formed with a membership of 4,81,733 women.

Meant for women (within 21-55 years of age) below the poverty line, preference is given to women-headed households, widows and destitutes. The democratic structure of the programme also encourages members to participate in the local body elections. The project has increased opportunities for disadvantaged women to come out of their homes and interact with institutions and people, including NGOs, loan officers, local authorities and others. The access to and control over resources by women has empowered them towards asserting their own rights. Although gender division in decision-making still persists in the project districts, there is an increase in the intra-household decision-making powers of women. This empowerment has percolated into decisions regarding credit activities, children's education, health care of family members and use of household assets.

More than 5,000 groups that were formed under the project, provide ample information on group formation and help to identify factors that are critical for effective group operations and sustainability. While about 50 per cent of the households engaged in the project reported a significant improvement in their income, only seven per cent of non-member households registered such an increase.

Replicability

The TNWDP has achieved much and has heralded an era of social change with respect to empowering women in rural communities. It has almost reached the quantitative targets of loans disbursed and has overachieved by 40 per cent the number of groups to be formed as specified in the appraisal report. However, its strongest point centres around the formation of cohesive women's groups who have been encouraged to develop the habit of systematic savings. There is evidence of considerable social impact of the project on women, especially in well-functioning, homogeneous groups of very poor women. It has helped consolidate their bargaining power and decision-making responsibilities towards the overall development of their communities. The distinct features, the various strategies and most importantly, the lessons to strengthen the TNWDP, clearly point towards its relevance for replicating the model to empower women in other states.

Contact

Tamil Nadu Corporation for Development of Women Ltd.
100, Anna Salai, Guindy
Chennai – 600 032, India
Tel.: +91-44-235 5904
Fax: +91-44-235 2751
E-mail: tncdw@satyam.net.in
Website: www.tamilnaduwomen.org

CHAPTER 19

Community-Owned Rural Internet Project

Gyandoot, Madhya Pradesh

Introduction

The use of information technology as a tool of governance is an efficient and transparent medium for the dissemination of information and the discharge of administrative activities. If used effectively, it has the potential to catalyse a social revolution benefiting millions around the world. It is a vital agent in the metamorphoses of isolated local communities into a world that seems increasingly like a 'global village'. As on December 2001, India had 330 lakh telephone connections and 30 lakh Internet users for its 100 crore people. Unfortunately, the use of information technology in daily life has been a preserve of the elite, with the fruits of its many advantages failing to trickle down to the masses. Further, more, most of these connections are confined to big cities. It is not monetarily feasible for Bharat Sanchar Nigam Limited (BSNL) to provide connections beyond these big cities. Small towns and rural areas, therefore, have very little connectivity.

In an attempt to bring the benefits of information and communication technologies (ICT) to the resource-poor, the Government of Madhya Pradesh launched an experimental intranet service on 1 January 2000, in the remote, tribal-dominated district of Dhar. The project, Gyandoot, was proposed as a low-cost, self-sustainable and community-owned rural intranet project. Through the unique people-centric approach, i.e., government-to-citizen model, the project has changed the lives of thousands of villagers across 311 Gram Panchayats and over 600 villages, affecting a population of around five lakh. Every second Gyandoot user is from a below poverty line-family; every sixth user is a woman; and every seventh user is an illiterate person (Rajora, 2002a).

Background

This tribal-dominated district of Dhar or Dharanagari boasts of a rich art and a flourishing soya market. Agriculture and industry are the twin mainstays of business here. Dhar handles close to Rs. 400 crore worth of agricultural commodities, principally soya, cotton and wheat.

Dhar began the new millennium with the installation of a low-cost, self-sustainable and community-owned rural intranet project. During the course of the project, computers in 20 village centres, in five blocks of the district were wired through an intranet network. Local rural youth were the *Soochaks* (entrepreneurs) who run the cyber cafes-cum-cyber offices on commercial lines, without a salary or a stipend. Computer networks called *Soochanalayas* (information kiosks) have been established in Gram Panchayats throughout the district. These Soochanalayas provide user-charge-based services and provide rural folk access to the internet.

This intranet system has been named Gyandoot or the Messenger of Information. In a span of two months, the entire intranet system has been installed and made operational for the villagers in the district of Dhar. The project has demonstrated a new model for more effective, accessible, prompt and transparent governance, which benefits not only the citizens but also the government by making the citizen an equal partner in the process of governance.

Objectives

The Gyandoot project aims to give marginalised citizens in one of India's most poverty-stricken rural areas, a chance to access knowledge with minimum investment. The objective of this project has been to establish a community-owned, innovative and sustainable source of information technology and cater to the social, economical and developmental needs of the villagers through an innovative G2C (government-to-citizen) model and consequently, to break down the digital divide.

The long-term objective of the project has been to use innovative e-governance, e-commerce and e-education techniques as tool for social change and development by means of wired village networks in the district.

The Gyandoot initiative sought to fulfil the following objectives:

- Create a cost-effective, replicable, economically self-reliant and financially viable model for development, taking the benefits of information technology to the rural masses.
- Implement a new grassroots entrepreneurial model with participation of groups of non-traditional entrepreneurs.
- Enhance participation in community affairs by the creative use of information technology.
- Improve the quality, speed and sensitivity of the state delivery apparatus towards the needs of local citizen-customers.
- Ensure equal access to emerging technologies for oppressed and exploited segments of the society.

Salient features

Project implementation

Services and facilities

While formulating the project proposal, a detailed survey was undertaken involving the villagers and rural communities. The selection of services proposed by the Gyandoot network was a result of this interactive exercise and was based upon the advice and the requirements of the villagers.

The services offered on the Gyandoot network included utilising the intranet network towards services related to economic, social, and governance related facilities available from the information technology.

- *Economic services:* Agriculture-produce auction centre rates (*Mandi Bhav*), access to copies of land records (*Bhu Abhilekh*), employment news (*Rozgardoot*), business facilities (*Nirmiti Kendra, Roopayan and Charm Vikas Parisar*), rural e-mail facility (*Gram Daak*), rural innovators (*Avishkarak*).
- *Social services:* Free e-mail facilities on social issues (*Samaj Seva*), e-education (*Shiksha Gyandoot and Gyanmitra*), access to village auction sites and on-line matrimonial sites (*Gram Haat and Vaivahiki*), net supported health services (*Swasthya Seva*).
- *Governance-related services:* On-line public grievance redressal (*Samasyain*), information regarding government programmes and schemes (*Suvidha*), access to application forms (*Avedan Patra*), Below Poverty Line list, transparency in government functioning (*Padarshita*).
- *Others:* Village newspaper (*Gaon ka Khabar*), online registration services, an interactive question and answer service (*Sawaliram se puchiye*), information on using the server space, information on setting up cyber cafes, advertisement opportunities, local weather report (*Meghdoot*), emergency services (*Teevra Doot*), e-newspaper (*e-samachar*).

Soochanalayas (information kiosks or cyber offices)

Soochanalayas are client sites/nodes, working as rural information kiosks. They are well-located and easily accessible to the villagers. They are established in the vicinity of Gram Panchayats, located either at block headquarters or at prominent *haat bazaars* (weekly markets in tribal areas) and on major roads in larger villages. Each Soochanalaya is envisioned to cater to approximately 15 Gram Panchayats and about 25–30 villages.

The Soochanalayas are equipped with a personal computer, modem, telephone connection, UPS and printer. The income of a Soochanalaya centre comes from providing services such as job-work, training and computer education, and desk-top publishing services.

Dhar district has a total of 31 Soochanalayas. The server/hub is a Remote Access Server (RAS) housed in the computer room in the Zilla Panchayat (district council). Each Soochanalaya provides access services to about 15 Gram Panchayats in 25–30 villages, covering a population base of 20,000–30,000 rural folk. The network covers five out of 13 blocks in the district and three out of seven tehsils in the district.

Soochak (operator)

The entrepreneur operating the Soochanalaya is a local matriculate and is called the Soochak. A Soochak has only basic computer maintenance knowledge and numeric data entry skills. Since most of the Intranet software is menu-driven, typing skills are not a requisite for manning the cyber office. The Soochaks for the initial 20 centres in Dhar were selected in an interactive process and jointly decided by the village committees and the local community. They were also given a one month operational training by the district council. Some of them were provided with stamp vending and petition writing powers.

A Soochak manages the Soochanalaya on commercial lines. He/she is the owner of the establishment and has, initially, a one-year agreement with the village committee. A Soochak does not receive any fixed remuneration and bears maintenance costs, electricity and telephone bills. He/she pays 10 per cent of income as commission to the Zilla Panchayat for maintaining the intranet and pays

Rs. 5,000 per annum as a license fee to the district council. Each Soochak is expected to earn a net minimum income of at least Rs. 36,000 per annum.

Software & connectivity

The main server of the Gyandoot network is located in the Zilla Panchayat premises. The server has five modems connected to five dedicated BSNL lines. Also a local area network (LAN) has been established in the collector's office premises, with connectivity to all the government departments to facilitate immediate receipt, action, monitoring and reply of grievances relating to their department. The intranet also provides the option of local e-mail in Hindi. The technical team of the Gyandoot Samiti makes daily content updates. The Soochanalayas (kiosks) are connected to the main server through a BSNL dial-up line, which provides access to information at a nominal cost.

The Gyandoot Samiti, a registered society to support the project, has developed software to run the intranet and its associated services. They offer a software, named 'Gyandoot Software', at a nominal price to any district administration, interested in replicating the model. It is very simple and menu-driven software, requiring minimum data entry at the client end. The software, which is in Hindi, has an elaborate administration mechanism to monitor node activities and maintain quality of services offered to the end-users. There is also a provision for some of the Gyandoot server space for local entrepreneur seeking to advertise their products. Offers for opening local cyber cafes are regularly solicited.

Financing

The Gyandoot network is financed entirely by the local rural community. The government does not contribute towards the installation or maintenance costs of the network. The various sources of funding for the project are:

- Private investments.
- Revenues earned by the village committee.
- The share of annual revenue of the village committee from the State Finance Commission.
- National social aid programme allotment available to the Zilla Panchayat.
- Participatory funding from the community.
- Advertisements on pre-printed stationery and website solicitations.

The network has been set up at a total cost of Rs. 25 lakh. The average cost incurred by the village committee and the rural user-community in establishing a single kiosk is Rs. 75,000. The system is very cost-effective (Box 19.1).

Gyandoot service users

As per a sample study conducted by Jafri *et al* (2002) most users of Gyandoot services were from the middle class and lower-income groups. A substantial proportion of the users are literate (Fig. 19.1). It is interesting to note that Gyandoot services are primarily used to obtain *mandi* rates, check the land records and to clarify grievance redressals (Fig. 19.2 and Box 19.2).

Box 19.1 **Sources of income of the kiosk manager**

The Soochak has the following sources of income generated through the management of kiosks in each village:

- Gyandoot services = Rs. 5–25 as user charge per service.
- Internet surfing = Rs. 50 per hour.
- Job work = Rs. 10–20 per page.
- Data entry = Rs. 10 per page.
- Computer training = Rs. 150–300 per student per month.
- Offset printing = Rs. 500–2,000 per contract.
- Video games = Rs. 10–20 per game.
- Preparation of horoscopes = Rs. 50–250 per horoscope.

Source: Rajesh Rajora, 2002, Bridging the Digital Divide, Gyandoot: The Model for Community Networks, Tata McGraw-Hill.

Fig. 19.1 **Literacy profile of Gyandoot users**

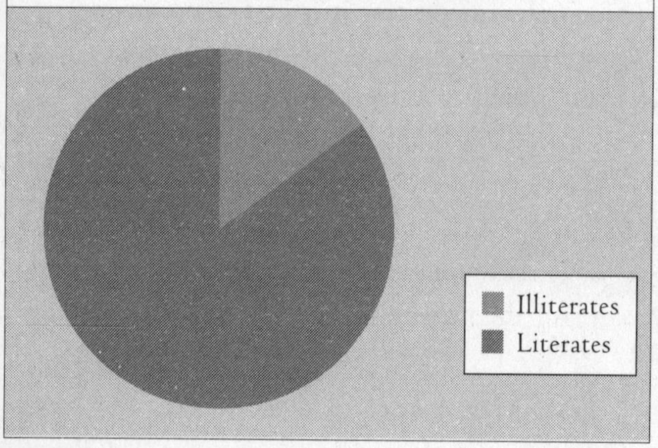

Fig. 19.2 **Service utilisation profile of users**

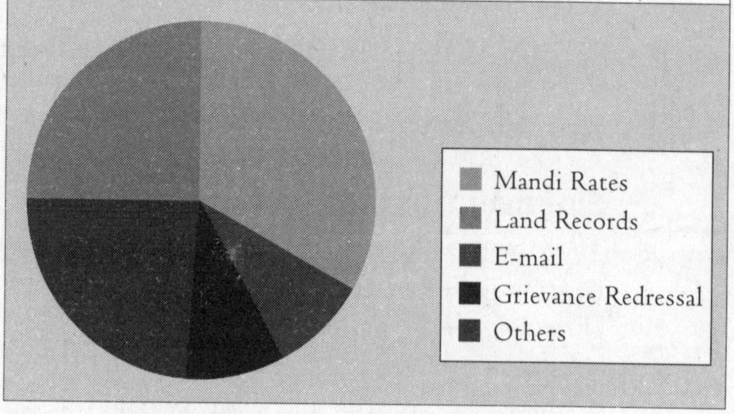

Box 19.2 **Avedan Patra: drinking water for a tribal hamlet**

A small hamlet, Baidi Awar of village Mafipura, has one handpump for clean drinking water for 39 households. The handpump had been out of order for six months and villagers had been fetching their drinking water from distances of over two km. Complaints to the concerned department remained unheeded. Subsequently, a villager, Ramesh Gobaria, went to the nearby Soochanalaya to lodge a complaint. Initially he was skeptical about the payment of Rs.10 for filing the complaint online. To the surprise of the villagers, a handpump mechanic reached the hamlet within two days of filing the complaint at the Soochanalaya, and the handpump was repaired within three hours. The incident has greatly boosted the confidence level of the villagers who have become regular users of Gyandoot services.

Source: http://gyandoot.nic.in/

There have been several interesting experiences of Gyandoot service users who have benefited economically and socially (Box 19.3). The online public grievance redressal and increasing government accountability enabled illiterate tribal women in the hinterland of the district to get prompt redressal of their problems without having to go to the district headquarters. Three old widows—Nandanbai, Punnibai and Ramibai—of Tirla, a tribal hamlet, placed a complaint to the District Magistrate through the nearby Soochanalaya, that eligible villagers had not received pensions for five months. Their complaint was promptly addressed and payment of dues made to all the eligible villagers. The District Magistrate ordered tightening of the pension delivery system, which functions through a three-tier hierarchy of local self-government bodies. The secretary of the Tirla village committee has also realised the importance of regular payment of the social security benefits and vowed to deliver the pension on time.

Box 19.3 **Auction action**

Farmers in Bagadi village were getting a rate of Rs. 300 per quintal from local traders for their potato crop. From the Soochanalaya, the farmers found that the current rate in the Indore *mandi* (auction centre) was Rs. 400 per quintal. They now take their potato produce to the Indore *mandi* directly.

Kalsingh of village Mirjapur wanted to sell his cow. He registered at the Soochanalaya of nearby Gunavad village to put up his offer of the animal online. He received four trade inquiries and finally sold his cow to the highest bidder, Premanarayan of village Dilwara. The auction facility of Gyandoot enables trading of commodities like milch animals, cultivable land, tractors, and agricultural tools, creating a virtual market place for villagers through expanded horizons and increased competitiveness. This is the first case of an e-commerce transaction in a rural area. The service is becoming very popular—it has deepened and widened the market for the villagers of the tribal hinterland and benefited them economically.

Hiralal sent an e-mail from Gunavad Soochanalaya that an epidemic had broken out amongst the milch cattle of village Kot Bhidota. A veterinary rescue team was sent on the same day by the district head of the veterinary department. Haemorrhagic septicemia was detected and the team promptly started curative treatment by vaccinating the rest of the animals against the disease. They also conducted a search and survey operation in the neighbouring villages for detection of similar symptoms and undertook preventive vaccination. Thus, 256 milch animals were vaccinated in one day. Teevra Doot facility of Gyandoot caters to natural calamities and epidemics providing instant information to the right government functionary. Instant relief and preventive measures are possible due to the timely availability of information.

Source: *http://gyandoot.nic.in/*

Earlier, village committees were unaware of whether the money had been deposited in their bank accounts. Ever since the committee was intimated through e-mail about the release of funds, it resulted in cutting down bureaucratic red-tapism. In the interior remote hamlets of Anandkhedi and Umrela village, the local *gurujis* (teachers) of the Education Guarantee Scheme centres had not received their honorarium for the period March–July 1999. When this complaint was brought to the notice of the authorities through the Soochanalaya, it was promptly rectified.

Strengthening and expansion of the project

To make the Soochanalayas economically viable entities and to constantly improve the functioning of the project, the following steps are being taken:

- Online linking of all government departments with the Gyandoot server.
- Implementation of wireless in local loop technology.
- E-education initiatives.

The future expansion plans of the Gyandoot network include starting cyber centres only in those villages with local telephone exchanges to ensure reasonably good connectivity of lines. New centres are to be created through increased private investment with additional services and facilities being introduced in phases. Additionally, certain novel steps are going to be initiated, like:

- E-news for the district.
- Distance education.
- Registration of property transaction.
- Feedback system on development programmes.
- Immediate access to medical facilities through the barefoot doctor initiative.

Wireless in local loop technology (WLL)

Gyandoot *Samiti* has recognised these issues and is currently working with the TelNet group of IIT Madras to roll out rural connectivity using indigenous technologies, as a social model amenable to future replication. The objectives of this ambitious project are:

- To provide internet and voice connectivity as a commercial service in every village of Dhar with at least one Soochanalaya in every village. This would facilitate greater coverage by the project and hence bring a larger number of rural communities together.
- To provide WLL connectivity that will facilitate simultaneous telephone and 35/70 KBPS internet connections to users at a per-line access cost of about Rs. 13,000–17,000 (in thinly populated rural areas).

The WLL arrangement would enable low-cost internet infrastructure and thus connect every village of Dhar district (wireless connectivity using CorDECT). The entire initiative will be divided into 3–4 access centres, ensuring coverage of the entire district. Each access centre will have two phases. Phase- I will cover all areas within a 10 km line of sight (LoS) radius from the access centre and Phase- II would cover all areas within a 25–30 km radius from the access centre. The first access centre will be located in the Zilla Panchayat computer room in the Collectorate Office premises. All the Soochanalayas that fall within Phase- I would be the first to get wireless connectivity. New Soochanalayas in every village within the 10 km range can be added under this phase. In Phase- II, all Soochanalayas that fall within a 25–30 km arial distance will get wireless connectivity. The Soochanalayas out of the wireless range will still be connected on the existing dial-up mode. The telephone charge would be the standard Department of Telecommunications (DOT) rates with appropriate discount, and the Internet charges will be approximately Rs. 15–20 per hour.

Action plan

A comprehensive and integrated multimedia mass campaign concentrating on information, education and communication strategies, has been launched in the district. The campaign focuses on penetration and propagation of the project in the hinterlands of the district. Several novel techniques have been employed to increase the levels of interaction between the villagers and the Soochanalayas. These include:

- Institution of the Gyandoot Medhavi Chhatra (talented students) Scholarship.
- Regular visits of school children to the nearest Soochanalaya.
- Ensuring that the Gram Sabha in the villages are located in the vicinity of the project area.
- Audio-visual campaigns.
- Introduction of Gyandoot Computer Clubs.
- Introduction of the Sir Ratan Tata Trust Healthy Child Competition (an award of Rs. 5,000 is made each year to the healthiest girl/boy child in the community, in collaboration with the Department of Women and Child Welfare).

Evaluation of the Gyandoot project

In mid-2001, a study was conducted by a combined team from Eklavya, an NGO, and the Indian Institute of Forest Management, in collaboration with the Overseas Development Institute Livelihoods Option Study (Jafri *et.al*, 2002). The objective of the study was to assess the impact of the Gyandoot project on the rural environment, taking into account the widespread disparities of caste, gender, economic status and educational levels. The study was carried out at three levels of participants: the villagers who use the services, the kiosk operators who provide the services and finally at the administration level, who implement the project. The methodology adopted was sample survey with the help of questionnaires.

The major findings of the study are as follows:

- Overall awareness level of the Gyandoot user-villages was found to be more than 50 per cent. However, the awareness was not consistent and was found lower among women, among people from remote areas and those with lower levels of education.
- The most frequently used services consisted of the ones used to obtain government records or certificates of various kinds, to make complaints about the quality of governance and to obtain market-related information.
- About 80 per cent user-respondents were satisfied with the services and the amount charged for the services was also seen to be reasonable.
- The administration was of the view that the mere awareness of the fact that complaints could be made through Gyandoot, has had a positive impact towards improving their performance.
- The study suggested that the issue of economic sustainability needs to be assessed from the point of view of kiosk owners. This issue of a viable rate of return to the owners might become crucial in case the government discontinues bearing the full investment cost of a kiosk.
- It recommended that services could be expanded for economies of scale and scope by providing more services like long-distance telephone services and Panchayat services under one roof, thereby providing a platform for small business development.

Summary

The Government of Madhya Pradesh launched an experimental intranet service on 1 January, 2000, in the remote, tribal-dominated district of Dhar as a low-cost, self-sustainable and community-owned rural intranet project. Through 'government-to-citizen' model, the project changed the lives of thousands of villagers across 311 Gram Panchayats and over 600 villages. In the words of Mr Digvijay Singh, Chief Minister of Madhya Pradesh, the Gyandoot experience has highlighted the fact that local content, appropriate technology and community participation are the fundamental pre-requisites for the socialisation of information technology. In a way, such knowledge networking serves as a mechanism to bridge the gap between micro-level activism and macro-level policy discourse.

The various services offered on the Gyandoot network included utilising the intranet network towards services related to economic, social, and governance related aspects as well as other facilities available from the information technology. The Soochaks or entrepreneurs of the Soochanalaya, were from the community who had basic education and were given one month operational training by the district council. These Soochak's managed the Soochanalaya on commercial lines, and paid 10 per cent of income as commission to the Zilla Panchayat for maintaining the intranet and paid, Rs. 5,000 per annum as a license fee to the district council. The Gyandoot network is financed entirely by the local rural community.

What is more interesting is that every second Gyandoot-user is from a below poverty line-family, every sixth user is a woman and every seventh user is an illiterate person. Gyandoot services are used primarily to obtain mandi rates, check the land records and to obtain clarifications for the various grievances, which were promptly rectified.

An independent study also pointed out that the overall awareness level of the Gyandoot user-villages was just over 50 per cent. The study also highlighted that the issue of economic sustainability needs to be assessed from the point of view kiosk owners, especially if the government discontinues bearing the full investment cost of a kiosk. Hence, it also recommended that services should be expanded for economies of scale and scope by providing more services like long-distance telephone services and Panchayat services under one roof, which might therefore form a basis for small business development.

Thus, while there is scope for improvement, the project has demonstrated a new model for more effective, accessible, prompt and transparent governance, which benefits not only the citizen but also the government by making the citizen an equal partner in the process of governance.

Replicability

The Gyandoot project of Dhar district has been awarded the prestigious Stockholm Challenge IT 2000 Award in the Public Service and Democracy category. The award is a worldwide recognition of pioneering information technology initiatives. The project was also awarded the CSI-TCS National IT Award 2000 for best IT usage, institutionalised by the Computer Society of India. The success of Gyandoot is largely attributable to its participatory approach, relevance to rural user-communities and financial sustainability. It has been instrumental in empowering the underprivileged, economically and socially disadvantaged groups as well as rural youth. But perhaps its greatest strength lies in the fact that it has been able to break new ground and adapt modern technologies to suit the everyday needs of a remote, tribal-dominated poverty-stricken district in Madhya Pradesh.

Future plans of the Gyandoot network, centre on extending its connectivity area to other districts in Madhya Pradesh and introducing user-specific services. These include providing commodity/ *mandi* marketing information systems, issuing income, caste and domicile certification, introducing e-mail facilities in Hindi and evolution of specific e-education modules for school children.

Contact

Collector
District Dhar
Madhya Pradesh, India
Tel.: +91-91-7292-347 02
Fax: +91-91-7292-347 11
E-mail: gyandoot@rediffmail.com
gyandoot@vsnl.com
Website: http://gyandoot.nic.in/

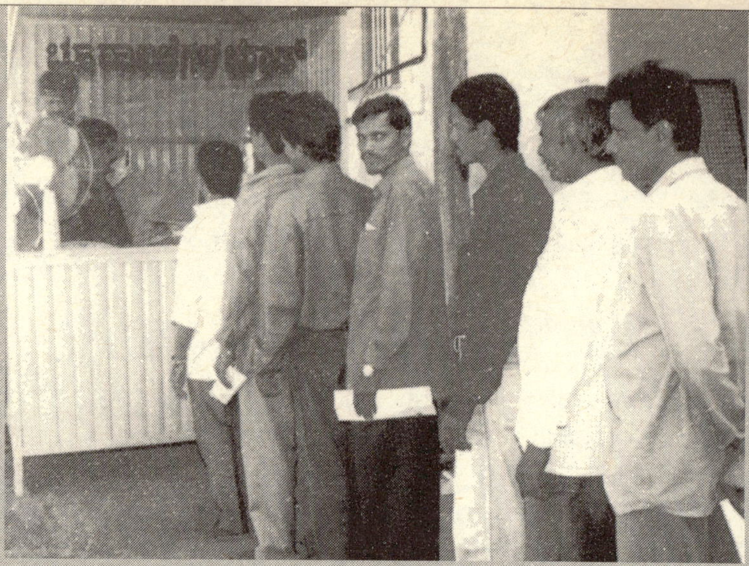

CHAPTER 20

E-Governance for Information Dissemination

Bhoomi, Karnataka

Introduction

In a country with over 70 per cent of the 100 crore population depending on agriculture, land is a very important source of income generation and economic security. Indian policy on taxation of land refers to the need to create, maintain and update the land information system which also helps towards better governance. The process of computerising land records in Karnataka started in 1991 when the first pilot study was conducted through a centrally sponsored scheme for Computerisation of Land Records. This was fully funded by the Government of India. However, lack of adequate computer facilities at the taluka level inhibited the operationalisation of the project. This posed a challenge in maintaining accurate and genuine land records system to further the objectives of land reforms, protection of legal rights over land and efficiency in maintenance and updation of these records.

Background

Land is a very precious source of livelihood and land records system must safeguard the rights of the legal owner of the land. The Government of Karnataka took the initiative to formulate a system of land records. The term 'land records' itself is a generic expression and could include, in Karnataka, records like the Register of Lands of Khetwar Patrika, Records of Rights, Tenancy and Crop Inspection Register (RTC, Form-16), Khata Register (Form-24), Khirdi (Form-25), Mutation Register (Form-12), Disputed Cases Register (Form-8) and the like.

The online updation of land records is performed through a Kannada interface software, appropriately named *Bhoomi* (land) which is user-friendly. Its technology is state-of-the-art. It has been completely designed in-house by the National Informatics Centre (NIC). It is a centrally sponsored scheme, implemented by the Government of Karnataka through the Revenue Department in all the 177 talukas of the state. This scheme is expected to cover more than two crore land records and more than 67 lakh landowners in the state.

In a people-friendly move, the Chief Minister of Karnataka launched the first of the Records of Rights, Tenancy and Cultivation (RTC) Information Kiosks in Maddur taluka of Mandya district on 6 February 2001. This initiative was taken by the Government of Karnataka under its declared information technology policy, better known as "Mahiti" or using information technology for rural development. Seventy such information kiosks are operational in the state.

The scope of the project includes:

- Facilitating easy maintenance and updation of land records after:
    - Irrigation/natural calamities/consolidation.
    - Legal changes like transfer of ownership.
- Providing comprehensive scrutiny to make land records tamper proof.
- Providing required support to implement developmental programmes which require data on distribution of landholdings.

Objectives

- To facilitate preparation of an annual set of records in mechanised processes such as collection of land revenue, updating of cropping pattern, etc.
- To facilitate a variety of standard and ad hoc queries on land data.
- Allow farmers easy access to their records through various kiosks and booths and through the web.
- To provide farmers an easy mechanism to lodge request for updation of land records.
- To facilitate usage of this database by courts, banks and various other government agencies.

Salient features

Project set-up

System design

The data entry software Bhoomi, developed by the NIC, Bangalore, is very comprehensive and takes into account all the divisional variations in land records maintenance. The initial data entry is done at the taluka level through private data entry agencies. The data entry agencies use the data entry software to enter data in offline. Once the data entry is completed, printouts are taken by the data entry agencies and then validated by the village accountants by comparing against their original land record books called RTC or Record of Rights, Tenancy and Cultivation. The data after correction is then ported to the Bhoomi software.

Bhoomi provides for printing of land records as and when required. It incorporates the process of online updation to ensure that the RTCs provided to the farmers are in sync with the time. When a change of ownership takes place through sale or inheritance, farmers can file for a mutation of the land record at the Bhoomi centre. All the mutations to the land records database are made directly on the computer so as to ensure that data on computer remain current. The Government of Karnataka has passed a rule that as and when the land records scheme is operationalised in a taluka, manually written land records or RTC will become null and void. Only computerised RTC, duly signed by the authorised signatory, will be valid for all legal purposes. A notification to the above effect would be issued in a taluka only when the scheme is firmly in place in that particular taluka.

Record kiosks

Land record kiosks are being set up in every taluka office in Karnataka. Landowners would be able to obtain copies of their land records on payment of Rs.15. The land records database will be connected to banks and lending institutions to facilitate the use of the database by these institutions for providing crop loans. The Government of Karnataka also plans to allow the high court and other district and taluka courts to use this database in their judicial and administrative work. In future, it also intends to permit private internet service providers (ISPs) to use this database as their value addition content and charge them a user-fee. This would help the Government of Karnataka make the land record project a self-financed scheme. The government also has plans to gradually let the information kiosks (which are proposed to be set up by private parties in Karnataka in rural areas) use these databases to provide land records at the farmers doorstep, although they may not be signed in the beginning by anybody and would be more for informative purposes only.

People's response at the taluka level has been overwhelming. Queues can be seen at the kiosks of the taluka centres where they have been operationalised and people are more than willing to pay the nominal fee of Rs.15 for getting a copy of the land records instantaneously.

Other features

- The software incorporates the state-of-the-art bio-logon metric system from Compaq, which authenticates various users on the basis of their fingerprint. This ensures that nobody can hack the system by imitating other users.
- The Bhoomi software has the provision to scan original mutation orders and notices served on interested groups by revenue inspectors who are the authorised personnel to pass such orders in the field. Both documents are scanned to ensure that future responsibility is fixed on revenue inspectors by showing the original documents signed by them, but interested parties cannot claim in court that they were not served with the necessary notice before the effect of mutation.
- Bhoomi enables the administrators to generate various type of reports on the type of soil, number of land owners owning land above a certain average, type of crops grown in a taluka and their percentage, etc. Such information enables administrators and policy-makers to make appropriate decisions.

Funding

The Computerisation of Land Records is a centrally sponsored scheme of the Ministry of Rural Development, Government of India. The total expenditure on the scheme is Rs. 2.9 lakh, which includes expenditures on the cost of computers, data entry and related costs. However, the fingerprint authenticating system and the touch-skin information kiosks are totally a Government of Karnataka initiative and have been installed at an additional cost of Rs. 4.9 lakh. Therefore the government's involvement is significant and the innovations introduced by the Revenue Department in Karnataka are a major effort to make land records completely transparent and easily accessible. The foolproof system makes the revenue officials accountable for all the entries made in the land records.

Coverage

The past and the targeted coverage of the Bhoomi project in its various phases is as follows[1]:

Phase 1–end-March 2001

- Captured about 50 lakh RTC data of 50 sub-districts on digital media.
- Operationalise the scheme in these 50 sub-districts.
- Trained about 8,000 revenue staff up to village accountant level on data entry operation.

Phase 2–end-March 2002

- Captured data on 1.5 crore RTCs of remaining 127 sub-districts in digital form.
- Operationalised the scheme in remaining 126+1 sub-districts.
- One of the kiosks is being used for additional cross-selling initiatives.
- Scheme decentralised to five sub-taluka (sub-sub districts) on experimental basis.

Phase 3–April 2002–March 2003

- Interlinking of sub-district level systems to district data centres and to web-enable this data.
- To use these data centres for disaster recovery.
- To manage the sub-district servers centrally from the district centres.
- To provide connectivity to banks and courts.
- To decentralise the scheme to about 100 sub-sub districts with private participation.
- To broadband the Bhoomi kiosks and use these for various cross-selling initiatives like provision of weather details, details of beneficiaries of government schemes, etc.

Phase 4–March 2003 onwards

- Interlinking of district-level data banks to the state-level data warehouse.
- To provide geographical information system (GIS) and other management information system (MIS) data using multidimensional RTC hyper cubes.
- To carry pilot projects on online mutation facility up to village-level.

Impact

Farmers

- Farmers have direct access to information about their properties at all times. All necessary records will be available to them without the long delays that accompany applications to village accountants.
- Records are available free of human arbitration.
- Land records can be easily updated by applying at the RTC information kiosks. Requests are directly registered into the land record database.
- Farmers are freed of harassment from government officials, touts, middlemen, and village-level leaders.
- Easily accessible facility to scan the field mutation order passed by revenue authorities and the notice served on the public.

---

[1] http:\\www.revdept.kar.nic.in

Box 20.1 **Bhoomi marks the take-off of e-governance in Karnataka**

"It is the best thing to happen for people like us," says Venkataram, a farmer from Kengeri, located about 20 km away from the country's Silicon Plateau, on receiving a computerised RTC certificate at an information kiosk in Bangalore, south taluka office premises. He received the RTC within a couple of minutes without any hassle or bribing the government officials. A dream come true!

Ramaiah, another farmer, was amazed when he found the details of his land on the touch-screen kiosk installed next to the RTC kiosk in the taluka office premises. "This is something very unusual. Earlier, the village accountant was the big man and did not bother to provide any information. To obtain an RTC, we had to wait for several days, apart from bribing him," said Ramaiah, who later procured the RTC certificate across the counter like a railway ticket.

Source: The Deccan Herald, 8 June 2001

Administrators

- Enables easy maintenance and updation of land record documents.
- Evolves tamper-proof land record database to reduce litigations and other disputes.
- Provides support for development programmes with the help of valuable land record data to departments like agriculture, industries and planning.
- Facilitates easy preparation of annual records like land revenue.
- Helps in monitoring government lands from encroachments.
- Helps in monitoring the land record work of subordinates and thereby enables better control over their sphere of work.

Summary

The Government of Karnataka started the Computerisation of Land Records through a project called Bhoomi. This project, which aimed at creating an online updation of land records, was performed through Kannada interface software, appropriately named *Bhoomi* (meaning land), which is user-friendly. It is a centrally sponsored scheme, being implemented by the state government through the Revenue Department in all the 177 talukas of the state.

The data entry software Bhoomi, is very comprehensive and takes into account all the divisional variations in land record maintenance. It provides for printing of land records as and when required

Box 20.2 **A record achievement**

The Bhoomi Project was given the silver at the 2002 CAPAM (Commonwealth Association of Public Administration and Management) awards function in Glasgow, Scotland. It is also among the final entries chosen for the prestigious Stockholm Challenge Award.

The estimated expenditure of the project is Rs. 19 crore. Bhoomi currently serves about 70 lakh farmers across more than 170 kiosks in the state. This inspiring project has taught the rest of the country that information technology can be taken to the rural areas. Thus, the efforts of the state government in taking information technology to rural areas has paid off.

Source: The Hindu, 23 September 2002

and incorporates the process of online updation to ensure that the RTCs provided to the farmers are in sync with the time. With a change of ownership through sale or inheritance, farmers are expected to file for a mutation of the land record at the Bhoomi centre. All the mutations to the land record database are done on the computer itself so as to ensure that the data remains current.

In order to help the land records process, the Government of Karnataka has passed a rule that as and when the land records scheme is operationalised in a taluka, manually written land records or RTC, will become null and void. Only computerised RTCs duly signed by the authorised signatory will be valid for all legal purposes. A notification to the above effect would be issued in a taluka only when the scheme is firmly in place in that particular taluka. The state government also aims to connect banks and lending institutions to this programme to facilitate the use of the database by these institutions for providing crop loans. Bhoomi enables the administrators to generate various types of reports on the type of soil, number of landowners owning land above a certain average, types of crops grown in a taluka and their percentage, etc. Such information enables administrators and policy-makers to make appropriate decisions.

The achievements of this project include the following:

- It presently serves 70 lakh farmers across more than 170 kiosks in the state.
- It has created transparency of records for the farmers and the administrators. Most farmers have direct access to information about their properties at all times. All necessary records are available to them without the long delays that usually accompany applications to village accountants.
- These records are available free of human arbitration and provide support for development programmes with the help of valuable land records data to departments like Agriculture, Industry and Planning.
- It facilitates easy preparation of annual records like land revenue.

Replicability

Land record management has always been a weak area in state administration. The centrally sponsored scheme of computerisation of land records is a significant step to strengthen land record management at the national level. Karnataka's Bhoomi represents an innovative approach in this direction by providing transparency as well as easy and quick access to land records, with an added advantage of security and reliability to the farmers. The Computerised Land Record System has succeeded in including all taluka-level revenue officials in the e-governance efforts of the Karnataka government. The system can be successfully replicated in other states, provided the Government of India considers enhancing the financial allocation to the states and the state governments too make a commitment to implement the system as has been done in Karnataka.

Contact

Rajeev Chavla
Additional Secretary, Department of Revenue
Government of Karnataka
VI Floor, M.S. Building, Ambedkar Road
Bangalore – 560 001
Phone: +91-80-226 2104
Fax : +91-80-226 2104
e-mail : as-lrf@revdept.kar.nic.in

Abbreviations

ADS : Area Development Society
AEO : Agricultural Extension Officer
AIDS : Acquired Immune Deficiency Syndrome
AO : Agricultural Officer
AP : Angan Pathshala
ARIASP : Assam Rural Infrastructure and Agricultural Services Project
BAS : Baseline Assessment Survey
BEMC : Block Education Management Committee
BEO : Block Education Officer
BPA : Block Plantation Approach
BPL : Below Poverty Line
BPO : Block Plantation Officer
BRC : Block Resource Centre
BSG : Block Steering Group
BSNL : Bharat Sanchar Nigam Limited
CEP : Community Empowerment Plan
CADD : Common Area Development Department
CAPAM : Commonwealth Association of Public Administration and Management
CDS : Community Development Society
CRC : Cluster Resource Centre
CRP : Cluster Co-ordinator and Resource Person
DEAR : Directorate of Evaluation and Research
DEO : District Education Officer
DIET : District Institute of Education and Training
DPAP : Drought Prone Areas Programme
DPEP : District Primary Education Programme
DPMU : District Project Management Unit
DRDA : District Rural Development Agency
DRP : District Resource Person
DWAC : District Watershed Advisory Committee
DWTC : District Watershed Technical Committee
EAS : Employment Assurance Scheme
ECCE : Early Childhood Care and Education
EFA : Education for All
EGS : Education Guarantee Scheme
FAO : Food and Agriculture Organisation
FMC : Field Management Committee
GDN : Global Development Network
GIS : Geographical Information System
GO : Government Organisation
GOI : Government of India
HESA : Hygiene Environmental Sanitation Awareness
HPEDS : Himachal Pradesh Eco- Development Society
IMA : Indian Medical Association
ICT : Information and Communication Technology
IFAD : International Fund for Agricultural Development
IGCEDP : Indo-German Changar Eco-Development Project
IIT : Indian Institute of Technology
ILO : International Labour Organisation
IRDP : Integrated Rural Development Programme
IRMP : Integrated Resource Management Plan
ISP : Internet Service Provider
IWDP : Integrated Watershed Development Programme
JFM : Joint Forest Management
JRY : Jawahar Rozgar Yojana
KBPS : Kilo Bytes Per Second
LAN : Local Area Network
LMT : Lakh Metric Tonnes
M&E : Monitoring & Evaluation
MP : Member of Parliament

MCL : Municipal Corporation of Ludhiana
MIS : Management Information System
MLA : Member of Legislative Assembly
MPEGS : Mahatma Phule Education Guarantee Scheme
MTA : Mother-Teacher Association
NABARD : National Bank for Agriculture and Rural Development
NFE : Non-Formal Education
NGO : Non-Governmental Organisation
NIC : National Informatics Centre
NRD : Natural Resource Development
NSAP : National Social Assistance Programme
NWDPRA : National Watershed Development Project for Rainfed Area
O&M : Operations & Maintenance
PIA : Project Implementation Agency
PMU : Project Management Unit
PO : Project Officer
PRA : Participatory Rural Appraisal
PRI : Panchayati Raj Institution
PRIP : Private Rural Initiative Programme
PROBE : Public Report on Basic Education
PTA : Parent-Teacher Association
R&D : Research & Development
RAS : Remote Access Server
RGWMM : Rajiv Gandhi Watershed Management Mission
RIDF : Rural Infrastructure Development Fund
RKS : Rogi Kalyan Samiti
RPS : Rubber Producers' Society
RTC : Rights, Tenancy and Cultivation
RVP : River Valley Project
RWS : Rural Water Supply
SC/ST : Scheduled Caste/Schedule Tribe
SCERT : State Council of Educational Research and Training
SHG : Self-Help Group
SK : Shiksha Karmi
SKB : Shiksha Karmi Board
SKP : Shiksha Karmi Project
SKS : Shiksha Karmi Sahyogi
SKY : Samridha Krishak Yojana
SLM : Self-Learning Material
SO : Support Organisation
SS : Sahaj Shiksha / Sikhna-Sikhana
SSA : Sarva Shiksha Abhiyan (National Education for All movement)
SSK : Shishu Shiksha Karmasuchi
STW : Shallow Tube Well
SWRC : Social Work and Research Centre
TANWA : Tamil Nadu Women in Agriculture
TFDPC : Tripura Forest Development Plantation Corporation
TLM : Teaching-Learning Material
TNWDP : Tamil Nadu Women's Development Project
UEE : Universalisation of Elementary Education
UN : United Nations
UNDP : United Nations Development Programme
UNESCO : United Nations Educational, Scientific and Cultural Organisation
UNFPA : United Nations Population Fund
UNICEF : United Nations Children's Fund
UPJN : Uttar Pradesh Jal Nigam
VCC : Village Construction Committee
VDC : Village Development Committee
VEAP : Village Environmental Action Plan
VEC : Village Education Committee
VER : Village Education Register
VMDF : Village Maintenance and Development Fund
VWSC : Village Water and Sanitation Committee
WDI : Women's Development Initiatives
WPG : Women's Production Group
WSS : Water Supply and Sanitation
WTCG : Water Thrift and Credit Group
WTG : Women Thrift Group

References

1. Chowdhury, Sumitra, 2000, *Universal Elementary Education in Rajasthan: A Study with Focus on Innovative Strategies*, Education for All- Year 2000 Assessment, Government of India, National Institute if Educational Planning and Administration (NIEPA), New Delhi

2. Collector, Nilgiri District, *Nilgiris Women and Children in Distress Survey and Rehabilitation Plan*, Nilgiri District, Tamil Nadu

3. Dr. Ommen, M.A., 1999, Impact of CDS in Kerala, Report Submitted to the Government of Kerala, Indian Institute of Social Science, New Delhi

4. Dreze, J. and Amartya Sen, 2002, *India Development and Participation*, New Delhi, Oxford University Press

5. Evaluation Committee and IFAD's Technical Advisory Division, 2000, *India- Completion Evaluation of The Tamil Nadu Women's Development Project: Five Lessons Learned*, Chennai

6. Fundaschool, 1998, 'M.P. Wins Award in Primary Education', in *The Hindu*, September 15, 1998, Education Guarantee Scheme in Madhya Pradesh, http:\\www.fundaschool.org

7. Government of India (GOI)-United Nations (UN) 2002d, *Report of Joint Mid-Term Review Report of Janshala Programme in Maharashtra*, dates: October 19-29, 2002

8. GOI-UNDP-UNICEF-UNFPA-ILO 2002c, *Shared Vision- Joint Government of India and UN System for Community Based Primary Education*, New Delhi

9. Gopalakrishnan, R. and Amita Sharma, 1998, 'Education Guarantee Scheme in Madhya Pradesh', *Economic and Political Weekly*, September, 26, pp. 2546-51

10. Government of Andhra Pradesh, *Functional Manual of Rythu Bazar*, Department of Marketing, Hyderabad

11. Government of Assam, 2001, *Evaluation Study on Samridha Krishak Yojana*, Evaluation and Monitoring Division, Planning and Development Department, Guwahati–6

12. Government of Karnataka, *Bhoomi: Online Delivery of Land Titles in Karnataka, India*, Bhoomi: In the Press, E-Government, Karnataka

13. Government of Kerala, *Kudumbashree (Poverty Eradication Mission)*, A Participatory Women-based Programme to Eradicate Absolute Poverty in Kerala by 2007 AD

14. Government of Madhya Pradesh, 2002, *Rajiv Gandhi Missions: Eight Years 1994-2002- Report of the People*, For a Mass Co-scripting of the Future, Rajiv Gandhi Prathmik Shiksha Mission

15. Government of Rajasthan, 2002, *Rajasthan Human Development Report- 2002*, Government of Rajasthan, Jaipur

16. Government of Tamil Nadu, 2002, *Status Report on TANWA*, Commissioner of Agriculture, Chennai

17. Government of Uttar Pradesh, *SWAJAL Project*, UP/Uttaranchal Rural Water Supply and Environmental Sanitation Project, Department of Rural Development, Government of Uttar Pradesh, LN 04056-IN, Lucknow

18. Government of Uttar Pradesh, *The SWAJAL Project,* UP Rural Water Supply and Environmental Sanitation Project Department of Rural Development, Lucknow

19. Indo-German Changar Eco-Development Project, 2001, Approaches to Participatory Natural Resource Management, Issue Nos. 1-6, Palampur

20. Jafri, A., A., Dongre, Tripathi, V.N. and S.Shrivastava, 2002, 'Information Communication Technologies and Governance: The Gyandoot Experiment in Dhar District of Madhya Pradesh, Working Paper, 160, Overseas Development Institute, London, March

21. Janshala (GOI-UN) Programme 2002a, *Working Towards a Common Goal: Innovations and Experiments in Janshala,* Department of Elementary Education & Literacy, Ministry of Human Resource Development, Government of India, New Delhi

22. Janshala (GOI-UN) Programme 2002b, *Janshala: Towards Empowered Community Schools,* Department of Elementary Education & Literacy, Ministry of Human Resource Development, Government of India, New Delhi

23. Jha, Jyotsna, 1998, *Education Guarantee Scheme and Alternative Schooling: Community- based Initiatives in Primary Education,* Rajiv Gandhi Prathmik Shiksha Mission, Government of Madhya Pradesh

24. Lok Jumbish Parishad, 2001, *Lok Jumbish-The Eighth Report: January 1998-December 1999,* Lok Jumbish Project, Jaipur

25. Lok Jumbish, 1998, *Lok Jumbish Phase III- 1998-2003,* Project Document, Lok Jumbish Project, Jaipur

26. Rajagopalan, Vijayalakshmi, 2001, *Hope and Vision: The Voices of TANWA Women Farmers,* Danish International Development Assistance (DANIDA), Chennai

27. Rajesh Rajora, 2002, *Bridging the Digital Divide, Gyandoot: The Model for Community Networks,* Tata McGraw-Hill

28. Rajiv Gandhi Mission, 2002, *Rajiv Gandhi Missions: Eighth Years 1994-2002,* Report to the People

29. Shanmugavelan, M., 2000, TANWA- Case Studies, DANIDA, Chennai

30. Srivastava, Ranjana, *Evaluation of Community-based Primary Schooling Initiatives in Madhya Pradesh: Education Guarantee Scheme and Alternative Schools,* Rajiv Gandhi Prathmik Shiksha Mission, Government of Madhya Pradesh

31. Tamil Nadu Corporation for Development of Women Ltd., 2000, *Credit Guidelines for Self-Help Groups: A Tool for SHG Credit Ratings,* Bangaru Ammaiyar Ninaivu Mahalir Thittam, Chennai

32. The PROBE team and Centre of Development Economics, 1998, *Public Report on Basic Education* in India, New Delhi

33. United Nations Development Programme (UNDP), 2002, *Human Development Report 2002: Deepening Democracy in a Fragmented World,* New York, Oxford University Press

Feedback Form

Sender's Name : ____________________

Organisation : ____________________

Designation : ____________________

Address : ____________________

____

E-mail : ____________________

(Please use extra sheets if the space here is not sufficient for your comments.)

1. Do you find the exercise attempted in the compendium informative/ useful?

____

____

2. Please provide your valuable comments on any/all of the case studies presented in the compendium.

____

____

3. Are there any other successful governance initiatives of which you are aware, that could be included in subsequent editions of this compendium? If yes, please send us the information or indicate the source from where we can find the information.

____

____

4. Do you have any other suggestions to improve the content/presentation of this compendium? Please specify.

____

____

Please send your feedback to either of the following addresses:

1. Director (State Plans-Coordination)
   Planning Commission
   Yojana Bhavan
   New Delhi-110001

2. Human Development Resource Centre
   United Nations Development Programme
   55, Lodhi Estate
   New Delhi-110003